# RELEASE THE
# REVIVAL FLOOD

## Gregory R. Frizzell

# Additional Books by Dr. Frizzell

# Available Church and Regionwide Conferences

Going Deeper With God Weekend

Developing Mountain-Moving Prayer,
and Intimacy with God

Journey to Holiness and Power

Church and Association-wide Revivals,
and Solemn Assemblies

Transformed Relationships, Healed Families,
and United Churches

Holiness and Power in Christian Leaders

Developing Powerful Prayer Meetings,
and Prayer Ministries

Powerful Prayer Meetings and
Evangelistic Prayer Ministries

Powerful Marriage and Family Prayer

Biblical and Historic Patterns of Spiritual Awakening

Escaping the Trap of Dead Religion

---

For information concerning conferences or resources contact
Dr. Frizzell:

Baptist General Convention of Oklahoma
3800 N. May Ave., Oklahoma City, OK 73112-6506
phone: 405.942.3800 e-mail: gfrizzell@bgco.org

# RELEASING THE REVIVAL FLOOD

A Churchwide Journey to Miraculous
Unity and God-Glorifying Fellowship

Revised with Study Questions

Gregory R. Frizzell

*Releasing the Revival Flood – A Churchwide Journey to Miraculous Unity and God-Glorifying Fellowship*
ISBN 978-1-930285-25-6

Copyright © 2005 by Gregory R. Frizzell
Published by The Master Design
   in cooperation with Master Design Ministries
      PO Box 569
      Union City, TN 38281-0569
      bookinfo@masterdesign.org
      www.masterdesign.org

Additional copies of this and other books by Dr. Frizzell may be ordered from:

Baptist General Convention of Oklahoma
3800 N. May Ave., Oklahoma City, OK 73112-6506
phone: 405.942.3800 e-mail: gfrizzell@bgco.org

or online at www.masterdesign.org

Printed by Bethany Press International in the USA.

JJ

# Table of Contents

# Preface

## God's Kingdom and Glory
## All About Relationships!

Welcome to a biblical journey of life-changing cleansing and surrender to God. While this book focuses on transforming church and family relationships, it focuses even more on our individual love and surrender to Christ! You may indeed be among the thousands desiring an explosion of God's holy presence in their hearts. Or perhaps you are among growing numbers desiring to see God's name hallowed and His glory flood their lives and churches. If you desire to encounter God in awesome new depth, I have great news. Our Lord promises to fill every hungry and seeking heart! (Jeremiah 29:13; Matthew 5:6)

Yet for the vast majority of modern believers, addressing strained relationships will surely be a vital part of drawing near to God. My friend, if you are seeking far greater closeness and surrender to God, you have come to the right journey. If you are weary of low spiritual power or relationship tensions, God can transform even the most hopeless situations. And be assured of one great truth — as we draw near to God for cleansing and purity, He will surely draw near to us! (James 4:8)

## A Hopeful Stirring in God's Remnant

Words can hardly express my excitement at growing signs of revival in God's small remnant! Without question, more and more saints are beginning to seek God in deeper prayer and repentance. Though it is still only a small minority of churches, personal and corporate prayers are definitely on the rise! And while God may yet have to seriously *judge* America and *shake* a sleeping, compromised Church, at last His remnant *is* stirring. This spiritual stirring is significant because God sends revival through just such remnants. In view of God's growing activity, *Releasing the Revival Flood* seeks to address one of the final barriers to the long-awaited flood of His holy presence.

While we can certainly rejoice in today's rising prayer movement, there is at least one crucial element yet to show much progress. *That crucial element is loving unity and God-glorifying fellowship among believers!* In fact concerning relationships, we not only have not seen much progress, we have witnessed a devastating collapse. One thing is certain — if we are to encounter God in revival, believers must reject today's divisive patterns and return to loving biblical fellowship (Acts 1:14; 2:1,42-47; 4:31-32).

This book is designed to show how God utterly transforms churches and families through restored relationships. But most of all, this study is about honoring God's name, exalting His Word and spreading His kingdom! Yet in a day of shallow, self-focused religion, it is crucial that believers learn to seek relationship transformation for the right foundational reason. Dear saints, we will never understand repentance, revival or loving God until we get our *motive* and *perspective* right. Make no mistake — the right perspective is a burning desire to **hallow** God's name and **spread His kingdom** in all the earth!


## Hallowing God's Name — Expanding His Kingdom
### The Central Motives for Seeking Unity
(Matthew 6:9,33; John 17:1-26; Acts 2:1-4; 42-44; 4:31-21)

Without question, it is extremely urgent that we return to a major focus on biblical love and unity. However, it is indeed important to approach it with the right *motive* and from God's *perspective! The foundational reason is simply obeying Jesus and exalting His holy name in all the earth.* Believers, we must not seek unity, love and forgiveness just so we'll be "happy and successful or avoid problems." While these issues are considerations, the far bigger issue is glorifying God's name and expanding His kingdom. We must realize the opposite of *hallowing* God's name is to *profane* our Lord. Like little else, anger, bickering and disunity "profanes" the holy name of our God! To profane (*khawla*) means to "make common, unclean or bring shame." Of course, this also devastates the Church's power in evangelism.

## The Biblical Urgency for Unity

Based on Scripture and history, guarding Christian fellowship is crucial for at least six reasons. (1) Loving fellowship is a primary way we hallow God's name and reflect His glory to all mankind (John 17:20-23). (2) Anger and disunity severely grieve the Holy Spirit and hinder God's presence in our midst (Ephesians 4:30; 1 Thessalonians 5:19). (3) Loving unity is essential for experiencing God's fullest power in evangelism and testimony of Christ (John 13:34-35; 17:21-23; Acts 2:1). (4) As God's eternal "family" we are to live in one accord (Ephesians 3:15). We are saved to function in "Christian community," not as lone rangers. In other words, this life is training and "dress rehearsal" for heaven. (5) One of God's central Kingdom purposes is believers' living in oneness with Him and each other (John 17:20-23; 1 Corinthians 14). (6) Loving each other is a foundational way we love and obey God's Great Commandments (Matthew 22:38; 1 John 2:8-11).

Dear saints, as we consider these crucial factors, one thing is clear — loving biblical fellowship is not some periphery side issue. It is absolutely central to our *being* God's people and *doing* His kingdom work! By way of definition, "one accord unity" is believers being utterly united in loving God, loving each other, spreading God's kingdom (evangelism) and glorifying His name (Acts 1:14; 2:1). May God grant us eyes to see the true kingdom priority of Christian love and one accord unity.

## Recognizing the Top Kingdom Priority
## of Love and Oneness
### (John 13:34-35; 17:1-26)

Loving one another is of such enormous kingdom priority, Jesus places it as one of only two Great Commandments (Matthew 22:37-38). Incredibly, Jesus even closely ties our power in evangelistic witness to love and unity among believers (John 13:34-35; 21:17). The issue is so vital, Scriptures state that no one can be unkind and unforgiving, yet still be right with God (Matthew 5:23-24; 6:15; 1 John 4:20). Like little else, unforgiveness and anger decimate our power in prayer (Mark 11:25). When it comes to exalting God's name and advancing His kingdom — *it really is "all about relationships!"*

Yet, in spite of God's intense focus on unity, divisive church conflict has risen to shocking levels! Though long-term research data is not exhaustive, current surveys leave no doubt that church splits, tensions and staff firings are at devastating highs. Virtually *nothing* more shames Christ's name or hinders His kingdom than church and denominational division. But let every reader take hope — God can transform the most divided believers and churches!

## Fellowship and Evangelistic Power
## A Direct Connection!
### (Acts 1:14; 2:1; 2:42-47; 4:31-32)

As we examine New Testament patterns, a profound truth becomes evident. *Unified fellowship is often directly connected to God's manifest presence and power!* It is extremely significant that many times when the Bible mentions unusual power and evangelism, unified fellowship and love are preeminent elements. Carefully read the following passages giving special attention to the sections in bold print.

"These all continued with **one accord in prayer and supplication**, with the women, and Mary the mother of Jesus, and with her brethren" (Acts 1:14). "And when the day of Pentecost was fully come, **they were all with one accord in one place**" (Acts 2:1). "And they continued steadfastly in the apostles' doctrine and **fellowship and in breaking of bread, and in prayers**. And fear came upon every soul: and many wonders and signs were done by the apostles. **And all that believed were together, and had all things common**: And sold their possessions and goods, and parted them to all men, as every man had need. And they, **continuing daily with one accord in the temple, and breaking bread from house to house, did eat their meat with gladness and singleness of heart**, Praising God, and having favor with all the people. And the Lord added to the church daily such as should be saved" (Acts 2:42-47). "And when they had prayed, the place was shaken where they were assembled together; and they were all filled with the Holy Ghost, and they spake the word of God with boldness. **And the multitude of them that believed were of one heart and of one soul; neither said any of them that ought of the things which he possessed was his own; but they had all things common**" (Acts 4:31-32).

Dear saint, do you see it? When it comes to New Testament power, the "fellowship connection" is incontrovertible. Make no mistake — loving Christian fellowship and spiritual power are inherently linked! In John 13 and 17, even our evangelistic witness and testimony are closely tied to loving fellowship. Given the overwhelming importance of this principle, we can only wonder, *"How could we possibly have missed it?"* And yet for the past fifty years, loving unity has definitely been more a side issue than a central emphasis. In fact, for both churches and denominations, it often seemsthe ends justify the most godless of relational means. No amount of supposed evangelistic fervor can excuse attitudes of prideful arrogance or slanderous unloving behavior toward others.

Considering the current level of church and denominational conflict, is it really any surprise that baptisms are so stagnant? Is it any wonder the world now looks at our message with higher levels of suspicion? One thing is clear — programs apart from unity are bound to lack full New Testament power! No wonder churches have gone through one study and program after another yet not seen true revival. Until we address relationships *biblically* and *thoroughly*, we are doomed to keep hitting the wall of low baptisms, spiritual apathy and high church dropout. To the praise of God's grace, more and more saints are weary of fighting and hungry for peace.

## Tired of the Tension — Hungry for Unity!

Even in today's flood of disunity, we see growing signs of hope. More and more believers are tired of all the fighting and hungry for God's solution. Increasingly they are asking, "*Why* is there such tension and how can we find peace?" While there are many causes, certainly one is a lack of strong emphases, clear preaching and Scripture-filled resources on this vital subject. Though there are thousands of sermons, books and strategies on evangelism, discipleship and nearly every other subject, serious focus on unity has seriously lagged behind. Unfortunately, the resources that do address unity often do so more from a humanistic psychological standpoint than the Word of God.

While the New Testament frequently addresses relational unity, modern congregations have been largely silent. The tragic result is thousands of churches and families paralyzed by tension and disunity. No wonder we are seeing low baptisms, exhausted pastors and a rash of church splits! Yet when we address relationships biblically, God brings glorious change in seemingly hopeless places!

Make no mistake — God's Word gives enormous hope for even the most battle-torn church and family. No doubt, some may wonder if their churches could ever see loving unity and revival. Some readers may so struggle with personal weariness, anger or bitterness they can hardly imagine a flood of love and power. Dear believer, please believe God *will* help you overcome even your severest relationship barriers. **Do not lose hope for your family or church!**

It is glorious to realize great revivals have often come to the most unlikely people and places. Thank God, His grace *is* greater than our greatest weakness! In fact, our Lord delights to show Himself strong in our greatest points of weakness. No matter how challenging your situation, it is not too hard for God. From long personal experience of serious illness and inheriting a pastorate in a grave, long-term battle, I assure you God can bring loving unity and revival *anywhere*!

## Victory in a "Chernobyl" Church Situation!

When I went to my first pastorate (where I served seventeen years) it was literally called the "Chernobyl" of the church world. Obviously, that's not a good sign and was top story television news for five years. Just before I accepted the call, the church was attacked in a massive scandal that cost nearly three million dollars and was front page news for five years. Furthermore, the church was severely divided and located in the worst gang-infested area of a major city. Yet with God, *nothing* is impossible! Though the biblical principles we fully describe in this book, God brought incredible revival, healing and evangelism. He ultimately gave this seemingly hopeless church a powerful multi-state radio program and a publishing ministry that touched people in many nations!

Whether you are in a strong church (that hasn't quite moved into revival) or a desperately divided congregation, God can help you recognize and remove your barriers to sweeping revival. And while it will certainly take prayer and repentance, the results will be worth it a million times over. Most of all, He receives glory and His kingdom expands through your church!

Thank God, more and more believers are saddened that their divisions have so profaned the name of Jesus. Increasingly, they are saying *"We are hungry for a mighty revival of loving fellowship and oneness!" Releasing the Revival Flood* is dedicated to removing the barriers and restoring deep intimacy with God. In this book, you will learn to move from "general confession" to the specific "biblical repentance" that brings healing. But more than being a book you merely *read*, this tool is an experiential journey of surrender to God Himself. In Section Two, we will pray through the twenty-four major patterns by which Satan divides God's people. Yet, in every step of the journey, God's grace will prove your constant companion. God's grace is sufficient for every need! (2 Corinthians 12:9; Philippians 4:13,19)

## God's Penetrating Insights — The Pruning that Heals
### (John 15:1-3)

Dear reader, as you journey through these pages, there may be times God speaks so specifically you will think someone has been spying on you or your church! Frankly, I have been astounded at the penetrating nature of some revelations God has surfaced in this study. With incisive clarity, the Scriptures unveil the devil's dark devices for dividing believers. My friend, when God lays bare the deepest secrets of your heart, you can know it is the work of His Spirit (1 Corinthians 14:15). Like a skillful surgeon, God prunes Christ's Church for His glorious name and eternal kingdom purpose (John 15:2).

Let me further state that no specific examples in this tool came from any particular church or people. I drew from hundreds of churches and mostly from God's Word. As I researched and prayed, I asked God the following simple question, *"Lord what is most breaking your heart and preventing revival in today's churches?"* I must confess I was somewhat surprised where that prayer would ultimately lead. In fact, I really did not set out to write this particular book. Yet God soon made it clear, the patterns in this book are indeed among the most serious (and largely unaddressed) hindrances to a modern revival flood. Today's rampant patterns of anger and disunity demonstrate an astounding lack of fear and reverence for the name of God. It is urgent that we now see these patterns through God's eyes.

## Hope for Every Believer and Church!

As I wrote this book, there were times God's piercing revelation become so real, it was almost frightening. In some sections, God's direction and presence seemed overwhelming. Without question, our Lord is deadly serious about addressing the relational patterns now dividing so many believers. But praise be unto God — even the worst situations can be reversed!

For every step of this journey, remember God's incredible grace and love. While no believer or church is anywhere near perfect, you *can* identify your main barriers and discover glorious new life. It is my fervent prayer that no reader settles for anything less than God's awesome manifest presence.

Above all, let us never forget, revival is not an *it* but rather a *He*. Revival is Jesus Christ Himself being free to manifest His awesome glory and power through His people! Dear saints, let us at last return to the kingdom reality that "loving God means loving each other." Before we can fully love God and shake a world, we must reject today's culture of division and learn again to fervently love one another. May God's name be hallowed and His kingdom advanced through His people!

Toward the Next Great Awakening

Your Brother and Friend,

# Section One
# Loving God Means
# Loving Each Other

## Vital Foundations for Glorifying God
## and Seeking His Kingdom
### (John 17:1-26)

## Introduction

Have you ever experienced the power of a mighty flooding river? Even if you have not, you have surely witnessed gripping news coverage of massive floods or tsunamis. When such flooding occurs, all normal activities cease and lives change forever. In the realm of nature, we all know the catastrophic life-altering effects of such events. But now I ask you to consider the possibility of an entirely different kind of flood. A flood that would bring miraculous and wonderful changes to your life, family, church and nation. Consider an event so huge that everything about your relationships and world change forever.

Please know that I am referring to something incredibly real and entirely possible. I am speaking of a sweeping revival flood of the manifest presence of God Himself (Isaiah 44:3; Acts 2:1-2). My friend, you can experience this miraculous flood of love, power and unity! To every reader let me stress the vital importance of prayerfully reading this foundational section. Though it has some length, take your time and carefully read Section One. In these pages, we fully deal with the biblical *why* and *how* of meeting God through this journey. If you grasp these simple foundations, God can totally revolutionize your life and church. But best of all, we learn to hallow His name and spread His glorious kingdom!

## A Flood of God's Presence is Truly Possible!

It is vital to understand that sweeping revival floods have happened many times and can surely happen again! Consider God's incredible imagery describing mighty outpourings of His Spirit. In Isaiah 44:3, God refers to sending forth His Spirit like "floods of water on dry ground and upon the thirsty." Jesus described His Spirit as "*rivers of living water flowing from our hearts*" (John 7:38). The unique Greek work (*patamos*) used here for rivers, implies a continual gushing torrent or flood of God's Spirit!

In Acts 2:2, God's manifest presence was the "sudden sound of a rushing, mighty wind and a fire that filled the disciples." Even our English word for "dynamite" comes from the Greek word "*dunamis*" which Jesus used to describe the mighty power to flow through His followers (Acts 1:8).

Dear reader, God wants you to believe He is ready and able to flood your life with His holy presence. Though God's mighty flood may not come overnight, it *will come* if you are willing to let Him remove your barriers! In fact, some of the most incredible transformations come to the most battered people and troubled churches. So how about it friend? Are you thirsty for a flood of God? One thing is certain — *no* repentant person or church is too far gone for God's mighty touch!

## Growing Signs of Hope

As I write these words, my heart fills with inexpressible excitement. At last, there are growing signs God is up to something not seen since the last Great Awakening. All across the land, we see evidence of growing spiritual hunger, increasing prayer and at last deepening repentance. While admittedly, this rising tide is only a very small percentage, it is growing!

We can take great hope in the fact God sends revival floods through the small percentage, *not* the lukewarm majority. And even if sweeping revival does not come to the whole nation, it can certainly come to your family and church! No matter how long you may have struggled, we serve the all-powerful, merciful God Who finishes what He starts (Philippians 1:6). Take heart dear reader, God is now calling us to a whole new level of closeness. We can learn to hallow and exalt God's name as never before!

Yet you may well be asking, "Where are these signs of a potential revival flood?" After all, dark clouds of moral collapse and spiritual decay abound on every hand. But remember a most encouraging truth — *revivals usually explode in times of darkness and trial, not comfort and ease.* Floods come to *dry* ground and great lights in times of *deepest darkness.* On that score one thing is obvious, it is getting gloriously dark! In fact, we are already under growing levels of judgment.

I must stress there are indeed signs God may yet have to send greater judgments to fully turn us to Himself. Let us remember the words of 1 Peter 4:17, "Judgment begins at the house of God." But even if God sends far greater chastisements, His ultimate desire is redemption and restoration for His own. God will likely do whatever it takes to hear the burdened prayers of millions He has now called to prayer. But even if it must begin with judgment, a God-glorifying revival is worth whatever breakings are required to see it!

## Learning to Seek the "Reviver" — Not Just Revival Glorifying His Name — Not Ours!

Without question, seeking a revival flood should be the burning passion of every saved person. Yet we must never lose sight of a one great truth. *The primary goal is **not** just seeking a revival flood, it is seeking the glory and will of the **Reviver Himself**.* At its heart, a true revival is simply a far greater love, deeper surrender and fuller closeness with God Himself! And friend, when you truly experience God, you experience life itself.

No amount of money, fame, success or blessing begins to compare with simply knowing God in tremendous depth and power. "Now this is eternal life: that they may know you, the only true God, and Jesus Christ, whom you have sent" (John 17:3). "The thief comes only to steal and to kill and to destroy: I have come that they may have life, and have it to the full" (John 10:10).

## So What Would True Revival Look Like?

Since our generation has seen no great revival, we might well ask, "What would a flood of God's Presence really look like?" Historic descriptions are absolutely mind-boggling. If America were to see another Great Awakening, between *twenty and thirty million* new converts would explode into churches within three to five years! Based on historic patterns, a church of one hundred in attendance would baptize between fifty and one hundred persons in a single year. A church of a thousand, would likely baptize between five hundred and a thousand. Best of all, most of these converts would still be present five years later (which is a huge switch from today's appalling dropout patterns!)

In true revival, even divided churches in tough surroundings would see miraculous growth and unity! The modern scourge of bickering would turn into floods of fellowship and love. Burned out, defeated leaders would receive glorious healing and renewal. Most of all, God's kingdom would expand rapidly with His name receiving great glory! In Great Awakenings, God is glorified, His Church cleansed and Christ's kingdom advances in mighty power.

## True Revival Means God-Glorifying Relationships
### (Acts 1:14; 2:1; 2:42-47; 4:31-32)

A flood of God's presence not only radically changes churches, but society as well. Ratios of crime and immorality immediately plummet. Patterns of serious family breakup improve dramatically. By the millions, broken lives and relationships see glorious healing. Social improvements and missions explode many-fold. In a great flood of revival, evangelism and global harvests explode through the roof! Best of all, God's name receives great glory.

Dear reader if all this sounds like a fairytale, I assure you it is not! These descriptions and percentages are exactly what God has done many times in history. Frankly, it may sound impossible to us because America has not witnessed such revival since the mid-1800's. Yet there is good news. Our God has not changed and He *can* do it again! (Hebrews 13:8) In fact, several places in the world are seeing mighty moves of God right now. Just because we have not yet seen a flood, does not mean we will not.

Since we know God *can* send revival the question is, "Why hasn't He?" The answer is three fold. *First*, most believers and churches have not met the conditions in prayer and repentance. *Second*, many are seeking the "blessings" of revival rather than the glory and hallowing of God's name. *Third*, relational barriers of anger and bickering are seriously blocking the Holy Spirit. But thank God, there *is* an answer and relational barriers *can* be addressed by renewed prayer and obedience. God then reveals Himself in phenomenal power!

## Revival Means an Explosion of Intimacy and Power with God

We now turn our attention to the greatest of all revival blessings — *an incredible closeness with God Himself!* For believers who often feel distant and find it hard to hear God's voice, His voice often becomes clearer than those of spouses and best friends! For those who struggle with areas of spiritual bondage or defeat, God's power begins to flow like a river (John 7:38). Impossible mountains begin to move and long awaited answers at last arrive. Churches and ministers long dry and weary suddenly burst forth with new life. God's name is exalted and His kingdom explodes forward by evangelistic harvest!

While a revival flood certainly does not remove all suffering, God's grace becomes so real we tend not to care. In fact, true revival often brings some level of persecution from those who oppose God. Yet truly revived believers are so full of God they actually *rejoice* in their persecutions and trials! (2 Corinthians 12:9; James 1:1-3)

Dear saint, if you are among the millions struggling to achieve a strong prayer life or intimacy with God, *please take hope*. Spiritual power is not out of reach and God definitely desires to help you remove your barriers. But even beyond personal blessings and closeness with God, there is another purpose greater than all other. That purpose is pleasing God and glorifying His name! Indeed, true revival is all about *Him*, not us.

## Increased Love and Unity Exalts God's Name!
### (John 17:1-26)

The greatest reason for seeking a revival flood involves a primary purpose of our existence. And what is that primary purpose? Put simply, it is to know, love and glorify God through seeking His kingdom and exalting His name. And without question, *loving one another* is a vital part of loving God and seeking His kingdom!

Believers, when we learn to seek first His kingdom and His righteousness, we find life itself! "But seek you first His kingdom and His righteousness, and all these things will be given to you" (Matthew 6:33). "Whoever loses his life for Me and for the gospel will save it" (Mark 8:35). Indeed life is all about knowing Him, surrendering to Jesus and walking humbly with our God (John 17:3). Jesus pulled it all together in His two Great Commandments. "Love the Lord your God with all your heart and with all your soul and with all your mind. This is the first and greatest commandment. And the second is like it — Love your neighbor as yourself" (Matthew 22:37-39).

The Bible leaves no doubt that loving God means loving each other (Matthew 22:37-38; John 13:34-35; 17:21). Today believers must re-discover a vital fact — *the two Great Commandments are inseparably linked!* In other words, no one can truly love God yet be unkind or bitter toward fellow Christians. In Matthew 5:23 and

6:14-15, Jesus made clear that anger and disunity among believers seriously blocks our relationships with Him. In fact, the entire chapter of John 17 closely ties God's glory and our witness to dynamic oneness among saints.

In terms of love and fellowship, today's Church is in a major crisis. Never has our nation seen such devastating disintegration of church and family relationships. In fact, what we have witnessed in family structure is no longer a decline, it is an unmitigated *collapse!* As much or more than any other factors, relational anger and unforgiveness are huge barriers to a modern day revival flood.

## Church and Family Conflict — "Preeminent" Barriers to Revival
### The Public Profaning of God's Name

In light of today's epidemic immorality and compromise, it may even sound strange to call disunity a "preeminent" revival hindrance. Yet surveys reveal divisive conflict and lack of love are even more prevalent than out-right immorality (at least in the church). According to Jesus, relationship sins are often even more spiritually offensive then some of the more outward sins of the flesh (Matthew 5:23; 6:14; John 13:34-35). Worse yet, they bring shame and dishonor to the holy name of God.

Dear saints, we must not miss the significance nearly *every* New Testament epistle contains strong commands for fervent love and unity among believers. Only the issue of salvation receives greater focus in New Testament writing. Without question, God is extremely serious about strong love and unity among Christians! This issue is absolutely central to God's kingdom purpose and to exalting His name.

Yet for all the biblical importance of loving unity, congregations hear astoundingly little detailed teaching on this subject. Unfortunately, teaching that does occur is often general and vague. Detailed descriptions like those in this resource are badly neglected. Yet this is exactly the kind of specific teaching required for deep conviction and healing in damaged relationships! Throughout revival history, restored relationships are significant in sweeping revivals. This tool is designed to heal divisions and recapture the long missing element of loving relationships

## Church Conflict and Disunity
### The Devil's Favorite Game — The Church's Great Shame

There is something unspeakably ugly about disunity, fighting and tension in churches. Not only do these patterns utterly quench God's Spirit, they badly damage our witness and power in evangelism! (John 13:34-35) Anger and disunity break the heart of the Savior who literally died to make us one. Believers, when we cannot get along in reasonable peace, we shame Christ's name and irreparably damage lives. While Jesus said the world would be *drawn* to Him by believers' love, they are instead being *repulsed* by their anger and bickering! (John 17:21-23) No wonder the enemy devotes so much effort to inflaming bitter battles between believers!

In today's Church, there is a growing scenario as predictable as clockwork. Throughout twenty years of pastoring, conferences, and research, I could not count the times I have heard the following anguished statement: "*Just when our church was really showing progress, we had an explosion of angry blowups and divisions — it seemed to come out of nowhere.*"

Should it really be any surprise that relationship eruptions often occur just when a church is starting to see real progress? Such timing is certainly no coincidence as our enemy constantly seeks to disrupt God's activity! And sadly enough, the devil knows just who he can count on to fuel church dissension. In most churches, the enemy always seems to have at least some who are ready to be his instruments of anger or controversy. (The instigators usually do not even realize who is guiding their speech.)

In order to hinder or stop churches, the devil continually seeks to exploit issues and divide believers (1 Peter 5:8). It is so predictable we should be prepared and ready with biblical tools for both prevention and correction. Paul confirmed this sentiment when he wrote that we should not be "ignorant of Satan's *devices* lest he gain the advantage" (2 Corinthians 2:11, KJV). *Releasing the Revival Flood* is designed to fully uncover the devil's "relational devices" in believers and churches. In this tool, God helps readers clearly recognize the devil's tactics.

## Uncovering the Relationship "Devices" of the Enemy
### We Wrestle Not Against Flesh and Blood
### (Ephesians 6:10-18)

As we might expect, Satan works best under a cover of darkness (Ephesians 6:10). Current studies show the very same patterns are tragically common in thousands of congregations. Again and again, the same exact barriers are preventing revival in untold numbers of churches. While names and faces are different, the destructive patterns vary little from church to church. Though these patterns are clearly wrong, such issues are often difficult to fully address in sermons or conflict resolution programs. If believers do not deal with relational issues biblically and thoroughly, they quickly escalate into bitter personal battles.

This tool is specifically designed to address problems through Scripture and sound spiritual principles. It is vital to realize damaged relational patterns are usually much more "spiritual battles" and "heart issues" than mere personality or psychological conflicts. Because the root battle is spiritual, most relationship patterns will not be solved by human resolution techniques alone. While such techniques are certainly helpful, they *must* be combined with the relational principles from Scripture. The patterns in this book are the heart of effective spiritual warfare. Let us ever remember the true source of our battles — "we wrestle not against flesh and blood" (Ephesians 6:12).

Even though we all know evil relational patterns are present, they are often much like the *"elephant in the room"* no one discusses directly or effectively. Make no mistake — until God's people are fully discipled and enlightened on the devil's relational devices, revival will remain an impossible dream for most churches and families. No matter how many evangelism, discipleship or prayer efforts we embrace, the Holy Spirit will remain significantly quenched by unresolved anger and bickering. Unless we understand and address the devil's wiles scripturally, we will remain dangerously vulnerable to his relational tactics.

## Letting God's Truth Set You Free
### (John 8:32)

In this book, God will help congregations clearly discern their unique relationship barriers to revival. Many saints are caught in harmful patterns without knowing God's truth on the particular practices. In John 8:32, Jesus tells of the vital importance of knowing His truth. "You will know the truth, and **the truth will set you free**" (John 8:32). One thing is certain — until believers and churches recognize God's truth about Satan's divisive relationship tactics, the devastating patterns will surely continue. This book shines God's Word of truth into the darkest corners of modern relational barriers.

In the coming pages, we will experience a Spirit-guided journey of cleansing and transformation. As God reveals several areas needing change, let us remember that His grace is sufficient for every change! Thank God there is hope for even the most troubled church or weakest Christian. How good to know we are "accepted" and "under grace" (even in our struggles.) It is truly glorious to know that we are "accepted in the Beloved" though our knees may be skinned from battles.

Because this tool deals with some deep long-standing issues, it is very important for believers to grasp several key truths. Readers should also be aware this book is not "casual reading." As countless believers and churches read through this study, some will sense they have struggles in almost every area. For this reason, every reader should remember two glorious truths.

First, God's grace is greater than all our weaknesses. Second, He still works in very imperfect people and churches (which includes us all.) No reader should become discouraged or overwhelmed if they see several areas that need God's touch. Remember, our Lord does not require perfection, just honest steps to start addressing the issues He reveals. Before you begin this journey, reflect on the following foundational truths. Embracing these steps will make this a life-changing encounter with God Himself!

## Vital Steps for Encountering God Through This Journey
### How to Let God Change Your Life

*(1) Embrace relationship transformation for the exalting of God's name and furtherance of His kingdom, not just to get blessings or solve problems.* Dear saints, we must ever remember that our primary purposes are loving God, glorifying His name and furthering His kingdom (Matthew 6:33; 22:37-39). In everything we do, the central motive is the hallowing of God's name and furtherance of His kingdom. We must always ask the *critical why* of what we are what we do. Seeking relationship transformation is no exception!

So why should we focus on biblical fellowship and loving unity among believers? We do it to love God, exalt His name and further Christ's kingdom! We do *not* seek unity mostly just to solve our problems or find temporal success. Though personal blessing and comfort is certainly *part* of our motive, it should not be our preeminent focus. The heart of our motive is to glorify God's name and kingdom. Without question, a huge part of fearing, loving and glorifying God is loving each other (John 13:34-35; 17:21)! As believers, we must be preeminently concerned with our testimony of God's glory before a lost and dying world. While believers' loving unity greatly glorifies God, angry bickering tragically profanes His name and hinders evangelism.

*(2)* *Let this journey point you straight to Jesus' grace and forgiveness, not to condemnation or discouragement.* (Romans 8:1; 1 John 1:9) As you read through the potential revival barriers, God may bring awareness and conviction of several sins previously unrealized. Please understand that God is convicting to bless and transform your life, not to hurt, condemn or discourage. Above all, do not let the devil turn God's conviction into condemnation or despair. Though we all have many areas needing work, God still views us as *"righteous through Jesus' blood."* My friend, as you begin to confess and forsake your sins, God will bless in ways you cannot even imagine. Though it likely will not happen overnight, stay with the process and never run from God's conviction. God loves you and seeks only your good and the glory of His name.

*(3)* *As God reveals spiritual barriers, immediately confess all sin and embrace concrete steps of repentance.* (Proverbs 28:13) It is vitally important both to *confess* and *forsake* the sins! It is crucial not only to "put off" sin but to "put on" Christ by faith (Colossians 3:8-10). It is vital to resist the fleshly tendency to become angry or defensive when God reveals your areas of need. Do not justify your sin by blaming others. Above all, do not try to excuse, minimize or rationalize your failures. It is also important to remember that God's specific conviction raises your accountability to repent many-fold. It is essential not to put God off or only partially repent. God warns that such blatant abuse of His grace eventually brings chastisement (Hebrews 10:26-31).

If you or your church has offended someone, get wise council and by all means ask forgiveness in the spirit of Matthew 5:23.

Conversely, if there are people you have not truly forgiven "from the heart," you must admit it and truly forgive them now! (Mark 11:25) And remember, forgiveness is a choice by God's grace, not some rosy feeling. Dear reader, *Releasing the Revival Flood* is not so much a book of lessons to be "studied" as Scriptures to be "obeyed." By so doing, you will experience phenomenal closeness and power with God.

(4) *As God reveals areas of needed change, by faith appropriate Christ's life as your victory.* (Romans 6:6, 14; Galatians 2:20; Colossians 2:6) Do not try to gain victory in your own strength or by legalistic efforts! Just as we are saved and declared righteous by faith, we also daily grow and change by faith. From the start to the finish of our walk as His children, God accepts us in the righteousness of His Son (Ephesians 1:6). Above all remember, you *do* have the ability to repent and change by the Christ Who lives within you. Never say you can't change when God says you can (Philippians 4:13)!

With each relationship pattern in this book, you will notice it ends with "*Putting On Christ — Putting Off the Flesh.*" It does so for a very important reason. Our victory comes from learning to let Christ live through us by faith, not our trying to live for Him by human effort. In this journey we do not just turn from sin, we turn *to* Christ. We don't just look at what is wrong — we learn to look at Jesus, "the author and finisher of our faith." Our purpose is not to wallow in sin and defeat but to move straight to victory and change. The prayers at the end of each pattern are designed to help us do just that!

(5) *Use this tool to bring consistent focus to loving unity as a "lifestyle," not a one-time study course we do and lay aside.* (1 Peter 4:8) The issues in this resource are not areas we read once and lay aside. At one reading God may speak in certain areas while later He reveals something totally different. This biblical journey is designed for *repeated use* as God's Spirit guides. Because Satan

13

so constantly seeks to damage relationships, churches should probably embrace a thorough relational checkup at least every two to three years. Since loving relational oneness is so crucial to God's kingdom purpose, we must devote continual focus to Christian fellowship.

*An especially powerful strategy is to print excerpts from various sections of this book in weekly church bulletins, newsletters or prayer sheets.* In this manner, a steady flow of strong relationship focus is kept before church members. A related pattern is to regularly observe a brief "relationship focus" in worship services or mid-week prayer meetings. The pastor takes 3-5 minutes, reads an appropriate section and leads the congregation in prayer for loving unity in the church and its families.

Whatever method we use, it is *vital* to consistently address relationship unity in the Body! The issue of love and unity is so urgent that it definitely warrants this type of consistent focus. If churches continue to neglect this crucial issue, God's Spirit will surely remain quenched and evangelism hindered. Believers, we simply cannot leave relational issues to happenstance.

*(6) Periodically use this book as a discipleship tool for "preventing" spiritual barriers as well as "addressing" problems that already exist. It is especially recommended as required reading for all deacons, elders, teachers and church committee heads!* (Psalms 119:11; 2 Corinthians 10:3-5) In essence, this resource is a practical tool for discipling believers in healthy church relationships. Studies show very few believers (or pastors and leaders) have had clear instruction in these specific issues. In a fair number of cases, believers honestly do not realize some of these patterns are as wrong as the Scriptures indicate. Perhaps the strongest use of this tool is making believers keenly aware of the relational dynamics that operate in our midst. Again, it is *especially critical* that every deacon, elder, teacher or committee leader fully understand these patterns.

When the penetrating light of God's truth shines into dark patterns, darkness loses its power. For this reason, it is crucial that we frequently teach the specific patterns that most hinder revival. If we regularly shine God's truth on fleshly patterns, God's Spirit will do the rest! Yet if we mostly avoid these issues, we open wide the door for Satanic attack. A tool like this is especially crucial for ongoing discipleship as well as prevention of relational battles.

(7) *Use this tool as a powerful Bible-based weapon for effective spiritual warfare. Because relational battles are mostly "spiritual," they must be fought with spiritual weapons!* (Ephesians 6:1-13; 2 Corinthians 10:3-5; James 4:7-8) Today a major problem is that many spiritual warfare tools deal mostly with principles and neglect to unmask the devil's specific, detailed tactics. While it is certainly essential to understand our theological foundations of victory, it is the devil's daily tactics that are destroying so many believers and churches. Simply knowing principles will not suffice. We must also be fully aware of his specific devices.

It is also true that much so-called Christian "conflict resolution" material focuses far more on inter-personal dynamics, personalities or psychological techniques than Bible-based spiritual principles. While understanding psychology and intra-personal techniques is certainly helpful, these are *not* the central source of most church conflict. Because the warfare is *spiritual*, so must be our training and weapons (2 Corinthians 10:3-5).

It is most disturbing that students can still go all the way through seminary and receive little detailed teaching about the dynamics now eating churches and ministers alive. Unfortunately, the patterns in this resource are exactly where many churches really live. For this reason, it is vital that we begin to teach the spiritual dynamics of relationship wars in churches! After all, it is the enemy we do not see that usually gets us. Use this tool as a practical, Bible-based strategy for helping our members fully recognize and reject the devil's specific devices in the churches and family relationships.

(8) *Understand this book is designed equally for spiritual cleansing in pastors, church leaders and laypeople.* (Romans 2:11; 14:10-13) While some of the barriers discussed rest more on the shoulders of leaders, others relate more to laypeople. This tool is not designed to target any group more than the other. It is also true that in any one of these issues, we as pastors and denominational leaders can be just as ensnared as laypeople. Every person should pray through this tool with your eyes on what God is saying to *you*, not what you think He might be saying to someone else!

*Above all, no one should use this tool as a weapon to beat someone else over the head.* Pastors, we must avoid addressing any of these issues with an angry, condemning spirit. As leaders and church members alike pray through this material, we must trust God to do His work in leaders as much as lay people. Thank God, if we thoroughly expose churches to God's Word about relational barriers, the Holy Spirit will do the rest. Indeed, it is the "truth" that sets us free (John 8:32).

(9) *Utilize this resource to "refocus" churches on kingdom priorities as well as "removing" their spiritual barriers.* (Matthew 6:33; 21:13; 28:16-18) In many ways, this tool is about a wide range of issues addressing *general church health.* Though it is mostly about relationships, the book also has key elements of adjusting church strategies. Major adjustments of focus are often necessary for God to send revival. Without question, a huge hindrance to revival is a neglect of the primary kingdom patterns by which God works. Two prime examples are abandoning prayer meetings and being more self-focused than kingdom-focused in strategic church visions. Our purpose is not only allowing God to *remove* patterns of sinful barriers but to *add* patterns of

kingdom focus. Because of this focus, a few points deal more with leadership and those who influence strategic vision. Readers should prepare to make whatever adjustments God reveals for priorities and vision.

*(10) Do not let the enemy convince you that your church is so problem ridden it is hopeless.* (Romans 8:1; Ephesians 2:8-10) Without question, one of the most encouraging books in the all the Bible is Paul's letters to the Corinthians. These epistles are particularly encouraging because the Corinthian Church had virtually every possible relationship problem. Yet God still loved and used them! As you read through this tool, God may reveal several areas for growth and change. In fact, some who read these pages will be troubled to see virtually every fleshly pattern at work in their midst. You may even be tempted to throw up your hands and run away. My friend, do not panic! God's grace is incredibly powerful and even when filled with problems, we are still His Church. Keep your eyes on God and what He *is* doing rather than obbessing on all that is wrong.

Be encouraged that our God is a wise and merciful Father who blesses by grace, not because we deserve it (which none of us do). Each reader should work on the areas God reveals and trust His grace to cover the rest. One thing is certain — even the most mature among us will always be a "work in progress." While we must take seriously the things God reveals, we should not fall victim to discouragement.

*(11) Understand that all conflict is not bad and is in fact a fairly normal part of growing together as Christians.* (1 Corinthians 12-14; Colossians 3:8-17) It is certainly true that no two people agree or have the same tastes in all things. Even husbands and wives have real differences yet they still share incredible unity. Indeed, a most vital part of Christian growth is for church members to commit to work through the ways we disagree.

Believers, we can definitely learn to disagree without becoming angry, condemning or disrespectful.

It is further true that mature saints can learn to disagree on many non-essentials without compromising essentials. No reader should think that revival requires church members to continually sit around and sing "kumbaya." Again, the grace of God is a wonderful thing! Thank God, He still works in our midst though we all have many areas needing growth.

*(12) Use this tool as a "scriptural mirror" or "plumb line" to help provide a clear vision of who we are to be as the unified Body of Christ.* (Amos 7:7-8; James 1:23-24) Above all, this tool is saturated with Scripture. As such it is designed to hold up the biblical mirror of the relationship characteristics of revived, New Testament churches. We examine both the positive patterns to *embrace* and the sinful patterns to *renounce*. The book also helps us clearly see the specific relational patterns hindering the revival flood. To illustrate the point, consider the physical analogy of looking in a mirror. If we never looked in a mirror, something about our appearance could be badly out of place yet we would never know it. Furthermore, if we looked in a mirror that was oily or distorted, our self image would be vague and unreliable.

*Releasing the Revival Flood* provides a clear mirror of specific patterns now hindering the flood of God's Spirit. While clear sight can at first be painful, the "godly sorrow" and "specific conviction" are necessary for revival floods. But saints, let us never fear our loving Father. He prunes for good and wounds only to heal (John 15:2). Be prepared to let God fully remove your barriers and release the flood of His Presence.

*(13) Along with other new member materials, consider giving this tool to all adults who join your church.* (Psalms 119:11; John 8:32) When someone joins, there is an excellent opportunity to stress the importance your church places on New Testament

unity. While you would certainly not suggest your church is anywhere near perfect, you would at least tell them of your church's serious commitment to love and unity.

Today we must face the fact that a significant percentage of people leave churches for precisely the reasons outlined in this book. They either actively caused some of these conditions or in many cases are seeking to escape those caused by others. Either way, the truths in this book will be important for them to read. Though you might not actually require its reading, you should at least strongly suggest it. Many churches will ask new members to read the entire book and turn in a brief synopsis of their impressions. *(This insures they actually read it.)* The time of their joining is an excellent time to address such issues before there is any personal history with the individuals. If churches ask all new members to read the material, no one is being singled out for special attention.

When it comes to church conflict, remember two axioms. (a) "It is much easier to address disunity and anger patterns *before* you are in the middle of a battle." (Yet God can still work in the middle of World War III!) (b) "When it comes to angry church conflict, "an ounce of *prevention* is worth a pound of *cure!*" Insisting that new members read this book is a very practical way to prevent or minimize problems before they can occur.

*(14) Be aware that major revival floods require the strong specific conviction that brings godly sorrow and thorough repentance.* (Proverbs 28:13; 2 Corinthians 6:14-7:1; Hebrews 12:14) Today's Church has a tendency to try and avoid deep conviction. Furthermore, when sin is addressed at all, it is often in general and vague terms. That pattern is especially true when it comes to relationship sins of anger and disunity. For this reason, believers seldom experience either the depth or specific type of conviction that brings real change. If we are to have any chance

of seeing a sweeping revival flood, there must be a return to the type of clear, detailed descriptions contained in this book.

Dear leaders, let us not be afraid to share spiritual meat with today's saints! For far too long most churches have heard only milk regarding the crucial subjects of this book. We must not fear deep Holy Spirit produced conviction because this alone leads to true repentance, healing and joy (2 Corinthians 7:10). In truth, a return to "godly sorrow" over specific sin is our only hope of a modern day revival flood. Confession that is general never brings the sweeping flood of God's presence.

*(15) We must be very careful not to harshly judge or devalue those who consistently perpetuate some of the relational conflicts in this tool.* (Galatians 6:1-4; Ephesians 4:29-32; 1 Peter 4:8) In the pages of this book, God will clearly unmask the true evil of certain patterns in churches. Yet it is vital not to become angry or condescending toward those ensnared in these sins. This tool is designed to reveal sinful patterns so they can be confessed and *healed*, not so we can harshly condemn fellow believers. Remember dear saint, we do not wrestle against "flesh and blood." *Do not* let your rightful abhorrence for harmful sin patterns cause you any abhorrence toward the "persons." As always, we are to hate the sin but love the sinner.

*(16) Use this tool to help believers embrace unity as a central on-going priority, not some secondary issue.* (John 13:34-35; 17:20-24; Ephesians 4:29-32) Without question, loving unity among believers is *not* a periphery issue we just leave to chance. Unity is absolutely central to God's kingdom purpose. As Christians, we truly are an eternal family and we must learn to live in that reality. Indeed, the very heart of our existence is to live in "*community* and *oneness*." God saved us to be one with Him and one with each other in love (John 17). Because love and unity are so crucial to God's purpose, anger and disunity profoundly grieves God's Spirit.

*(17) Use this resource to teach the appropriate fear of God and aware-
ness of His chastisement upon serious, persistent sin (especially
blatant sins of anger, disunity and unkindness.)* (Ecclesiastes
12:13-14; 1 Corinthians 5:11; 11:28-34) A desperate need in
today's Church is to return believers to a biblical fear and reverence for holy God. In overwhelming numbers of churches,
believers simply are not taught a biblical view of God. He is
typically portrayed as all-loving and forgiving with no judgments upon persistent, willful sin.

As a result of today's casual view of God and sin, many saints
routinely gossip and slander other believers with no thought
of consequences. Yet, the New Testament clearly warns of the
enormous danger for those who damage the purity and unity
of Christ's Church. In fact, in Corinth the primary element of
Lord's Supper abuse related to believer's disunity and selfish
mistreatment of one another. These believers had a blatant
disregard for the fellowship, love and unity of Christ's Church.
The direct result was *many* sicknesses and deaths among the
offending believers (1 Corinthians 11:30)! It is worth noting
these believers apparently had no idea their sicknesses and
deaths were a result of God's judgment. Paul had to tell them!
Since the Bible tells us "God doesn't change," we must assume
similar patterns are in effect today (Malachi 3:6; James 1:17).

According to Scripture, few sins put Christians at greater risk
of chastisement (or even removal) than persistent damage to the
bond of love and peace in Christ's Body. If any believer thinks
this statement is severe, let him or her read of the Corinthian
church, Ananias and Sapphira and the churches of Ephesus
and Laodicea (1 Corinthians 11:28-34; Acts 5:1-5; Revelation
2:1-3:15). There can be no question that God deals strongly
with blatant sin in the church. God will not forever tolerate
blatant damage to His Church or the public profaning of His
name. (Take a moment and read Appendix E.)

As leaders, we do our people a grave disservice if we fail to warn of the seriousness of harming the loving unity of Christ's Body. It is this author's opinion that many churches are teetering on the brink of serious judgment or "removal of their candlestick" (Revelation 2:4). *Releasing the Revival Flood* is prayerfully dedicated to help heal churches and deliver some from the very brink of destruction.

*(18) Use Releasing the Revival Flood to facilitate prayer groups targeting relationship healing and revival.* (Matthew 5:23-24; 6:15-17; James 5:16) While the book contains study questions after each pattern addressed, the most powerful effect will come from small group confession, prayer and repentance. In James 5:16, the process is stated concisely. *"Confess your trespasses to one another, and pray for one another, that you may be healed. The effective, fervent prayer of a righteous man avails much."* Church prayer groups can do just that!

A powerful option is to establish weekly *study/prayer groups* which meet to discuss that week's material and pray for one another in areas of needed growth or repentance. Such prayer groups are relatively easy to facilitate and the results are phenomenal! To facilitate the discussions and prayer, simply summarize the Scripture truths of that week's material and ask each group member to share what God revealed to his or her heart. **Appendix D** is provided as a clear guide for conducting prayer groups focused on revival and transformation.

Because *Releasing the Revival Flood* is Scripture-filled, such meetings quickly turn into confession and repentance. When each person shares, the group simply prays for that person's growth, healing and repentance. Toward the end of the session, the group prays for revival and evangelism in the whole church. This type of prayer releases enormous power for fellowship, relational healing and biblical repentance! The group leader then shares with the larger church body the cleansing and victory God has wrought. (Using discretion, this is done in the worship service.) Needless to say, this type of prayer and confession is essential to genuine biblical revival!

## Church — A Dress Rehearsal for Heaven!

Dear saints, we are going to be together forever and we must learn to act like it now. In other words, this life is a "dress rehearsal" for heaven! A huge part of Christian growth comes in the challenge of learning to function together in spite of many differing likes and dislikes. *Releasing the Revival Flood* is a tool to help us discover and correct key points of broken fellowship. Through these pages, we learn practical ways to grow together as one. Above all, we learn to treat loving unity as an absolute top priority, *not* some secondary side issue.

One thing is for sure — none of us are completely without sin when it comes to the patterns in this book. And even when we cannot help but notice serious patterns of error in some, we all should remember, "*There go I but by the grace of God.*" Believers, we must show love and patience to erring believers. Remember, we are never more like God than when we love those who do not love us. While there will surely be times we must squarely address serious sins of speech, we are to do so in love and humility. Through that spirit, God sends enormous healing and reconciliation. In the spirit of loving humility, He unleashes the flood of His Presence!

## God's Glorious Invitation to All

In James 4:8-10, God issues an awesome invitation to every reader. "*Come near to God and he will come near to you. Wash your hands, you sinners, and purify your hearts, you double-minded. Grieve, mourn and wail. Change your laughter to mourning and your joy to gloom. Humble yourselves before the Lord, and he will lift you up.*" God not only promises to "draw near," He tells us exactly how to approach Him. We come to Him by "cleansing our hands and purifying our hearts." My friend, that is exactly what will happen as you journey through this book. And because of God's wonderful grace, you already know the outcome. God is going to remove your barriers and release the flood of His Presence! As you embrace your journey with God, I have three final suggestions.

(1) *Each time you prepare to read a portion of this book, pause and ask God to speak to your heart.* Ask Him to help you avoid the fleshly reaction of anger or defensiveness when He convicts of a need for change. Obviously this book can do nothing without the mighty anointing and power of the Holy Spirit (Zechariah 4:6). If this study is being done churchwide, you should have special prayer meetings or prayer groups praying for God's power to change hearts. Obviously your faith is not in this book, it is in the power of God to bring powerful conviction and change.

When God convicts about areas of sin, we generally have one of two reactions. (a) People who are lost or backslidden typically react with anger, defensiveness or rationalizations to excuse their sins. (b) Those with hearts after God, become broken, contrite and repentant. They immediately experience glorious forgiveness, healing and blessing! The differing reactions of kings David and Saul are powerful biblical examples. Saul tried to *defend* his sin and was destroyed (1 Samuel 15:26). In utter brokenness, David fully *confessed* his sin and though there were tragic consequences, he was fully forgiven (2 Samuel 12:13-14). *Dear reader in terms of your response to conviction, please be a David, not a Saul!*

(2) *Let this journey help you revolutionize your own daily prayer life and power by learning to better abide in Christ.* Many precious saints are defeated and struggling because no one ever taught them how to daily abide in Christ by powerful prayer and cleansing! Obviously no one can walk in spiritual victory, power or love without the daily fullness of the Holy Spirit. And one thing is certain — no one can have fullness without strong daily prayer and cleansing.

Dear reader, I have great news for you. Once you understand the biblical pattern for abiding, anyone can walk in powerful daily prayer, cleansing and power! Even if you have never established any level of regular quiet time, all that can change right now. At some point in this journey, I encourage you to turn to page 240 and prayerfully work through Appendix C, **How to Experience Powerful Daily Prayer and Bible Reading.** You will be amazed how dynamic power and closeness with God is so possible for every believer.

*(3) If at any point in this journey you have the slightest doubt about your salvation, immediately pray through Appendix A — He will surely guide you to genuine peace!* Based on Scripture and strong statistical evidence, today's Church has disturbingly high numbers of lost members. According to the clear teaching of Jesus, lost church members are very common and most have no idea they are lost (Matthew 7:21-25). In the vast majority of cases, these dear people certainly did not mean to join the church without receiving the new birth. In fact, many were somewhat let down by their churches' thorough lack of biblical counseling or clear instruction.

If at any point in this journey you doubt your salvation, *do not* be ashamed to address it! After all, no one means to join the church without receiving Christ. Be assured that God wants to give you true salvation and the glorious confidence that you have it! Even now, if you know you have been struggling with doubt, go to Appendix A and seek God for the assurance He so longs to impart.

My friend, you do not have to live in doubt and defeat! God can make this journey a glorious turning point in your life. Let Him do it! So how about it? Are you ready to draw near to God? One thing is certain — He is certainly ready to draw near to you (James 4:8). Let this be the beginning of your own revival flood!

# Section Two

## Removing the Barriers — Releasing the Flood!
### Addressing Twenty-Four Most Common Hindrances

As a writer, I am ever more convinced only one opinion counts and it certainly isn't mine! There is surely nothing as powerful as God's Words straight from Scripture. For that reason, every part of the journey is drawn directly from Scripture. As we begin, it is vitally important to carefully pray through key selected Scriptures. The following Scriptures directly target the crucial subjects we now address. Please carefully and prayerfully read these direct words of God. Before you read the verses below, pause and ask God to speak to your heart.

## God's Powerful Commands for Fellowship and Unity
### Recognizing Christ's All-Important Command!

Proverbs 6:16 – "These six things doth the Lord hate: yea, seven are an **abomination** unto him: A proud look, a lying tongue, and hands that shed innocent blood, an heart that deviseth wicked imaginations, feet that be swift in running to mischief, a false witness that speaketh lies, **and he that soweth discord among brethren.**"

Matthew 5:23-24; 6:14-15 – "Therefore if thou bring they gift to the altar, and there rememberest that thy brother hath ought against thee: leave there thy gift before the altar, and go thy way; first be reconciled to thy brother, and then come and offer thy gift…For if you forgive men their trespasses, your heavenly Father will also forgive you: But if you forgive not men their trespasses, neither will your Father forgive your trespasses."

John 13:34-35; 17:20-22 - "A new commandment I give unto you, that you love one another; as I have loved you, that you also love one another. By this shall all men know that you are my disciples if you have love one to another… Neither pray I for these alone, but for them also which shall believe on me through their word; That they all may be one as thou, Father, art in me, and I in thee, that they also may be one in us; that the world may believe that thou hast sent me. And the glory which thou gavest me I have given them; that they may be one, even as we are one."

1 Corinthians 1:10; 3:1-3 - "Now I beseech you, brethren, by the name of our Lord Jesus Christ, that you all speak the same thing, and that there be no divisions among you; but that you be perfectly joined together in the same mind and in the same judgment... And I brethren, could not speak unto you as unto spiritual, but as unto carnal, even as unto babes in Christ. I have fed you with milk, and not with meat: for hitherto you were not able to bear it, neither yet now are you able. For you are yet carnal: for whereas there is among you envying, and strife, and divisions, are you not carnal, and walk as men?"

Ephesians 4:3 – "With all lowliness and meekness and longsuffering, forbearing one another in love; Endeavoring to keep the unity of the Spirit in the bond of peace."

Ephesians 4:29-32 – "Do not let any unwholesome talk come out of your mouths, but only what is helpful for building others up according to their needs, that it may benefit those who listen. And do not grieve the Holy Spirit of God, with whom you were sealed for the day of redemption. Get rid of all bitterness, rage and anger, brawling and slander, along with every form of malice. Be kind and compassionate to one another, forgiving each other, just as in Christ God forgave you."

Titus 3:10–11 – "A man that is a slanderer after the first and second admonition reject; knowing that he that is such is subverted, and sinneth, being condemned of himself."

James 4:11-12; 5:9 – "Speak not evil one of another, brethren. He that speaketh evil of his brother, and judgeth his brother, speaketh evil of the law, and judgeth the law: but if thou judge the law, thou art not a doer of the law, but a judge. There is one lawgiver, who is able to save and to destroy: who art thou that judgest another? …Grumble not one against another, brethren, lest you be condemned; behold, the judge standeth before the door."

1 Peter 4:8-9 – "And above all things have fervent love among yourselves: for love shall cover the multitude of sins. Use hospitality one to another without grudging."

1 John 3:10-15 – "In this the children of God are manifest, and the children of the devil: whosoever doeth not righteousness is not of God, neither he that loves not his brother. For this is the message that you heard from the beginning, that we should love one another… We know that we have passed from death unto life, because we love the brethren. He that loves not his brother abides in death. Whosoever hates his brother is a murderer: and you know that no murderer hath eternal life abiding in him."

1 John 4:7-8 – "Beloved, let us love one another: for love is of God; and every one that loveth is born of God, and knoweth God. He that loveth not knoweth not God; for God is love."

## The Biblical Commands of Loving Respect for Christian Leaders

Psalms 105:15 – "Touch not mine anointed, and do my prophets no harm."

1 Corinthians 1:10 – "I appeal to you, brothers, in the name of our Lord Jesus Christ, that all of you agree with one another so that their may be no divisions among you and that you may be perfectly united in mind and thought."

Ephesians 4:2-3 – "Be completely humble and gentle; be patient, bearing with one another in love. Endeavoring to keep the unity of the Spirit in the bond of peace."

1 Thessalonians 5:12 - 13 - "And we beseech you, brethren, recognize them which labor among you, and are over you in the Lord, and admonish you; and to esteem them very highly in love for their work's sake. And be at peace among yourselves."

1 Timothy 5:17 - "Let the elders that rule well be counted worthy of double honor, especially they who labor in the word and doctrine."

Hebrews 13:17 – "Obey them that have the rule over you, and submit yourselves: for they watch for your souls, as they that must give an account, that they may do it with joy, and not with grief; for that is unprofitable for you."

## Getting Ready for Relationship Miracles!

In the next section, we will carefully examine twenty-four of the most common revival hindrances that come from within congregations. While a few of the descriptive titles may seem a bit lighthearted, be assured God finds nothing humorous in these conditions. As you read each one, ask God to show whether you or your church has any of these significant patterns. Most of all, ask God whether you are in any way part of these devastating patterns. God is so ready to cleanse and heal your life. Let Him do His wonderful work.

Dear reader, as you embrace this journey it is crucial to be completely honest with yourself and with God. Remember, God convicts because He loves you and wants to work mightily in your life! If you heed His voice, great blessing and mercy will shower your life and church. *Yet if you resist His words, lost blessing and corrective judgments must eventually follow.*

My fervent prayer is that every reader will choose life and mercy, not chastisement and forfeited blessing. As you prepare to read the following pages, pause and ask God to speak directly to your heart. As He speaks immediately confess every sin, forsake all wrongs and make whatever restitution God directs. And know beyond doubt, God *will* transform your life, family and entire church!

# Pattern One
# Angry Attitudes, Buried Bitterness and
# False Forgiveness

## Loving God Means Loving Each Other!
(Matthew 6:14-15; 18:21-35; Mark 11:25; Luke 6:37; John
13:34-35; 17:21-23; 1 Corinthians 13:1-8; Ephesians 4:29-32)

*In light of today's shocking church battles, surely among the most devastating of all revival hindrances is unforgiveness and critical, unloving attitudes among believers.* In a day of rampant immorality, it may even sound strange to say relational bitterness and unkindness are actually the biggest hindrances. Yet surveys leave no doubt that relationship barriers are even far more common than immorality.

According to Scripture, there is little worse in God's eyes than believers harboring bitterness or unkindness toward other believers! Dear saints, if that statement sounds exaggerated, please carefully read the specific Bible references under this section's heading. The Bible is crystal clear that nothing more displeases God or quenches spiritual power than underlying bitterness and unkindness to others!

## Christian Anger and Bitterness
### The Dishonoring and Profaning of God's Name

In fact, God considers angry, divisive attitudes more than mere sin — He calls it an *abomination* (Proverbs 6:16d)! Paul actually places unkind abusive speech in exactly the same category as idolatry and gross immorality (1 Corinthians 5:11). When believers are negative, critical and unkind, God is profoundly displeased. If some believers barely speak and avoid one another, the Holy Spirit is seriously grieved and quenched (Ephesians 4:30; 1 Thessalonians 5:19). To ignore rifts between fellow believers is to literally make a mockery of Christ's death and purpose — to make us one in His love!

Yet tragically, most modern believers more or less ignore this issue. In fact, many view anger and damaged relationships as somewhat normal and unavoidable. There is no area in which the devil has more tragically pulled the wool over the eyes of God's children. Many saints simply do not treat forgiveness, kindness and unity with real seriousness. Many think as long as they are avoiding physical immorality and outward aggression, their spiritual bases are covered. Nothing could be further from the truth! Jesus said the "main thing" (alongside evangelism) is fervent heart-felt love toward God and loving forgiveness to others.

## Forgiveness and Love Among Believers — An Essential Kingdom Focus

While the Great Commission is obviously the "main thing" of what we *do*, the two Great Commandments are the main things of what we *are*. When our *hearts* are right with God and each other, evangelism and missions will explode through the roof. Yet to try and pray or conduct evangelism without deep love and forgiveness assures little power and small success. But even worse, our unforgiveness and anger deeply grieves Jesus' heart and shames His name before a lost world. After all, He literally gave His life that we would "love one another" and "be as one!"

In John 13:34-35 and 17:21, Jesus flatly states that Christian love and unity are absolutely central to our evangelistic witness. Today we certainly see the results of neglecting these central commands — dry divided churches, broken families, little prayer power, low baptisms and lost joy! Thank God, there is a remedy to today's deadly patterns of anger, bitterness and disunity. My friend, no matter how long these may have characterized your life or church, you can see miraculous change!

## Unforgiveness Toward Others —
## The Sin That Imprisons You!

It is most significant that Paul described several of the works of the flesh as wrong attitudes and harsh words toward others! In most cases, we develop underlying angry and bitter attitudes because we have not "from the heart" forgiven others. Furthermore, we will often "say" we have forgiven or "let something go" when we really have not. This is why Jesus added that all-important phrase, we must forgive "from the heart" (Matthew 18:35). Make no mistake — when we don't truly forgive, our prayers are greatly hindered and we lose God's power. But even worse, we grieve God's Spirit and tread on the Son of God (Ephesians 4:30; Hebrews 10:26-31).

One thing is certain — in this life we have all been wronged and will almost certainly be wronged again. That is why Jesus said if we are to be His followers, we must forgive others "as He has forgiven us." And how does He forgive us? He forgives with a rich, "unconditional" love. Even if people will not admit their wrong or ask our forgiveness, we can and must still take the "position" of loving them in Christ. This attitude is essential to preventing the devastating poison of internalized bitterness.

Forgiveness does not mean we minimize what others have done. Neither does it mean we must "feel" warm and gushy about the situation or the wrongs themselves. It is wonderful to realize that true forgiveness is a "choice" and is not dependent on our feelings. We forgive by trusting Christ for the power to forgive and overcome the anger that would otherwise control us. Yes as humans, we will certainly feel the pain of a wrong. But through Jesus, we can daily "choose" to forgive and not be imprisoned by anger.

When we begin to make the consistent choice to forgive, healing and deliverance can then begin in our emotions. Yet, until we genuinely choose forgiveness, we grieve God's Spirit and remain trapped in our pain. But friends there is good news — the One

Who literally forgave as He hung on a cross lives within us and can forgive through us. Our part is to daily make the sincere "choice" to forgive and show kindness, His power will do the rest!

## Counseling Center Miracles and Church Transformations

While doing an internship in a professional counseling center and nearly two decades of pastoring, I noticed a glorious key to transformed lives. We often asked people to prayerfully read Matthew 6:14-15; 18:21-35 and Ephesians 4:29-32. They were then urged to take a few days and prayerfully list every person against who they harbored the slightest bitterness or anger.

At first, most counselees they could only think of a few they needed to forgive. Yet, as they prayerfully reflected and *waited* before God, they soon realized there were *many* against whom they had buried bitterness! Believers, this sin so subtly slips into our lives we often do not even realize it is happening. Unless we periodically allow God to do a thorough inventory, we are probably not serious about keeping our hearts totally yielded to Christ.

In reliance on Christ's strength, we asked them to choose forgiveness and take daily steps to actually pray for the persons who had hurt them. Miracles come when believers let God search the *depths* of their hearts, not just the surface. While with some it certainly took time and several steps, the miracles were indescribable! Their joy returned, God was glorified and the Holy Spirit began a mighty new work in hearts, families and churches. But always there was one huge key — they had to become *honest* about their unforgiveness, *stop justifying* it and *choose* to daily forgive through Christ's indwelling power. My friend, you must do the same thing. And by God's grace, you *can* change and overcome your weaknesses! (2 Corinthians 12:9; Philippians 4:13)

## Learning to Renounce Angry Attitudes
### Agreeing to Disagree Agreeably

Closely related to bitterness, is the problem of believers with angry, critical attitudes. Again we see in God's Word, there is little more displeasing to God or hindering to the Holy Spirit. *Furthermore, a huge percentage of church conflict and division can be traced to members with angry, critical attitudes.* While as believers we certainly do not agree on everything, we can and must learn to "disagree agreeably." To do anything less horribly profanes and dishonors God's name! Little else could bring believers and churches into greater risk of God's chastisement.

Friends, if we simply resolve to treat each other with kindness and respect, it is amazing how many battles and conflicts quickly melt away. It is astounding how many battles would never occur in the first place! Yet there is good news to report — some believers and churches are getting so weary of the battle, they are truly ready to change. And by God's grace, they are changing!

But again, let there be no mistake as to what God is telling His Church. Plain and simple, it is an *abomination* for believers to harbor serious anger and unkindness toward one another! (Proverbs 6:16d) God's heart is profoundly grieved when some members will barely speak to certain other members. It is even more damaging when Church leaders are not speaking to other leaders!

Without question, God is deeply grieved and offended when some members go out of their way to avoid being around other members. Unkind words and attitudes are the very opposite of God's purpose for His people. If such patterns are allowed to persist, even our very worship and prayers become an empty ritual. Believers, when we deny, ignore or minimize damaged relationships, we utterly reject the Lordship of Christ. By so doing, we grieve God's heart and seriously quench His Spirit (Ephesians 4:31-32).

## Little Rifts — Not So Little to God

Based on Scripture, how could we think God is anything but profoundly grieved in any church where disunity is widespread and continuous? In fact, these angry attitudes and so-called "little rifts" can often be even more hindering to God's Spirit than more outward sins of the flesh. Oh dear reader, *please* be honest with yourself and honest with God about these matters. If you will be honest and take the clear steps revealed in Scripture, God will surely touch your life, family and church (John 6:37)!

It is glorious to realize God does not require perfection, just a willingness to be honest, stop making excuses and take some basic steps of repentance. Neither does revival require everyone in the church being willing to change. If only a few will begin to obey, it is astounding what God can do to eventually touch the others. His grace is certainly greater than the sin of anyone willing to stop making excuses and take basic steps to obey.

## We Can All Change!
### (Romans 6:14; Philippians 4:13)

No doubt many reading these pages are very weary, wounded and war-torn. You may be struggling with bitterness and unforgiveness because of some truly horrible experiences. My friend, God's compassion and grace especially goes out to you. Above all, *do not panic* about yourself or your church! God is incredibly caring and truly touched by the depth of your pain (Hebrews 4:15). By God's grace, you can begin to see change!

On the other hand, you may have long had a quick temper and often seem to hurt those around you. Though you have often desired to be different, change seems elusive. Even now God is stirring your heart with a real desire to change. Regardless of your circumstance, God's grace is sufficient to help you now become an incredibly kind and forgiving person. I have seen it happen in some of the most angry, negative people!

But it is essential that we all take this very seriously. It is no accident we began our look at revival hindrances with the issues of unforgiveness and angry unloving attitudes. *Virtually all the other battles in churches stem from these foundational sins.* As you work through the rest of this book, virtually all the other barriers come from these roots. Yet be encouraged — God is stronger than our strongest sins!

Dear reader, please go before God and consider whether He is already leading you to some key steps of confession and repentance. Above all, start by simply embracing a more loving, forgiving attitude. Believe me, you and your church will never be the same! However, it is vital that you be very specific in your confession and repentance. Confession that is general and vague simply will not suffice. Confession that does not involve specific steps of repentance is nothing but a subtle cop-out. Stopping with general confession is often an unconscious attempt to salve our conscious without taking the serious steps of specific change. God is not fooled by such deceptive games.

## Biblical Steps for Obedience and Repentance

1) *Fully confess and ask God's forgiveness for specific patterns of unforgiveness, anger or unkindness toward others.* Take significant time and let Him truly *search* your heart (Psalms 139:23-24). Do not rush this process or minimize your sins. Do not in any way justify or rationalize your sins. You must fully confess and forsake them now (Proverbs 28:13; 1 John 1:9)!

2) *If you know you have been unkind toward specific people, fully confess and forsake this most grievous sin to God.* Do not try to rationalize or convince yourself you do not need to go to those you have definitely offended. As God leads, you must go in love and humbly ask their forgiveness. Do not let the fact their attitude may have been wrong convince you that you do not need to go. You are going to confess *your* sin, not theirs. Fur-

thermore, you must make whatever restitution may be needed (Matthew 5:23-24).

*However*, if your relationship situation is in any way volatile, by all means get wise pastoral counsel for the best way to seek forgiveness. Be thoughtful and prayerful in what you do. Seek God's wisdom for the best method and timing. (But do not let this become a subtle ploy for endless delay!) Remember, our flesh and pride can be incredibly creative in coming up with ways to convince us not to seek forgiveness.

3) *Ask God to help you fully forgive "from the heart" all who have wronged you.* Be sure to go way back into the past and be very specific. I strongly encourage finding a godly counselor or prayer partner to help with the process. Read Matthew 18:15 and go to people if that applies to your situation. However, a general principle of maturity is to simply forgive and overlook most offenses that come our way. We should not run around constantly confronting people over smaller issues. (On the other hand, if we are the one who has done the offending, we should always err on the side of caution in asking other to forgive us. In other words, do not avoid asking forgiveness by saying, "Oh, it's just a little thing." It may well not be little to the one offended!)

In cases where an offense against us is serious, ongoing or doing real harm, we then follow the pattern of Malachi 18:15-17. When situations are in the more serious realm, we are in fact *obligated* to go to the offending party. To do less would be plain disobedience. With moderate and smaller offences, we should be mature and big enough to just forgive and "let it go." The writer of James beautifully summarizes this principle, "Love covers a multitude of sins" (James 5:20). I encourage every reader to immediately purchase and read *The PeaceMaker* by Ken Sande. It will provide complete biblical guidance for virtually all issues of forgiveness and reconciliation.

4) *Claim God's total forgiveness and forgive yourself!* My friend, we are all sinners and you must do with your failures what God does — He removes them as far as the east from the west! He chooses to remember them no more (Hebrews 8:12). "There is therefore no condemnation to those why are in Christ Jesus; who do not walk according to the flesh, but according to the Spirit" (Romans 8:1). Be aware that working on relationships is a life-long process not a one-time program. Getting over deep hurts and wounds will indeed be a process. Do not beat yourself up because feelings of anger and hurt may not instantly disappear. This will come with time and God's grace covers your whole journey. Be secure in His love!

## Don't be Overwhelmed
### A New Day Will Dawn!

It is important to understand that your miraculous change of heart will almost certainly be an ongoing process. By all means, do not be discouraged if you do not see mountain-moving miracles overnight. Continue in daily resolving to make loving-kindness and forgiveness a top priority. Just keep trusting God and repenting through every up and down in your journey. And know for a certainty — you are "accepted" in the Beloved. His grace is sufficient for you to become incredibly loving, kind and forgiving (Ephesians 1:6; Philippians 4:13). Above all, let us embrace love and forgiveness for God's glory and His kingdom. Only in this way do we live as the people of God exalting His name before all the earth.

I close this crucial first pattern with a final request. If unkindness and bitterness have been a significant pattern in your life, I strongly urge you to read Appendix B before proceeding. Many people struggle because God simply doesn't seem very real in their daily life. As a result, they lack assurance of their salvation. When God is not real to us, anger and bitterness tend to be far more of a problem. It is quite impossible to make much progress until the assurance issue is effectively solved. Oh dear reader, please let God give you deep assurance. He definitely wants to become far more real in your daily life. And know this for certain — when God is real in your daily life, love and forgiveness will fill your heart!

## Pictures of Grace and Hope

Over many years of pastoring and professional counseling, I have been privileged to watch miraculous changes in countless peoples' lives. In many individuals God so changed their attitudes and personalities, it is hard to believe they are even the same people! Some of the most angry, bitter people have become incredibly loving and kind. People long known as hot tempered and harsh have become truly gentle and patient. Believers who have feuded for years, at last dropped their pride and humbly asked forgiveness. Their healing and transformation has been astounding!

When believers confessed underlying anger and bitterness, the effect on their church was simply awesome. People whose attitudes have long hindered revival, soon became the very agents for a sweeping revival flood! As churches witnessed deep confession and change in certain people, whole congregations saw glorious revivals of love and unity. Churches with long reputations of being "volatile and troubled" became widely known as loving and peaceful. When even *some* of the separated saints forgave one another, God's presence soon gloriously touched many others.

Dear believer, do you sense God speaking to your own heart? Does your church and family need just such a miracle? Could revival now hinge upon you forgiving and asking forgiveness of someone else? Have you been waiting on someone else to change and take the first step? My friend, God is waiting on you. Delay no longer — His grace is more than sufficient and you will be changed!

## Putting On Christ — Putting Off the Flesh
### Steps for Repentance and Victory

If God has revealed a need for repentance, you must take this *very* seriously. Carefully consider the sample prayer below. If you would by willing to pray a similar prayer, please pause and do it now. Ask God to grant you sincerity and take all the steps of repentance His will requires. For many this will mean asking others (possibly including the whole church) to forgive you. But always remember, His grace is greater than your very deepest need! Furthermore, you will be amazed how your humble repentance can release a flood of God's Spirit in your whole church. Even more, your repentance will greatly honor and exalt the holy name of God. Yet if you ignore God's voice, the Holy Spirit is even far more quenched than before!

*A Prayer of Cleansing and Transformation* — "Father, I fully confess the anger and resentment I have harbored in my heart. I also confess the ways I have neglected to go to those I have offended. Forgive me for justifying my offenses or my anger. Dear God, please forgive me for my wrong attitudes and actions (be specific). By Your grace, I now resolve to forgive all whom have offended me and seek forgiveness from those I have offended. God, please fill me with Your Spirit and change my heart for Your name sake!"

> *As study or prayer groups work through the discussion questions at the end of each pattern, remember to stay very focused on God's grace and hope for change. No church or person should forget that God convicts to change us, not to condemn or discourage. In discussing areas for change, do not call peoples' names and stay positive. Let God's revelations lead you straight to prayer and faith for change, not criticism or gossip.

## *Pattern One*
## *Questions for Prayer and Study Groups*

(for individuals, small groups or churchwide studies)

(1)  Carefully read Matthew 6:14-15 and Mark 11:25. What is the result of a believer harboring any degree of anger or bitterness in his or her heart? How will harbored bitterness affect God hearing our prayers?

(2)  Based on Ephesians 4:32, why should we be willing to forgive others? Based on Philippians 4:13, where do we get our strength to forgive and love others?

(3)  Read Ephesians 4:29-32. In the Ephesian text, what specific sin especially grieved the Holy Spirit? What effect would the Spirit's grieving have on a believer or church?

(4)  Carefully read Matthew 5:23-24. In the Matthew text, "coming to the altar could certainly include prayer or worship as well as bringing a gift. Why did God say "don't bring the gift" without first going to reconcile with an offended brother? How would the arrogance and pride of ignoring our need to go and ask forgiveness affect our prayers and worship? On a scale of 1-10, how urgent is getting fully right with one another?

(5)  Based on John 13:34-35 and John 17:20-22, why is Christian love and unity so essential to honoring God's name and reaching a lost world?

Conduct a James 5:16 Transformation Prayer Group
   (Follow the Prayer Group Pattern of Confession, Intercession and Repentance Fully Outlined in Appendix D)

# Pattern Two
# Gossip, Innuendo and Slander

(Matthew 18:15; Ephesians 4:29-32; Titus 3:10-11)

*There is absolutely no doubt that patterns of church gossip, division and verbal slander are at crisis levels in today's Church.* Sadly, the same must be said of many denominations and religious organizations. Yet, as we prepare to let God deal with patterns needing change, it is vital to remember a glorious truth. Our Lord convicts to point us to Himself in grace and hope, *not* to ourselves in condemnation and despair!

Even as you see several significant patterns needing change, please know that our Lord brings "godly sorrow" to produce transformation, *not* hopeless guilt. Let us rejoice in the fact God's grace is greater than the greatest sins of anyone willing to repent. And best of all, He even gives the grace to repent!

## Addressing a Modern Epidemic

As I have researched factors hindering revival in today's churches, it is obvious that gossip, slander and division are near epidemic! It is also true that sins of speech have taken ever more vicious forms. Unfortunately, some of these patterns are very subtle and people can become ensnared without clear awareness it is even happening. One of the most common and deceptive is a subtle misuse of the so-called "*prayer concern.*"

While legitimate prayer requests are always important, some turn prayer concerns into a very damaging form of gossip. People with this tendency frequently spread gossip and slander under the guise of sharing a "prayer burden." It seems they are always needing to share some "concern" that usually ends up being much more a discussion of salacious rumors than actual prayer.

45

Still others become lighting quick to widely spread gossip, slander or problems under the excuse of "concern for the church." All the while they completely miss the fact God clearly says we are to first take issues or problems to someone privately and *not* to anyone else! (Matthew 18:15) Yet people with this pattern do just about everything but go to someone privately. Or if they finally do go to someone, they've usually gone to everyone else first. And after they've gone, they tell everyone else every word of the conversation. (Does this sound familiar?) People ensnared in this sin also ignore the fact God strongly condemns repeating rumors and tales in any form (Proverbs 11:13). He also warns of dire consequences to repeated abusers.

## The Neglected End-All Cure for Gossip

Ninety-five percent of gossip and slander would immediately cease if believers simply obeyed the crystal clear command of Matthew 18:15-17. "If your brother sins against you, go and show him his fault just **between the two of you.** If he listens to you, you have won your brother. But if he will not hear thee, then take with thee one or two more, that in the mouth of two or three witnesses every word may be established. And if he shall neglect to hear them, tell it unto the church; but if he neglect to hear the church, let him be unto thee as an heathen man and a publican." These commands of Christ leave absolutely no doubt as to how we are to address grievances or concerns between believers. Scores of other Scriptures clearly forbid gossip, speculation and all forms of rumor mongering. One thing is certain — following God's command puts an immediate stop to virtually all forms of talking about people behind their back!

Because Matthew 18:15 is so plain, if anyone starts telling you critical or suggestive things about someone else, you know *immediately* they are directly sinning against God. Indeed if we find ourselves often sitting and speculating about sins in other people's lives, we are already in major sin. No matter who they are or how "sweet" and "sincere" their tone of voice, gossips commit a most serious and damaging sin. In fact, in many cases God actually considers what they are doing (gossip and slander) far worse than the supposed sin of the person they are discussing!

It is sad but true that some people have a near obsessive fascination with hearing and sharing rumors and speculations. Their ears are like radar always searching for the latest bit of salacious news. Friends, it is absolutely crucial that we come to see gossip and slander for what they are — *vile sins* against God, people and the sacred unity of Christ's Church.

## Don't Be a "Gossip Magnet"

*We see a further disturbing symptom when people say, "Well, I don't know why, but people are just always coming to me to share complaints and gripes."* Those individuals often even seem to take a certain pride in the fact people come to them with complaints and concerns. While in one sense it may suggest they have people's confidence, it also suggests something of profound concern. It suggests others know they will listen to their gossip and will *not* follow the biblical injunctions! Complainers and gossips tend to know who will not insist on adhering to the biblical principles for discussing others.

Certain people are usually "gossip magnets" for one reason. People know they will not hold them accountable to obey God's clear command in Matthew 18:15! If a believer is committed to follow God's pattern of holiness, it is amazing how quickly gossips stop seeking them out. Yet if we are willing ears, they will come to us in droves. It definitely is *not* a good sign when grumblers and gossips consider us a friendly ear. Make no mistake — willfully receiving ungodly speech is nothing less than direct disobedience to God (1 Corinthians 5:11; 2 Thessalonians 3:11-14).

## Rash Judgments and Premature Assumptions

*We observe an especially damaging pattern in church members prone to make snap assumptions and premature judgments about people or situations.* These individuals typically form opinions on very little information and make quick assumptions that often prove to be wrong. Yet they continually voice their opinions "as facts" to virtually anyone who will listen. No doubt this is why God inspired the writing of the following three verses. "In the multitude of words there wanteth not sin; but he that refraineth his lips is wise" (Proverbs 10:19). "Seest thou a man that is hasty in his words? There is more hope of a fool than of him" (Proverbs 29:20). "Wherefore, my beloved brethren, let every man be swift to hear, slow to speak, slow to wrath" (James 3:5-6).

Untold damage is done when church members judge others without making sure they really know the facts. These patterns are tragically common and become a fertile breeding ground for broken relationships and slanderous gossip. Little more hinders God's Spirit than those who draw quick conclusions then widely voice their thoughts and suspicions. Even when suspicious prove true, there is absolutely no excuse for going beyond Matthew 18:15.

## The Devilish Art of "Innuendo"

*Another of the most devilish forms of gossip and slander is the wicked art of "innuendo."* In this form of evil, the perpetrators make statements that simply plant subtle seeds of doubt about someone's character or competence. While they may not come out and make a direct accusation, they are very adept at simply raising questions that cast suspicion. They know just the right questions to create a cloud of doubt about someone's character or competence.

An additional common ploy is to say "*I heard such and such*" when in fact, the question really came from their own mind. Yet another evil pattern is when they say "*Lots of people are saying*" when in fact, the only comments are from them and one or two others in whom they themselves initiated the questions! When you hear these telltale phrases of gossips, that is a huge red flag of concern. No matter who is doing the speaking, you should immediately suspect, "This person is not speaking from the Holy Spirit." While such statements do not always represent exaggeration, slander and gossip, most of the time they do. Such phrases are *not* words from the Holy Spirit.

## Secret Whisperings and Unfounded Speculations

A further suspicious pattern is when someone often takes you aside and says "I hesitate to say this but I need to share something confidential." (Yet you have the awareness they are likely sharing this with many more besides you!) When they begin their quiet whispering, keep in mind the following questions. "Are they sharing absolute facts or is some part speculation? Have they gone to the person they are discussing or are they spreading things behind their back? Is this conversation in line with Mathew 18:15 or does it clearly violate the biblical patterns? I suggest that you specifically ask if they have gone to the persons they are discussing. If the answers to these questions do not coincide with biblical principles, you must strongly suspect the conversation is not guided by the Holy Spirit (no matter who is sharing it.)

*In actuality, innuendo is often just a sneaky, indirect (somewhat cowardly) way of attack and gossip.* Under the guise of simply "sharing a concern" or "seeking information," people are actually spreading damaging suspicions and rumors. Of course, there are times when carefully sharing concerns or information is legitimate and necessary. But when this becomes a "pattern" and is more about speculative talk than prayer, something is seriously wrong. Satan is indeed a master at planting small doubts and skillfully fanning them into raging fires. These fires then damage reputations and decimate peace in the church.

## The Tongue — A Raging Fire and World of Evil
### (James 3:6-13)

It is truly astounding to see the enormous damage that often comes from simply raising a few suggestive questions. Small suggestions can easily become a sweeping wildfire of gossip and rumor. Sadly enough, some know just where to drop an innuendo to see it quickly race through the grapevine. It is like a well-placed time bomb — they know just who to tell to see it explode through the entire church.

In most churches we so commonly hear the same sad statement, "If you tell so and so, it's as good as putting it on the six o'clock news." Such statements would be humorous if they were not so tragically true. In many ways, the devil's most reliable and destructive tool is the willing tongue of a gossip (James 3:5-6). Godly people must in no way lend an ear to those who consistently exhibit these vile patterns of speech. Yet today, far too many believers fail to treat gossip and innuendo with the utter seriousness they deserve.

A related variation of evil speech occurs when people make hurtful or accusatory statements and then say, "Oh, I was only kidding." Some individuals are quite adept at making negative insinuations or verbal jabs under the guise of "making fun." Typically they will also say, "Well I really did not mean anything by it." That is about as absurd as willfully slicing someone with a knife and trying to defend it by saying, "I didn't mean any harm." Just because someone smiles when they malign or criticize makes it no less harmful. In fact, such evil "humor" is an especially devious and subtle form of slander. This form of deceptive malicious speech fools no one and is certainly not funny to God. In Proverbs 26:18, God likens this type of joking to a "*madman throwing burning wood at people.*"

## Negative Speech — No Laughing Matter!

Shamefully, such unbiblical patterns typically persist in churches because godly members sit back and say little. There is a disturbing tendency for churches to more or less "tolerate" people who spread malicious gossip. Members may try to laugh it off and say, "That's just old so and so, don't pay him (or her) any mind." But the problem is people *do* pay them mind.

Make no mistake — negative speech does enormous harm and seriously grieves the Holy Spirit. Worse yet, people who gossip in the church, typically share the same poisons out in the community. Their habits thus do severe damage to the witness and testimony of God's people. Be assured, God finds absolutely nothing humorous or insignificant about gossip and negative speech. He views this sin with extreme seriousness and so too must believers and churches.

Still another variation of excusing damaging behavior is when people say, "Oh that's just old so and so, don't pay any attention, *he or she has always been that way.*" Yet one thing is certain — the fact someone has long had a pattern of angry, negative or slanderous speech is no reason to excuse it! The fact they have been excused is a major reason they continue their ungodly patterns. It is time for God's people to change, *not* continue to justify or downplay their harm to church unity. While overlooking a minor flaw is one thing, tolerating damaging speech is quite another. God *never* views sins of speech lightly and neither must we!

If churches are to move into spiritual health, they simply cannot continue to view these issues as mostly the pastor's concern. Until the church body starts dealing with gossip biblically, the deadly cycles will surely continue. When churches ignore or down-play serious gossip, these wicked patterns continue year after year! Believers, if we let obvious evil triumph because we're afraid to "cause a controversy," we are ashamed to stand for Christ and His Church. Often believers say, "I just don't want to stir trouble," when they are really saying "I would rather avoid the discomfort of dealing with vindictive personalities." To consistently take the path of least resistance is a real form of "denying Christ" and "avoiding His cross."

## Diligently Guarding Peace
## The Job of Every Church Member
(Ephesians 4:3)

Without question, it is *every member's* responsibility to guard the fellowship and unity of their church! If any member hears someone spreading gossip, innuendo or negative speech, they must lovingly (but firmly) ask them to stop the conversation and immediately follow Matthew 18:15. Be prepared to read the passage and urge their compliance. If they refuse and persist in malicious gossip, get witnesses to go with you, write down what they are saying and take it straight to key church leadership.

When people are quickly held accountable for what they spread, most will soon reduce the pattern. If gossips know they are going to be held accountable before deacons, church leaders and an entire church, they are far less likely to spread their verbal poisons. However, you may also find they will frequently deny what they said or say that is not what they meant. That is why documentation and witnesses are often important in getting to the truth.

Dear saint, if you have any degree of spiritual depth, God may well be counting on you to help deal with such ungodly patterns in your church. A quote from Edmond Burke most clearly captures this important truth. "The only thing necessary for the triumph of evil is for good men to do nothing." Thank God, more and more churches are embracing written covenants to avoid gossip and to squarely address it when it occurs. In light of today's conditions, it is vital that congregations periodically pray through a cleansing resource, to correct any drift toward gossip and disunity. Occasional special emphases are often vital to helping individuals and whole churches renew their covenants to loving, unified fellowship.

# Peacekeeping —
# Leaders' Vital Role in Honoring God's Name

Needless to say, guarding the bond of peace is especially critical for pastors, staff and church leaders. Peace and unity are among the very first responsibilities of deacons, elders, teachers and committee members. For this reason, it is enormously damaging when gossip and negative speech originate or have free flow among pastor, staff or deacons. Those leaders are to be the guardians of fellowship and unity, *not* their destroyers! In terms of damage, a close second occurs when Sunday School classes spend more of their time in gossip than actual Bible study. Little could be a more wicked perversion of this special time reserved for the study of God's Holy Word.

Yet even now, we note some early signs of positive change. Growing numbers of leaders are beginning to take love and unity much more seriously. More and more pastors, deacons and teaches are seeking God's principles for "guarding the bond of peace" (Ephesians 4:3). While positive change is yet only a small minority, it is a growing minority! And thank God, He is well able to transform the most troubled church into a unified family of love and peace.

Yet, as churches or individuals address patterns of gossip, it is always crucial to carefully seek God's wisdom for *when* and *how* to deal with these conditions. It is never wise to confront or make judgments of others rashly. Neither is it advisable to just "up and do something" without much prayer, careful thought and godly council. To act apart from God's method, timing and wisdom could easily create even worse problems.

Let us never forget the truth of James' powerful statement. "For man's anger does not bring about the righteous life that God desires" (James 1:20). There are actually some very simple things believers can do to greatly lessen the incidence of slanderous gossip. Among the most effective is simply turning a deaf ear and denying an audience to gossip and innuendo. To do less is to aid and abet the spread of hurtful, negative speech. Remember the clear command of God in Ephesians 5:11. "And have no fellowship with the unfruitful works of darkness, but rather expose them."

## Carefully Avoid the "Aiding and Abetting" Syndrome

A common way we inadvertently encourage gossip is by giving a willing ear to one who consistently questions and slanders others. Though they may tell you, "I need to talk," you are *not* helping by letting them endlessly vent angry or slanderous talk behind someone's back. The truth is, people who tend to gossip often cease their habit if others stop listening! People with this sin pattern typically want an audience quite badly. Yet, when you give them a sympathetic ear, you definitely become an enabler, encourager and accomplice in the sinful pattern.

We must also be aware that people with this habit usually do not see themselves as gossips. It is amazing how they think what they are doing is somehow "different" and not really gossip. *They will often even gossip about how bad old so and so gossips!* People caught in this cycle often have a real blindspot to what they are causing in the lives of others. For this reason, these individuals need your prayers and loving Scripture-based rebuke, but not your tacit participation. In 1 Corinthians 5:11, Paul commanded believers to have nothing to do with a believer who is a "reviler." A reviler is one who is verbally abusive or seriously slanderous toward others. Sadly, we must also note that many do not have a blindspot — they know *exactly* what they are doing!

## When "Listening" Makes You an Accomplice

Please understand, if you choose to sit and passively listen to a slanderous person, you in a direct sense participate in their evil. Without meaning to, you are actually aiding and abetting these damaging sin patterns. The scriptural approach is to lovingly (but firmly) *stop* them and say, let's immediately follow Matthew 18:15 and go to the individual you're now taking about. If done in the right spirit, you may help the erring one see their wrong and repent. You may also help them move to a point of reconciliation and healing.

Unfortunately, in many cases people ensnared in gossip have little desire to actually take the biblical steps. Sadly, they usually just want to talk behind the person's back. If you suggest the biblical course of reconciliation and they refuse or change the subject, you can generally conclude this person is not interested in truly obeying God.

While slanderous gossip is tragically common, it is only one of many forms of evil now sweeping countless churches. To our shame, we live in a day when attacks on pastors, staff, lay-leaders and church fellowship are taking ever more varied and vicious forms. Concerning this point, we must all remember one vital truth. *"When we attack fellow believers, we are directly attacking the unity and love of Christ's Church.* Scriptures leave no doubt that to attack the unity of Christ's Church is to attack Christ!"

If so, you indeed have a deep and immediate need for full confession and repentance. If God is speaking to the depths of your heart, I am confident you sense His voice. Please do not become defensive or resist His Word! Remember, God always receives the broken and contrite but always resists the proud (Psalms 101:5). Reflect on His voice through these closing words.

## Grace to Claim
### (1 John 1:9)

As you read this section, did God bring specific patterns to your mind you need to confess and forsake? Please take a moment and look back through the different headings in this section. What very specific things do you need to confess? Be very specific and thorough. I suggest that you write them down. Above all, rest in the assurance that Jesus' blood is greater than your greatest sins! "Therefore there is now no condemnation for those who are in Christ Jesus" (Romans 8:1).

# Steps to Take
## (Proverbs 28:13)

**First, it is vital to understand that confession alone is not repentance.** In fact, confession doesn't become complete without the elements of repentance, restitution and reconciliation. "He who conceals his sins does not prosper: but whoever **confesses** and **forsakes** them finds mercy" (Proverbs 28:13). "Therefore if you are offering your gift at the altar and there remember that your brother has something against you, leave your gift there in front of the altar. First go and be reconciled to your brother; then come and offer your gift" (Matthew 5:23-24). "For if you forgive men when they sin against you, your heavenly Father will also forgive you: But if you do not forgive men their sins, your Father will not forgive your sins" (Matthew 6:14-15). My friend, do not despair, God will surely give you grace to make your necessary steps of change.

**Second, God will surely lead us to ask forgiveness of particular people we have in some way hurt or offended (either directly or indirectly).** An excellent way to know if you need to go to someone is by considering the following question. *When other church members read some of these sections, do you believe you came to the minds of certain people?* Dear saint, if your honest answer is yes, you just received your answer for badly needed steps of reconciliation. If fellow church or family members think of you when they read these sections, you can *know* you have an urgent need for change.

Ask God for wisdom and get spiritual council as you prepare to seek forgiveness and reconciliation from others. If you carefully follow God's leading, you will be amazed at the incredible sense of peace in following His guidance. Above all, remember His wonderful grace and acceptance even now. He is with you from the first moment you resolve to seek and do His will! Obey His voice and rest in His glorious love and grace!

## Putting On Christ — Putting Off the Flesh
### Steps for Repentance and Change

If God has indeed spoken to your heart, you must not deny it or ignore His voice! Carefully consider the prayer listed below. If you are willing to pray a similar prayer, please pause and do it now. Ask God to help you mean it and take whatever steps of repentance His will requires. And remember, God's grace never abandons a repentant heart.

*A Prayer of Cleansing and Transformation* — "Father, I fully confess my sins of gossip, innuendo and slander. Please forgive me for patterns I now see are very harmful and wrong. By Your grace, I resolve to repent and repair the damage I have done. Please fill me with Your Spirit and grant me a heart of godly speech."

## Comforting Words of Hope and Life

Proverbs 28:13 – "He that covers his sins shall not prosper: but whoso confesess and forsakes them shall have mercy."

Isaiah 1:18 – "Come now and let us reason together, says the Lord; though your sins be as scarlet, they shall be as white as snow; though they be red like crimson, they shall be as wool."

Joel 2:12-13 (KJV) – "Therefore also now, saith the Lord, Turn ye even to me with all your heart, and with fasting, and with weeping, and with mourning: And rend your heart, and not your garments, and turn unto the Lord your God: for He is gracious and merciful, slow to anger, and of great kindness, and repenteth him of the evil."

I John 1:9 – "If we confess our sins, He is faithful and just to forgive us our sins, and to cleanse us from all unrighteousness."

## Pattern Two
## Questions for Prayer and Study Groups

(for individuals, small group or churchwide studies)

(1) Based on Matthew 18:15-17, what should a believer do if someone causes them serious offense and harm? How would simply going *first* to the person (and not anyone else) stop most gossip?

(2) In 1 Corinthians 5:11, Paul lists a "reviler" in the same category as adulterers and idolaters. A reviler is someone who is slanderous or verbally abusive. Paul even said such persons shall be "put out of the Church." Based on the clear teaching of God's Word, how serious is the sin of gossip and slander?

(3) How can sharing the "prayer burden" become a subtle way of spreading gossip and salacious rumors?

(4) In your own words, describe the meaning of being a "gossip magnet." How could we get sucked into aiding and abetting a person with patterns of gossip? How does continually listening to a gossip or slanderer make you an accomplice?

(5) In your own words, describe the meaning of innuendo. Describe the meaning of rash judgment and premature assumptions. Define unfounded speculations.

(6) Based on Ephesians 4:3, why is "guarding the bond of peace" the job of every church member? List some ways laymen and leaders can guard the bond of peace.

# Pattern Three
# Revolving Door Pastors and
# Disappearing Members

(Psalms 105:15; 1 Corinthians 1:10;
1 Thessalonians 5:12-13; 1 Timothy 5:17)

*In some churches, there is a disturbing and repeating pattern of getting rid of preachers or staff after only a short tenure.* Make no mistake — a long history of "being hard" on leaders is strong indication of profound spiritual problems. Indeed, little could be more unscriptural or detrimental to kingdom work. Virtually nothing brings greater shame to the name of Christ and His Church.

Not only does unloving behavior devastate people in the church, it presents a horrible witness to the unchurched community. While Jesus said the world would know we are His by our love and unity, they are instead utterly repulsed by our anger and division (John 13:34-35). When we cannot even treat God's servants with civility, it rightly makes us an object of derision and scorn to the lost world. But again let me stress hope — even the bitterest, long-term patterns can be reversed! I encourage every church with serious patterns of conflict to immediately seek God's guidance in addressing these damaging cycles. Do not be ashamed to ask guidance from your association, state or national convention. God will surely guide you to help and healing!

> *Author's note: Fellow believers, I deeply wish this was not a section I was required to write. I assure you it is written with many tears and the most prayerful of deliberations. As I researched this matter, I have felt something of God's utter heartbreak over this troubling issue. While every revival hindrance is serious, little more grieves God's heart than bitter battles between church members and their pastors or leaders. Yet in recent years, there has been a shocking explosion of mistreating Christian leaders over smaller and often subjective issues. One thing is certain — revival will

surely tarry until believers fully address these patterns and seek reconciliation for past offenses.

However, I have great news for even the most discouraged church or reader. God is at work and some pastors and churches *are* finding reconciliation! Best of all, some are finding glorious victory by seeking forgiveness and healing for past battles. Concerning this point one thing is clear — *no one can fully move forward until they have addressed the past!* Yet, to God's praise, even the most seemingly hopeless people and churches can find incredible transformation.

For balance, I also state we are seeing far too many instances where pastors or leaders committed such major offenses their churches were forced to address them. *The conditions we address in the coming paragraphs, do not include those situations in which pastors or leaders were in such error their churches truly had to act.* Laypersons in such situations have God's deepest compassion and support.

In over twenty years of conferences I have known many godly laypersons that God mightily used to get churches through stormy waters and unavoidable leadership changes. But in every case they carefully followed biblical principles, moved with loving caution and many sought wise council from denominational leaders. These dear lay-leaders are to be much admired. The patterns addressed in the following section in no way refer to those who had no choice but to address blatant sinfulness in their leaders. No believer reading these pages should throw up their hands and run because they see serious sin patterns in their midst. Thank God, His grace is sufficient for whatever conditions we face in our churches. There *is* definitely hope for every person and church!

# Church Fights, Firings and Free-for-All's
## A Public Profaning of God's Name

We now examine one of the most dangerous hindrances in today's Church — unscriptural treatment of God's servants! *Little more blasphemes God's name than public fights to fire pastors or staff!* (Conversely, nothing more blasphemes God than pastors or leaders who sin blatantly and require dismissal.) Friends, this next section is especially crucial. Let us all embrace the honesty to hear and promptly obey whatever God reveals to our hearts.

Before examining these specific hindrances, we should note that some have certainly become involved in wrong patterns with no actual intent of doing harm. In some cases, people have never been taught the biblical patterns of leading ministers to and from churches. Sometimes those who end up harming churches and ministers truly had good intentions at the outset. Satan is indeed a master at deceiving us into doing his bidding without our even knowing it is happening. *This section is designed to fully unmask specific patterns that are definitely not from God.*

## The Time for Change is Now!

Remember dear reader, if God opens your eyes to formally unrealized areas of sin, He is doing it primarily to lift you up, not hurt you. In fact, He knows some were honestly just trying to do the right thing. Humbly and honestly confess whatever wrong He reveals and you will find glorious grace and restoration. However, most of the patterns described in this section are so obviously evil, *no one* could do them innocently! It is especially urgent that you immediately confess and forsake any such patterns. To do less is to virtually guarantee God's strong intervention. When it comes to the issue we now address, God is deadly serious about immediate change. As He begins to purify His Bride, the days of toleration may well be nearing an end.

As we study nation-wide trends of mistreating leaders, a few distinct patterns have become rampant. Surveys show unscriptural patterns usually revolve around a relatively small power group who take it upon themselves to decide when preachers come and go. Unfortunately, this most damaging behavior follows an all-too predictable pattern. Based on extensive study and conference experience, I must report the following scenario is almost as predictable as clockwork.

## Describing a Tragic, Repeating Pattern

Relatively soon after the pastor or staff person's arrival, there will be some area of disagreement or shortcoming (real or supposed.) Of course, sooner or later we all disagree on something. But rather than displaying the godly maturity to lovingly work through areas of disagreement, the power group quickly comes to their usual solution — "Let's just get rid of him!" (Sadly, I must add that some pastors can take this attitude toward staff.)

As shocking as it may seem, the group usually turns on the leader over relatively small issues. Usually, the pastor or leader make a suggestion for improvement or asks someone to make some type of change. If persons have oversensitive, proud or rebellious attitudes, the immediate reaction is one of extreme anger. The underlying attitude is, "Who are *you* to try and tell *us* what to do?" Rather than working though issues in Christian love, the attitude is one of immediate all-out war. With incredible speed they "turn on" a pastor or leader. Sadly, even the most basic biblical concepts of pastoral authority are utterly foreign in the minds of those who cause this ugly repeating pattern in churches. The devilish progression now enters phase two.

## The Camp-Building, Fault-Finding Phase

The group now enters what is known as the *"fault-finding, camp-building"* phase. This is a time of seeking to find numerous "faults" with the minister or staff person. The group promptly initiates a phone and gossip campaign to drain away his support. To those individuals, the leader just cannot seem to do anything right and they promote that view to all who will listen. They continually look for ways to *magnify* his faults (which every minister and church member certainly has) and *minimize* his positives.

During the camp-building phase certain people relentlessly pick apart the target's every move. The goal is to persuade as many people as possible to "side" with them against the pastor or targeted staff person. Before you know it, their efforts turn the church into something resembling "two camps" gearing up for battle. A growing tension overshadows all activities as little groups increasingly cluster and whisper in hushed tones. Amazingly, they do their clustering just before or after – of all things – *worshiping the Prince of Peace.* Of course, worship then largely becomes a sham as peoples' minds are now on "the problem" rather than God.

## The "Camps" Gear Up for Battle

Though it sounds unbelievable, it is not at all uncommon for some people to literally trump up false accusations or start rumors. Once they have decided they do not like a pastor, staff person or lay-leader, they adopt what could only be called a "scorched earth" policy. To get their way, they are often willing to seriously damage or destroy the reputations of virtually anyone and everyone in their path. Even the target's wives and children are often subjected to a ruthless barrage of criticism and fault-finding. The wife and children now become somewhat ostracized as many treat them with coldness and downright harshness.

Naturally all this godless behavior causes more and more church members to start "taking sides." Tension rises and people who have known one another for years begin to act like enemies. Wholly forgotten is God's direct warning from James 1:20. "The wrath of man works not the righteousness of God." People abandon anything even resembling biblical principles for addressing conflict and soon the "fight is on." The hellish cycle is now fully in motion and the damage is just beginning.

According to Scripture, such obvious wickedness puts people at escalated risk of God's correction. We should also understand that at least the *principle* of "touching not God's anointed" may extend to attacking laypersons who are being much used of the Lord. Yet, rather than developing the spiritual maturity to biblically work through areas of conflict, the godless approach is to quickly dump fellow believers or abruptly cut-off relationships so we can supposedly "move on and start afresh." Nothing could be more unbiblical or opposite to the ways of God! After all, Jesus said believers' love and unity is crucial to our evangelistic witness and representation of God to a lost world (John 13:34-35; 17:21). Like little else, angry attitudes break God's heart, shame His name and devastate His work in a church.

## "It's Just Time for a Change"

An especially sad form of this condition occurs when a minister has been with a church for some years and a small power group decides *"It's just time for a change."* Under that little phrase a literal world of ungodly behavior is committed against pastors, staff, lay-leaders and the church itself. And even though grievances against a pastor are often relatively minor and subjective, God's servant is essentially handed his walking papers. Though he may have faithfully led and suffered with the people through many valleys, all of that is easily forgotten.

A sign of deep modern wickedness is the fact many now view God's ministers as "expendable hired hand we can fire at will." Very little could be more contrary to biblical teachings or less like the attitude of Christ. God will not indefinitely tolerate such carnal, unscriptural patterns for treating His servants or conducting church. Sooner or later, serious chastisement comes to churches or individuals who persistently practice such godless patterns. God's holiness and concern for kingdom work cannot allow such conditions to continue indefinitely. While no pastor or leader is anywhere near perfect, the position and call is to be respected (1 Thessalonians 5:12-13; Hebrew 13:17)! *God-called servants are not just "hired hands."*

Of course, there are many instances when God does direct leaders to and from churches. But one thing is certain — the above patterns are the direct opposite of God's way for leading ministers to and from churches. They are also opposite of anything even remotely resembling loving or mature Christian behavior. Furthermore, if believers stubbornly persist in the more extreme forms of these sinful patterns, they run serious risk of God's intervention (especially after God convicts them.) Yet because of deep spiritual blindness, it never crosses their minds that God may deal severely with those who continually cause such major problems in churches (1 Corinthians 11:30; Acts 5:1-11).

## God's Toleration is not Endless!

It would likely shock us to realize the times God had to deal strongly with people for hindering His work in a church. While it certainly grieves Him to intervene, His holiness and concern for Christ's Church often requires an eventual response. After years of nationwide research, I could publish a massive book comprised solely of sobering reports where God apparently intervened to stop persons seriously damaging unity in His Church. Of course, I would never publish such a book because only God knows for certain which events are judgment and which are not. But one thing *is* certain — the Bible leaves *no doubt* that God will not indefinitely tolerate such obviously damaging, ungodly behavior in a local congregation (Acts 5:1-11; 1 Corinthians 11:28-34; Hebrews 10:26,31).

People must never think the fact they seem to have gotten away with harmful patterns is any sign they will continue to go un-judged. God's judgment may grind slowly but it grinds *surely* (Galatians 6:7; 1 Peter 4:17). Furthermore when God brings clear attention to a particular sin, His potential judgment just drew considerably closer (Luke 12:48). Once we fully recognize something as sin and *then* stubbornly resist obedience, consequences are much more certain and serious!

Dear readers, it is very dangerous to make excuses or try and explain away God's clear conviction. If He has revealed areas of sin, please do not resist God or be angered by His reproof. Humble yourself and you will be blessed beyond measure! Remember — God *never* rejects the broken and contrite but *always* resists those who justify their sin (Psalms 51:17; James 4:6).

## For Many — A Critical Moment of Decision

As stated earlier, I certainly take no pleasure in describing this tragic pattern in thousands of churches. Yet, I have the strongest sense God led me to address this issue for a vital reason. I believe there are growing indications our Lord is about to send a revival. But contrary to popular understanding, revivals often begin with increased cleansing and judgment among believers (1 Peter 4:17)! Profound breaking and cleansing usually precede genuine revival floods.

In writing this section, I am haunted by a sobering sense these words may for some be a "last warning" before God is forced to deal with patterns long harmful to Christ's Church (Proverbs 29:1). I pen these words with the deepest compassion and earnest prayer that *no one* hardens their heart against God. Now is the time for brokenness, honesty and repentance, not continued anger and self-justification. Please do not ignore God or put off obedience.

## Ending the "Fruit Basket Turn Over" Syndrome

*A final related symptom of a spiritually troubled church is rapid turnover of members.* Where unloving attitudes are prevalent, people that join the church often quickly stop attending or soon move their membership. Conversely, when people sense love and unity in a church, they usually want to establish relationships and get involved. However, if they do not sense love and warmth, they either drop out of regular attendance or quickly leave the church. If a church has a lot of "fruit basket turnover," it is very important to ask why. While high turnover is not always the fault of a church, it usually suggests a major problem of attitude and fellowship.

Again, I remind readers not to be overwhelmed if they see many problems in their church. Take comfort in the incredible grace of

God! He never fully abandons Christ's Church even in serious failures. Keep your eyes on God and trust Him for grace as you pray for miraculous changes in your midst. Ask God to guide you to clear steps for repentance and change.

## Questions for Prayerful Reflection

Dear friend, has God convicted you of any of the patterns in this section? Such patterns are an *extreme abomination* to the holy name of God! Has God indicated an area to address? If so, you must utterly reject the predictable sinful tendency to become defensive or argue with God. Remember, these principles come straight from Scripture, not from the opinion of men. When we argue with Scripture, we argue with God. One thing is certain — when we knowingly resist God we never win. In fact, we lose every time and the consequences may well be severe.

Let every reader again remember God's reason for conviction. *He loves you and seeks to bring repentance and transformation!* If you heed His voice, miraculous change and growth will surely occur. When you go to those you may have wronged, healing can begin to flow. However, if you now try to ignore God's voice or in any way justify sin, you leave God little choice (Hebrews 10:26-31). While our God does not willingly chastise His children, He cannot indefinitely tolerate blatant willful sin (Lamentations 3:33). Neither will He tolerate a belligerent pride that refuses to admit and confess an error! Let us seek God while He may yet be found (Isaiah 55:6).

## Putting On Christ — Putting Off the Flesh
### Steps for Repentance and Victory

If God has indeed spoken to your heart, you must take this with deadly seriousness! God is not playing games with these issues. Carefully consider the prayer below. If you would be willing to pray a prayer similar to the one below, please do it now. Ask God to help you mean it and take whatever steps of repentance His will requires.

And remember, His grace is greater than our greatest failures (and we have all failed!)

With this particular sin, some will definitely need to ask their church to forgive them. But make no mistake — your act of obedience may well be the spark that brings revival! Instead of bringing harm, you could now bring enormous healing to your church and many others. (I've seen it happen!) Do not be ashamed to admit an error and don't let pride keep you from obeying God. Oh friend, He loves you! Please let Him bless you and your whole church.

*A Prayer of Cleansing and Transformation* — "Father, I fully confess the ways I have mistreated Your servants and conducted Your work in unscriptural ways. Please forgive me for my angry actions and unkind words that are wrong. By Your grace, I now resolve to repent and seek forgiveness from those I have offended. Please fill me with Your Spirit and grant me a heart of humility, obedience and love."

## *Pattern Three*
## *Questions for Prayer and Study Groups*

(for individuals, small groups or churchwide studies)

(1)   Carefully read 1 Thessalonians 5:12-13, 1 Timothy 5:17 and Hebrews 13:17. Based on these Scriptures, what is to be believers' attitude toward spiritual leaders in their church?

(2)   Based on Psalms 105:15, does God give a serious warning to those who would harm His prophets and anointed servants? Why do you think this is so urgent to God?

(3)   Do you think God will forever tolerate those whose attitudes harm His work and His servants? Why or why not?

(4)   Please read John 13:34-35 and 17:21. Why does fighting in church profane God's name before a watching world? What does bickering and fighting do to church evangelism?

(5)   In 1 Corinthians 11:28-34, we clearly see that God brought severe judgments on believers who took the Lord's Supper "unworthily" by being unkind and divisive toward fellow believers. Do you think mistreating God's leaders and servants would also bring God's judgment? Why or why not?

(6)   Based on Philippians 4:13, do you think churches and people who have long patterns of fighting and bickering can still change?

(7)   What does it say about people or churches if they have a long history of controversy and angry conflict? If a sin or weakness becomes a long-term pattern, it is a spiritual stronghold. Read 2 Corinthians 10:3-5. Can spiritual strongholds be broken? Why or why not? What are our primary weapons?

## Pattern Four
## The "They're not Our Kind" Syndrome

(Matthew 28:16-18; James 2:1-4: 1 John 4:7-8)

*An especially shocking revival barrier is when some members actually attack pastors or staff who are leading a church to significant evangelism and growth.* It is utterly astounding that some long-standing members attack church growth by statements such as "they're just not our kind." It is deeply disturbing that any believer would actually say such a thing. Since Jesus said our whole purpose is to reach *all* people, this attitude is nothing less than an *abomination*! According to James 2:1-5, it is difficult to imagine how any saved person could do anything but rejoice when people are being reached (regardless of their kind.) Such attitudes represent profound immaturity, spiritual blindness or worse.

Just about the most spiritually dangerous things anyone can do is attack or hinder someone who is reaching souls for Christ. When someone is attacking evangelism, outreach or missions, there can be little doubt who is the real author of that attack. And it certainly isn't the Holy Spirit! Mark this well — God will have little or nothing to do with any church (or person) that draws a circle and only wants to minister to "certain people." Even the slightest hint of such an attitude is against all that Christ represents! Mark this well — *no one* walking with God could ever embrace blatant partiality or prejudice (James 2:1-9). Such attitudes are the direct opposite of Christ's heart of love for all people!

Still others harshly attack successful leaders because in their words, "*things are changing in our church.*" While it is certainly true that not all change is good, reaching large numbers of new people always means some level of change. The fact is, we cannot stay frozen in time and growth is simply going to bring some differences. Yet some people are so self-focused and set in their ways, they demand everything to stay just like they want it. To them, the desires, needs and tastes of others simply do not matter. Even if they see the church reaching far more people by making some changes, they really don't care. People with this problem often become very vicious in their attitudes toward those leaders who "brought the changes."

## It's Just Not "Our" Church Anymore

*Yet another reason some attack a successful leader is when a power group fears a "loss of control."* Many churches are plagued by those who really do not want pastors or staff to be "too successful" because it may lessen their (power group's) influence. Such reasoning is in no way biblical or Spirit-guided! Sadly enough, when a power group fears a pastor or leader is becoming "too popular" they often start magnifying his faults or exaggerating problems to make them seem worse. They hardly notice good points and dwell continually on real or imagined faults.

In far too many cases, we even hear of people finding subtle ways to sabotage people's ministries and relationships. If they cannot "snare him" in some serious error or flaw, they seek simply to make him and his family or supporters so miserable that he finally just leaves. All the while, these ungodly attitudes and behaviors devastate God's activity in their congregation.

Some people are so utterly godless and jealous of power, they are not above *inventing* scandal or crises to try and drive off a leader. Another tragically common pattern is relentless attack and pressure upon his family. In the minds of such people, even their children are fair game! It speaks volumes about the character of anyone who would be harsh and unkind to children. It is extremely doubtful that any truly saved person would ever commit such blatant, willful evil. If a Christian ever did sink to such wickedness, the Bible clearly teaches that he or she should *expect* strong chastisement from God.

Anyone involved in such patterns should take Psalms 105:15 very seriously (especially if God is now clearly speaking to your heart). "Do not touch My anointed ones, And do My prophets no harm"

(Psalms 105:15). According to Hebrews 10:26-31, continuing in willful sin after knowing better is to literally *stomp* on the precious blood of Jesus. My friend, God has gone to great lengths to place this book in your hands. If the Lord has clearly spoken to your heart, it is *essential* that you immediately heed His voice.

# Questions for Reflection

Is there any sense in which you have exhibited prejudice toward certain persons or groups? Have you drawn distinctions and sought only to reach people you consider more desirable? God's Word leaves no doubt as to His attitude toward "selective" ministry. These behaviors draw God's severest displeasure and reprimand. In such cases, God says we have become "judges with evil thoughts" (James 2:4).

Have you in any way attacked or criticized church leaders for reaching certain people or leading your church to growth? While it is certainly true that change and growth are challenging, this gives no one the right to become bitter or unkind toward others. Remember, the glory of God's name and furtherance of His kingdom is far above all personal preferences.

Dear saint if God has convicted you in any of these areas, please do not become angry or defensive. The only proper response is that of David (brokenness and repentant) not Saul (defensive and self-justifying). Remember, God is convicting to point you to forgiveness, healing and transformation. Yet, if we become angry or self-justifying at God's conviction, we run a most profound and serious risk. It is vital to humbly confess all sin and trust God for grace to change. Instead of a hindrance, we then become a powerful catalyst for revival! Will we be defensive and self-justifying or broken and repentant? The choice is yours — please choose wisely and seek God now.

## Putting On Christ — Putting Off the Flesh
### Steps for Repentance and Victory

Carefully consider the prayer below. If God has spoken and you are willing to pray a similar prayer, please take this very serious and do it now. God is definitely watching your response. Ask Him to help you mean your prayer and take whatever steps of repentance His will requires. And remember friend, God convicts to transform *not* condemn.

*A Prayer of Cleansing and Transformation* — "Father, please forgive me for showing prejudice and seeing some as more desirable than others. Forgive me for my selfish unwillingness to change. By Your grace, I now repent of all attitudes that are haughty and unloving. Help me go to those I have offended. Lord, please fill me with Your Spirit and grant me a heart of love for all peoples."

## *Pattern Four*
## *Questions for Prayer and Study Groups*

(for individuals, small groups or churchwide studies)

(1)   Please read James 2:1-4. Does God want us to value some people over others? Why or why not?

(2)   Read James 2:4. What do you think James means by "evil judges?" How would Jesus view a person or church that excluded people based on their color or social status?

(3)   Based on James 2:9, would Jesus bless a church that showed prejudice? On a scale of 1-10, how serious is the sin of deciding not to love and reach out to certain people? Would Jesus likely bring judgment on a people that practiced willful prejudice or exclusivity?

# Pattern Five
# Attack and Resistance
# Toward the "New People"

---

(John 17:20-22; Acts 2:1, 42-47: Romans 15:5-7)

*Another form of attack is long-term members expressing hostility or resistance toward newer people who take positions of leadership.* In some churches, long-standing members seek to maintain "control" at all costs. This can be an especially serious problem in smaller churches when one or two families may seek to tightly control everything. Mature believers rejoice when God grows their church and are thrilled for others to share leadership. Yet pastors and other leaders are often angrily attacked simply for seeking to involve a broader group in leadership. Little could be more selfish, prideful or ungodly. But for just such reasons, godly leaders are increasingly under fire.

Churches with this pattern tend to exhibit a distinct cliquishness among longer term members. Rather than following God's command to function as a loving family and unified body, they make it difficult for new members to fully feel a part. While admittedly assimilating new members takes real effort and loving patience, it is among the most vital elements of our calling as Christ's Church. In fact, we must totally commit to welcome and involve new members, not make them feel marginalized. Little worse could be said of a church than it is unloving or cold to visitors and new members. Again, a vital part of God's purpose is believers functioning as a unified, loving body (John 13:34-35; 17:20-22).

## Love Means Open Hearts to Others

Whether or not they realize it, people are badly hindering God's Spirit when they resist involving qualified newer members in the heart of church life. A church is to function as a body with many people using their gifts in service. It is not to be a monopoly with only a few people doing everything. However, in churches where no one will step up to the plate of service, a few people may indeed have to do it all. In such cases these people are to be much admired, not criticized.

People who will not work have no right to criticize those who at least get up and try. Yet it is amazing how some people will sit on the sidelines and continually criticize those who actually do the heavy lifting. These critics are typically full of advice and instructions *until* the question turns to the possibility of their actually shouldering a major work load themselves. In that case, they usually quickly change the subject, conveniently disappear or recite some of the best excuses ever known to man.

Dear believer, have you resisted God's command to welcome and embrace new members in your church? Without question, we are to work at assimilating new members in the ministry of Christ's Church. Have you in any sense been jealous or possessive of power? Do you at all exhibit a "we - they" attitude in the body of Christ? Divisive cliques and factions should have no place in the Church! In fact, this was the exact attitude that caused God to severely judge several members of the Corinthian church (1 Corinthians 11:28-34). May God grant us the wisdom to live and love as one family.

## Putting On Christ — Putting Off the Flesh
### Steps for Repentance and Victory

Carefully consider the prayer below. If God has spoken and you are willing to pray a similar prayer, please pause and do it now. Above all, ask God to help you mean it and take any steps of repentance His will requires. Remember, Jesus is worth our total repentance.

*A Prayer of Cleansing and Transformation* — "Father, please forgive me for hindering the oneness and love of my church. By Your grace, I repent of division and will seek to love and work with all members of my church family. Please fill me with Your Spirit and grant me a heart of loving patience."

## *Pattern Five*
## *Questions for Discussion and Study*

(for individuals, small groups or churchwide studies)

(1) Based on John 17:20-23, what should be believers' attitudes toward new members that God sends into the church body? How much priority should we give to welcoming and including new members into the church?

(2) What part do you think "maintaining control" might play in not wanting to include others? (Of course, it is wisdom to get to know new member's maturity and gifts before giving them key roles.)

(3) Based on Acts 2:1 and 42-47, how important is it to work at developing and maintaining the unity and fellowship of the church? Read Ephesians 4:29-32. According to these Scriptures, what is a primary way we "grieve the Holy Spirit?" Why is strong fellowship necessary for the full power of the Holy Spirit to work through a church?

# Pattern Six
# Worship Wars and Generational Battles

(Romans 12:9(a), 16-18; 1 Corinthians 3:1-3; 12:25-27)

*A most serious hindrance is the tendency for some to angrily attack others when music style is not always what ministers most to them.* This exceptionally damaging pattern is nothing short of epidemic in the modern Church. Church leadership has the difficult task of seeking ways to lead the widest range of people into genuine worship. While it is not wrong to respectfully share your personal preferences, it is utterly wrong to be angry and demanding. When we care only about our own desires and needs, we show gross selfishness and immaturity. For believers, the central issue should always be, "What is best for the kingdom and the widest range of people." Yet for the carnal and immature the central issue always revolves around, "How can I have everything exactly like I want it."

While attacks on worship style are often couched in spiritual or doctrinal objections, the real issues are usually personal taste and plain selfishness (though there are exceptions when objections are indeed doctrinal and legitimate.) It is my conviction that far extremes on either end of the scale should generally be avoided. If each group shows love and basic maturity, we can almost always meet peacefully somewhere in the middle. Yet, if each group is determined to have it all "their way," the fight is on! There is something profoundly sad about believers angrily dividing and fighting over of all things — *worshiping* the Prince of Peace! Indeed, what does it do to God's name when we fight over worship?

## Rejecting the "We-They" Mentality

Generational battles usually occur when young and old view one another with a general attitude of criticism and suspicion. While some natural generational tensions are to be expected, it can easily move into sinful attitudes of disrespect (both ways). We must all remember that different generations have had very varied experiences so some of their tastes and views will naturally be different. Yet rather than seeking to understand and accept some of these differences, each group more or less writes off the other as "unspiritual" or "out of touch." Battles lines are drawn and each group becomes antagonistic and withdraws from the other.

Bitter generational battles are completely opposite from the principle of unity in diversity as described in Scripture (1 Corinthians 12-14). It is healthy for diverse age groups and cultures to work through the process of developing the maturity to abide together in peace. Spiritual maturity definitely requires "give and take" from each group. Yet today, many want to selfishly draw a circle and only be around those just like themselves. This is clearly *not* the New Testament pattern and actually robs us of an essential element of spiritual growth.

## Different Generations Need One Another!

Serious age-related battles are especially sad because each group actually has so very much to give to the other. The truth is we really do need each other! Today's young desperately need the loving encouragement and guidance of senior adults, *not* their harsh condemnation. On the other hand, seniors deserve the honor, respect and ministry of younger generations. Clearly, God calls both groups to work at being loving and understanding toward the other. It is a great tragedy to see issues like music or cultural styles bring anger, suspicion and unnecessary separation.

An increasingly common failure is when seniors harshly over-criticize children and youth who are somewhat unruly in church. It is vital to remember many of these children come from chaotic schools and dysfunctional families with no church background whatsoever. How could we possibly expect them to automatically know how to act in church? While we certainly cannot give up on maintaining reasonable order, we must show love and patience toward today's youth. The very last thing they need is to attend church and experience anger, harshness and condemnation from older believers. If their first brief encounters in church are decidedly negative, they will likely reject Christ and never return to *any* church. Dear saints, our attitudes may well be the first (and potentially last) impression many ever receive of the Savior.

## Love Overcomes Music Styles and Hair-Do's

Reaching today's unchurched generation is indeed a challenging venture. They often come to our churches deeply wounded with no biblical knowledge and filled with sinful bondage. However, if we draw self-righteous robes around ourselves and mostly meet them with harsh condemnation, we could not be acting less like Christ.

While we certainly cannot compromise biblical standards or truth, we simply must show love and understanding in guiding younger generations toward spiritual growth. It is essential that older believers show the maturity and patience to love generations whose cultures differ vastly from our own. Let us ever remember that "love covers a multitude of sins" and crosses an ocean of barriers (1 Peter 4:8). In other words, love sees past earrings and purple hair to the precious souls that need God's touch!

*At the same time, it is equally vital for churches to teach children and youth to greatly honor and respect senior adults.* Youth leaders must work hard at helping youth appreciate the strengths and wisdom of older generations. After all, honoring seniors is a primary biblical command! Furthermore, it is the dear seniors who built most of our churches and pay many of the bills. It is today's seniors who set the example in strong marriages, faithful tithing and loyal church attendance. For any number of reasons, they deserve our honor and respect!

Our younger generations should be taught to consider and respect the feelings of seniors, not willfully flaunt offensive behaviors in their faces. Rather than ignoring their feelings, younger generations should avoid disrespect and insensitivity toward their elders. It is indeed a central command of God. Of course, God's command includes humble, loving-kindness from each age group to the other.

## Meeting "Somewhere in the Middle"

Though cultures, music and tastes are starkly different, young and old must both work at showing loving consideration for the other. Christ's love and unity demands that different generations work at meeting somewhere in the middle. "Each of you should look not only to your own interests, but also to the interests of others" (Philippians 2:4). Glorifying God's name demands that we immediately cease our fighting over selfish personal preferences!

As Christians, we are seldom more like Christ than when we move past our comfort zones to love those who are different. Conversely, we are seldom more like the devil than when we selfishly demand our way and ignore the needs of others. It is wonderful to note that some groups of senior adults and youth are working at loving one another in spite of differences. People who love step out of comfort zones, cross barriers and go to others rather than waiting for others to come to them. Is this happening in your church or are battle lines still drawn?

My friend, why wait on others to make the first move? God is almost certainly calling *you* to deny yourself and take steps to seek peace for the good of Christ's Church. One thing is certain —no believer can afford to shut off dialogue with other parts of the body of Christ. When we follow that path, we all lose and Christ's name is shamed before a watching world.

## Putting On Christ — Putting Off the Flesh
### Steps for Repentance and Victory

Carefully consider the prayer below. If God has spoken and you are willing to pray a similar prayer, please pause and do it now. Ask

God to help you mean it and take the steps of repentance His will requires. Thank God for His grace to help you change!

*A Prayer of Cleansing and Transformation* — "Father, I fully confess ways I have demanded my own preferences with little concern for the whole Body of Christ. Please forgive me for unloving, selfish attitudes and actions. By Your grace, I now resolve to repent and seek forgiveness from those I have offended. I commit to be more loving, patient and accepting of those who are different. Please fill me with Your Spirit and grant me a heart of humility and love."

## *Pattern Six*
## *Questions for Prayer and Study Groups*

(for individuals, small groups or churchwide studies)

(1)  Carefully read Philippians 2:3-4. How would looking to the interests of others lessen or prevent many worship wars over personal preferences in music styles?

(2)  Based on 1 Peter 4:8-9, how would an attitude of love and acceptance enable different age groups to view each other with less suspicion and greater love?

(3)  Please reflect on James 4:1-4. Do you think the basic root of most worship wars and generational battles are actual doctrinal disagreement or personal preferences and self-interest?

(4)  What do you think it means to say different groups can usually find reasonable peace "somewhere in the middle?"

(5)  Read 1 Corinthians chapter fourteen. Do you think one part of the body can afford to disregard and "write-off" another part as insignificant? Why or why not? Do you think unity automatically occurs between various groups and ages or does it require constant prayerful work? What part do you think "dying to self" and putting others first will play in building loving churches and families?

# Pattern Seven
# Clock Watching, Fleshly Complaining and Spiritual Insensitivity

## The Sin of Insulting the Holy Spirit!
(John 4:23-24; Ephesians 4:30; 1 Thessalonians 5:19-20)

*A disturbing modern evil is angry grumbling against leadership when worship services run a few minutes beyond the normal time.* Imagine the utter absurdity of telling the Holy Spirit, "You must enter and exit precisely on our time cue." One thing is certain — no great move of God has *ever* come with people closely watching a clock. Yet it is clear some have the attitude we're really doing God a favor by giving Him an hour on Sunday. God forbid that we should actually be made to sit for an extra few minutes of hearing His Word. And Lord help the person who would dare make us ten minutes late for lunch!

When individuals gripe and complain over such matters, they reveal a truly shocking level of carnality. The implications of such attitudes are deeply disturbing. Indeed, what does it say about a person's spirituality (or total lack thereof) when they find it difficult to "endure" even a few extra moments of Scripture and worship? How would they be able to tolerate the continuous praise of heaven? Without question, they would be extremely out of place in the atmosphere of heaven. Such an astoundingly shallow attitude suggests serious concern for someone's spiritual condition. It is frankly hard to imagine any truly saved person exhibiting such attitudes.

## Recapturing Reverence for the Preached Word
(Isaiah 66:5)

Another pattern of this sin is great insensitivity to the Holy Spirit *during* worship services. Especially as we move toward decision time, some people begin to shift around, look at their watches or even get up and leave. Anyone remotely sensitive to God knows the invitation (decision time) is absolutely crucial. Especially during that time, the only proper response is to remain utterly quiet, earnestly praying for yourself and those who may need to make decisions. Any other response becomes a tool Satan uses to seriously distract others and grieve the Holy Spirit.

Little is more distracting or hindering to God's Spirit than people shuffling around or leaving while a minister is trying to lead souls to a life or death choice. What does it say about someone if all he or she can think of is "getting out" while people are being asked to make eternal decisions? It can only say they are completely and totally out of touch with God's Spirit! If people are that concerned with getting to lunch or beating others to the parking lot, something is tragically wrong in their souls.

## We Must Return to the "Biblical Fear of God!"
### (Proverbs 1:7; Ecclesiastes 12:13-14)

We can tell much about believers' fear of God (or lack thereof) by how they treat times of worship and hearing Scripture. Though it sounds unbelievable, it is also not uncommon to hear of adults talking or doing other things *during* worship services. They seem oblivious to the serious purpose of worship and preaching God's word. There are also somewhat oblivious to the fact they are being heard by others.

Closely related is the tragically common pattern of church members talking and laughing in the foyer or hall just outside the sanctuary. Though we may be tempted to view this as a something of a minor annoyance, in many cases it is by no means "minor." Such actions can seriously distract and speak volumes about the attitudes of those doing the distracting. Needless to say, such patterns are real hindrances to the Spirit. Worse yet, these actions demonstrate a profound lack of the biblical fear (reverence) of Holy God. No one with proper reverence could ever practice these patterns!

For balance and grace, let me note that some believers may have committed these patterns without realizing how seriously they hinder the Holy Spirit. My friend, if that is your case, God is gracious and knows you did not intend to hinder His Spirit. But now that you know, you must take this very seriously. Simply confess this wrong and resolve to be more sensitive in the future. On the other hand, there are some who know full-well these patterns hinder God's Spirit and really don't care. There is grave concern for the soul of anyone so blatantly indifferent to God and people.

## Rejecting the "Worship Spectator" Attitude

A hindrance often overlooked is when believers are mentally and spiritually disengaged while the Word is preached and people are making decisions. In other words, they develop a "worship spectator" attitude. We become worship spectators when we sing music or listen to sermons without a change of heart. God definitely intends for all believers to be spiritual *participants* and not just passive *spectators* in a worship service.

When we are present in worship, God expects us to *participate* in three crucial ways. (1) By listening intently to His Word. (2) By responding immediately to what God says to your heart. (3) By praying for others as the Word is preached. To do less, is to hinder the moving of God's Spirit. Yet, many believers seem unaware they hinder God's Spirit by daydreaming instead of responding or praying for others. While this hindrance is not as direct and overt as moving around or leaving early, it is nonetheless significant.

In conclusion, I must also stress the enormous importance of believers immediately obeying whatever prompting God gives in a worship service. Surveys show many believers have settled into a passive, non-response pattern in worship services. Yet, if we are truly listening and sensitive, God will often prompt us to go to the altar to pray, go to someone needing prayer, commit to some area of repentance or share a testimony or prayer burden. When a church body settles into a continual pattern of doing nothing in response to God's Word, the Holy Spirit is seriously quenched. Failure to respond usually comes from apathy, pride or both. *The moment God speaks, believers must be sensitive to act in obedience!* To ignore that prompting profoundly quenches God's Spirit in the atmosphere of the church.

## Tearing Down the "Spiritual Wall of Resistance"

Preachers and evangelists go into some churches and immediately sense that all too familiar oppressive "wall of resistance." Experienced conference leaders and revivalists often dub this phenomena "the invisible wall." On the other hand, when church members are sensitive and quickly responsive, it is far easier for others to make much needed public decisions. This creates a spiritual freedom in the very atmosphere. In such churches, there is a far greater sense of God's Presence and wonderful freedom for people to respond. It is amazing how one person's obedience frees obedience in many others. Sadly, it is also true that one person's disobedience can hinder and quench God's Spirit in a whole congregation. May God help us return to a proper reverence and sensitivity to His Holy Presence.

Without question, corporate worship, preaching and prayer services are most crucial times of kingdom activity. Believers are to approach each of these events with an awe of God's Presence. If we are to see revival, saints must return to the proper respect of God's holy presence. We are commanded to adopt a humble attitude of brokenness and *tremble* before His Word (Isaiah 66:5). In worship and hearing God's Word, our attitude is to be one of careful listening to fully obey whatever God reveals. If we embrace such reverence, fleshly complaining, distracting behaviors and insensitivity will immediately cease in our services! May God help us return to instant obedience to His smallest prompting. As King of Kings and Lord of Lords, He surely deserves our full attention, deepest reverence and quick obedience.

## Returning to the Biblical Fear and Reverence of God
### (Proverbs 1:7; Ecclesiastes 12:13-14; Matthew 6:9)

Another form of hindering worship is to focus on the messenger rather than the message. To sit and over-analyze a preacher's appearance, clothing or style is to ignore God's voice. Our focus is to be on what God is saying, *not* the personality or style of the speaker. To focus on how a speaker or singer looks and sounds instead of the message is to utterly grieve the Holy Spirit. As worshipers, our responsibility is to focus on God, not the particular characteristics of the messenger. Worship is all about God, not the delivery person. People should leave services talking of the greatness and glory of God, not the speaker or singer. God shares His glory with no man, woman or program (Isaiah 42:3; 1 Corinthians 1:29).

Even before worship begins, congregations should embrace an attitude of preparing to enter the presence of Almighty God. The very heart of worship is the sincere bowing of hearts in utter surrender and loving obedience. It is not a good sign when people are boisterously laughing and talking while choirs are beginning a call to worship. It is equally disturbing when people loudly talk in the sanctuary foyer during worship. Not only are such patterns hindering to God's Spirit, they reflect a gross disrespect for the awesome importance of meeting with God. Yet concerning this point, there is some good news to report. Growing numbers of believers and churches are returning to a greater awe of Holy God. While it is yet a very small minority, it is a growing minority!

Dear reader, has God convicted you of any tendency to daydream or neglect prayer during worship services? Have you hindered God's Spirit by moving around or distracting others? Are there times you resist God's clear prompting to go to the altar or pray with your pastor? If you now resolve to revere His Word and promptly respond to His Spirit, neither you nor your church will ever be the same! Yet be aware of one vital truth. "Greater awareness not only brings greater potential for blessing, it *vastly increases* your level of accountability!"

Now that you know how to respond to God in corporate worship, it is infinitely more urgent that you obey.

## Putting On Christ — Putting Off the Flesh
### Steps for Repentance and Victory

Carefully consider the prayer below. If God has revealed a need and you are willing to pray a similar prayer, please pause and do it now. Ask God to help you mean it and take all the steps of repentance His will requires. Let us again learn to hallow and revere the presence of Holy God.

*A Prayer of Cleansing and Transformation* — "Father, I fully confess the ways I have hindered Your Spirit and dishonored Your Presence during worship services. Please forgive me for fleshly attitudes of insensitivity and irreverence. By Your grace, I now resolve to reverence Your Word and heed Your Spirit. Please fill me with the Spirit of holy reverence and genuine worship."

## *Pattern Seven*
## *Questions for Prayer and Study Groups*

(for individuals, small groups or churchwide studies)

(1)  Please reflect on John 4:23-24. Since we worship God in Spirit and in truth, do you think He is grieved by people who are inattentive or distracting in the midst of a worship service? On a scale of 1-10, what kind of disrespect does this show to God and others?

(2)  In Isaiah 66:5, the prophet said we are to "tremble before the Word of God." What does it say about our level of fearing God if we daydream or distract others while the Word is preached?

(3)  What does it say about the spiritual condition of anyone who would actually gripe and complain if worship runs a bit beyond the regular time? How does God view a person who finds it difficult to "endure" even a few extra moments of worship or preaching?

(4)  Carefully read James 1:22. What is the only proper response to God's Word when He reveals something about which we should repent?

(5)  How would it grieve and quench the Holy Spirit if hearers refused to respond or go to the altar for prayer if God so leads?

(6)  In your own words, why do you think there is a "spiritual wall of resistance" to God's activity in many modern congregations? Name at least three things that hinder God's Spirit in our churches.

# Pattern Eight
# Prayer Meeting Boycotts
# and Fleshly Resistance

(Matthew 21:13; Mark 11:17; Acts 2:1; 4:31)

*The most tragic of hindrances sometimes occurs when a church chooses to embrace a genuine weekly prayer meeting.* It is sad but true that most "church prayer meetings" long ago ceased to be actual prayer meetings. Generally, they became Bible studies with a brief hospital list prayer at the end. Virtually no prayer is given to the eternal issues of evangelism, missions or revival. Yet to God's praise, a glorious return to prayer meetings is underway! But unbelievably, some church members strongly attack and resist Christ's foremost command for churches to be "houses of prayer" (Matthew 21:13; Mark 11:17).

Frankly, it is astounding that any believer would actually attack and complain over establishing a weekly meeting that is predominantly prayer. Make no mistake — *to resist the greater emphasis and strengthening of prayer meetings is to attack the very heart and purpose of God!* But nonetheless, such fleshly resistance is disturbingly common. It truly shows how far a generation has fallen when believers will actually demean and resist the very heart of corporately walking with God.

Many may object to a weekly churchwide prayer meeting with statements such as the following. "I want Bible study so I can grow — we can pray at home. Our preacher's job is to preach and teach, we can all pray on our own. We pay our preacher to preach, not pray. There is no need to have a whole service to pray, we can just say a prayer at the end. I am not good at praying aloud so I will just stop attending if all we're going to do is pray." (Yet no one is required to pray aloud and praying is precisely how we learn to pray more effectively.) Furthermore, teaching his flock to pray is most definitely a major part of a pastor's job. And make no mistake — we teach and learn prayer primarily by *doing* it!

While some of today's common objections may be sincere, they are utterly contrary to Scripture and the practice of the New Testament Church! They are also completely out of touch with The Spirit of God. Such sentiments are the very opposite of any generation that ever saw a great spiritual awakening. If any readers have expressed these sentiments, they probably did it in ignorance and God will certainly forgive. However, immediate repentance is absolutely essential!

## Church Prayer Meetings
## A New Testament Fundamental!

Without question, *every* church should embrace a strong pattern of powerful churchwide prayer meetings! Both the Old and New Testaments leave no doubt that strong corporate praying is essential to being the people of God. Jesus made this utterly clear with His powerful statement in Matthew 21:13(KJV). *"My house shall be called a house of prayer."* There is no question that the whole practice and power of the New Testament Church centered around corporate prayer (Acts 1:4; 2:1; 4:31; 6:4,12). Furthermore, every Great Awakening centered around corporate prayer, strong biblical preaching and deep repentance.

It is vital to understand that a New Testament church is not defined by doctrine alone! It is defined by doctrine and *practice.* Though a church may have the right doctrine on prayer, it must also be reflected in practice before the church can truly call itself "New Testament." How could any church honestly call itself a "New Testament church" if serious corporate prayer meetings are not a predominant practice? After all, was not corporate prayer a central preeminent practice of New Testament Churches? Indeed it was! According to the book of Acts, early churches spent so much time in corporate prayer you could almost say they *were* a prayer meeting!

Given the clear pattern of Scripture and history, is it not utterly astounding that so many modern churches decided they could no longer devote even one weekly service given mostly to prayer? Friends, it is not only astounding, it is unquestionably a primary cause of declining baptisms, rising disunity and collapsing morals! Even churches with solid expository preaching fall far short of Great Awakening power if they neglect the crucial element of dynamic corporate prayer. If you doubt this, study the conversion rates of today's Bible-preaching churches. Tragically few are little better than today's appallingly low baptism averages. Virtually none are even close to New Testament and Great Awakening patterns. The conclusion is clear —we either do church God's way or we do without much of His presence and power. Without question, God's way includes a major emphasis on powerful corporate prayer and repentance *alongside* biblical preaching and evangelism.

## A Modern Day Organizational Arrogance?

Very little could be more unbiblical (or arrogant) than to assume we can do fine without a major emphasis on churchwide prayer meetings. In modern religious life, we can immediately tell what we deem important by observing what we *plan, promote* and *organize.* The fact most churches do everything in the world *but* serious corporate prayer speaks volumes about our true perspectives and priorities. In light of today's devastating trends, do we really still think our activities and strategies can replace prayer meetings? Based on observed actions and priorities, many clearly do.

Dear saints, have we not taken an honest look at the obvious track record from fifty years of quality programs but shallow prayer? One honest look at facts and trends leave no doubt *something* needs to change in a major fashion. We do not need just a little program tweaking, stronger preaching or a better promotional phrase. Neither do we just need to pedal faster and try harder as many promotional emphases imply. The problem is not the programs as many are reasonably solid. The problem is a lack of serious corporate prayer and cleansing *alongside* them!

## Actions Speak Louder Than Words
### We Promote and Practice our "Real" Priorities

Today's typical practice tells us thousands of churches obviously still believe programs, activities and preaching can replace humbling ourselves in fervent, united prayer. In essence, we are telling God, "We don't need prayer meetings, we've got programs, good preaching technique and exciting activities!" Though we have not verbally stated such a position, we may as well have done so. After all, God watches what we "do" not what we "say." According to Judges 7:2, over-emphasizing our abilities is totally unacceptable in the eyes of God.

Friends, it doesn't matter how much we "say" prayer is a priority if we do not practice strong personal and corporate prayer. While we say prayer is a top priority, it is actually only a periphery part of most modern churches and strategies. *Saying* prayer and humility before God are top priorities does not make it so!

One thing is certain — God has *never* sent sweeping revival to any generation that thought itself "beyond" the need for consistently humbling itself in fervent, corporate prayer. If corporate prayer and repentance is the primary way we humble ourselves before God (and it is) then the consistent neglect of serious corporate prayer is the very height of prideful arrogance.

Surely it is no coincidence the abandonment of corporate prayer perfectly coincides with today's shocking decline of baptisms and morals. Make no mistake — *corporate prayer is the primary way we humble ourselves before God.* Until we return to God's fundamental principle, we will continue to lack full New Testament power. Yet at long last, there are growing signs of hope. Concerning prayer meetings, there is a cloud the size of a man's hand on the horizon!

# A Coming Wave of Prayer Meetings!

Even as I write these words, we gladly note a growing minority of churches returning to powerful weekly prayer meetings and periodic solemn assemblies. Without question, God is at work and hundreds of churches are returning to corporate prayer and deeper repentance! After fifty years of nearly total silence, some seminaries are showing signs of increasing emphasis on these crucial practices. I believe today's increasing prayer meetings and solemn assemblies represent the single greatest sign of a potential coming revival.

Yet sadly, some church members actually attack and criticize pastors for doing the one thing that can bring revival — church prayer meetings! Even more unbelievable, some pastors and denominational leaders actually down-play and resist the need for much deeper prayer! They typically resist by saying, "Oh, we're already doing that." To suggest current prayer patterns are adequate shows a serious lack of awareness of New Testament and Great Awakening prayer practice. Worse yet, it may suggest the prideful attitude of saying "how dare anyone imply that our programs could possibly be improved by a greater prayer component." It raises real concern when people resist stronger prayer meetings or defend today's status quo. After all, prayer meetings are the very *heart* of Christians' spiritual power, fellowship and contrition before God (2 Chronicles 7:14; Joel 2:12-18; Matthew 21:13; Acts 1-4).

For sake of balance and fairness, let me state that some prayer meeting resistance comes out of honest misunderstanding or fear. Since most laypeople have never been taught these truths, many truly do not understand *why* church prayer meetings are so important. Still others are insecure and intimidated by a prayer meeting simply because they've never been *taught* to pray effectively.

As leaders, we cannot expect our people to automatically understand the significance of prayer meetings if we haven't clearly taught them! Indeed, how could we expect them to be comfortable or proficient at praying together if we have not modeled it or instructed them? While attacking or boycotting prayer meetings is a truly egregious sin, pastors must show patience in lovingly leading our people toward deeper prayer and understanding. Toward that purpose, I highly recommend that every pastor read *And the Place Was Shaken* by John Franklin. This book is an excellent tool for establishing effective prayer meetings in local churches.

To prepare and motivate churches to embrace prayer meetings, pastors are encouraged to have their entire congregations read the book, *Biblical Patterns for Powerful Church Prayer Meetings*. This concise, inexpensive book is designed to fully convince believers of the importance and practicality of conducting powerful prayer meetings. It is very inexpensively prices so pastors can easily have their whole church read it. If congregations can fully understand why prayer meetings are so vital, they are far less likely to resist efforts to embrace corporate prayer. In fact, once they see the enormous power of effective prayer meetings, they will often be quite *excited* about the changes!

Pastors are also encouraged to copy this section *(Prayer Meeting Boycotts and Fleshly Resistance)* and have their congregations read it. This can have a massive impact toward lessening resistance and motivating churches to support the weekly prayer meeting! A related book is entitled *Seeking the Reviver—Not Just Revival, "Personal and Corporate Prayers that Please God and Bring Awakening."* A third book, *How to Develop an Evangelistic, Kingdom-focused Church Prayer Ministry* also addresses the subject of powerful corporate prayer and cleansing.

The last three books can be secured from the Oklahoma Baptist General Convention for very nominal costs. Once church members truly understand the biblical necessity and awesome benefits of corporate prayer meetings, they will be more than ready to embrace them. To the praise of God, thousands of churches are beginning to do just that!

## Putting On Christ — Putting Off the Flesh
### Steps for Repentance and Victory

Dear reader, it is essential to take this issue seriously. You must not boycott or resist prayer meetings! Carefully consider the prayer below. If God has spoken and you are willing to pray a similar prayer, please pause and do it now. Ask God to grant you sincerity and take the steps of repentance His will requires. And remember, His grace is greater than your deepest need!

*A Prayer of Cleansing and Transformation* — "Father, I confess my fleshly resistance to our church becoming more a house of prayer. Please forgive me for resisting the very heart of our closeness, humility and power before You. By Your grace, I now repent and ask You to teach me to pray. Please fill me with the Holy Spirit and true passion to seek Your face. Lord, I ask these things in Jesus' holy name."

## *Pattern Eight*
## *Questions for Prayer and Study Groups*

(for individuals, small groups or churchwide studies)

(1) Prayerfully read Acts 1:14; 2:1,42-47; 4:31-32. Was corporate prayer central to the priorities of the New Testament Church or was it periphery?

(2) Since the early Church had none of our nice buildings, education, organizations or program, why do you think their spiritual power was so much greater than ours?

(3) According to 2 Chronicles 7:14, what is the primary way we humble ourselves and seek God's face? Remember, all the Old Testament revivals were in the context of *corporate* prayer and repentance.

(4) Carefully read Judges 7:1-2. In what way is it unwise to plan and promote everything in the world *except* humbling ourselves before God in consistent united prayer? What does it say when we think all we need is a "little casual prayer" thrown in around our programs?

(5) Why do you think every great revival and evangelistic explosion in history was centered in powerful corporate prayer meetings (alongside biblical preaching and evangelism)?

(6) Do you think resistance to establishing regular corporate prayer meetings and solemn assemblies could possibly be coming from the Holy Spirit? Why or why not? Do you think it is possible that some leaders might give lip-service to needing more prayer yet either not change or do it half-heartedly?

# Pattern Nine
# Business Meeting Ambushes
# and "Get Out the Vote" Power Plays

(Proverbs 6:16d; Matthew 5:9; 1 Thessalonians 5:13b-15)

*An especially damaging form of spiritual attack is when church members wait for a public meeting to "spring" some issue or grievance on their leadership in a churchwide setting.* I call this pattern "the business meeting ambush." Not only does this totally violate Matthew 18:15, it is usually just a sneaky attempt to force an agenda or attack, belittle and embarrass church leaders. After all, we are commanded to deal with issues privately if at all possible.

Yet instead of going to church leaders and discussing or informing them of a matter beforehand, some individuals purposely wait in order to make a public scene. It becomes an evil game of trying to "blindside" or "out-maneuver" leaders by catching them off guard. Little could be more unbiblical or contrary to the Spirit of Christ.

Closely related is the very ungodly behavior of the phone campaign to get inactive members to come to that one meeting and back a particular position. It is frankly hard to imagine how non-attendees would even have the gall to show up and then of course promptly disappear again. To assure they "get their way," words and motions are carefully preplanned down to who will quickly jump up, second the motion and call for the vote.

## The Surprise Attack!
### Vacation-Time Ambushes and Out of Town Take-Overs

Some actually plan devious ways to keep potential opposition from being in the meeting. They may even orchestrate a "surprise" business meeting when key opposing leaders are out of town. People who commit such deceits are often so utterly out of touch with God, they will even *brag* about these tactics and congratulate themselves for what they think is clever maneuvering. It is difficult to imagine how any Christian would think such behavior is the way to conduct God's business? Yet today, such fleshly machinations are all too common. The resulting damage is both severe and long-lasting. Ugly memories and emotional scars are often etched into the very depths of people's souls.

Of course these fleshly behaviors often lead to angry, bitter battles in business meetings. If battles do not erupt in the actual meeting, these patterns surely lead to serious anger and divisiveness under the surface. Even more serious, such practices profoundly quench and grieve the Holy Spirit (Ephesians 4:30). Business meetings and decisions of these types set back churches' ministries for months or even years. These behaviors greatly damage our ability to evangelize and are an absolute disgrace to the name of Christ (John 13:34-35; 17:21). Make no mistake—God is deeply offended by such blatant godlessness committed in His name. The Bible is clear that Holy God cannot forever tolerate such fleshly patterns in His Church. *Worse yet, these ungodly patterns are a most dangerous profaning of God's name before the world!*

## Angry Division Devastates Evangelism and Profanes God's Name!

Without question, the most devastating impact of this wickedness is a devastated testimony to the community at large. Again, we must soberly reflect on Jesus' powerful words, "the world will know you are mine by the way you love and remain in unity with one another" (author's paraphrase of John 13:34-35 and 17:21). Believers, if a huge part of our witness is loving unity, then countless thousands surely reject Jesus because of our fighting! Indeed, why should a lost world listen to us if they often actually get along better than we do? They not only don't listen, they laugh at such churches in scornful derision. (And who could blame them?)

Dear saints, if such are our patterns, we must *weep* before God in utter brokenness and repentance. If ever there was an issue over which the priests (leaders) should *"weep between the porch and the altar,"* surely this is one! (Joel 2:17) Even more there must be brokenness over the shame this brings to God's holy name! But thank God, there is forgiveness! Let us see these evils for the abominations they are and immediately repent. The name of God and power of our evangelism are surely at stake.

Though this subject is painful, God assures us of mercy if we genuinely repent. Indeed, there may be several reading this section who were never taught the serious error of the behaviors we have chronicled. It is entirely possible you have seen church conducted in these ways from your earliest memory. Through no fault of your own, you really didn't know better on some of these matters. God is especially merciful to those who sinned unintentionally. Yet with several of these patterns, *no one* could do them in innocence.

My friend, God is so ready to forgive, heal and restore! Whatever you do, please do not make excuses, resist the Spirit or become angry at His reproof. Again, if God has opened your eyes to sin, He has done it for one reason — to forgive you and change your life! But also be aware, when He clearly speaks, our *accountability* to obey rises many fold. If after clear conviction we stubbornly resist God and justify our actions, we are in a sense *treading* on the Son of God (Hebrews 10:26-31). God cannot let such rebellion go forever unaddressed. As God's Spirit speaks, the choice is yours — rebellion or revival. Oh dear saint, *please* let it be revival.

## Putting On Christ — Putting Off the Flesh
### Steps for Repentance and Victory

It is very important that you carefully consider the prayer below. If God has spoken and you are willing to pray a similar prayer, please pause and do it now. Ask God to help you mean it and take the steps of repentance His will requires. And remember, God never loses a case that is fully laid at His feet.

*A Prayer of Cleansing and Transformation* — "Father, I fully confess my role in angry and divisive church politics. Please forgive me for using the world's ways and shaming the gospel of my blessed Savior. By Your grace, I repent of these patterns and resolve to seek the forgiveness of those I have harmed. Please fill me with the Holy Spirit of humility, love and repentance."

## *Pattern Nine*
## *Questions for Prayer and Study Groups*

(for individuals, small groups or churchwide studies)

(1)  Please read Ephesians 4:1-3 and 4:29-32. Why do you think angry bickering, disunity and unkindness so severely grieves God's Spirit? Do you think God will forever tolerate the actions of those who consistently stir controversy in a church? Why or why not?

(2)  Carefully reflect on 1 John 4:7-8. What is a major indicator that someone may not be born again? Can anyone right with God consistently exhibit an angry or unkind attitude toward others?

(3)  On a scale of 1-10, how urgent is the need for change in someone who always seem to be negative or unkind about something or someone? In other words, how big a priority is an attitude of forgiveness and loving-kindness? Try to think of Scriptures that explain your answer.

(4)  Read Proverbs 6:16d. When something is called an "abomination," it is a major step *beyond* basic sin. Is it significant that God included divisive actions among believers as an abomination? Why or why not?

(5)  Based on Matthew 5:23-24, if someone has committed public anger and ungodliness in a church setting, can they be fully right with God without asking forgiveness of those they have offended? Based on Proverbs 28:13, what must we do besides confession to again be right with God?

# Pattern Ten
# Pot Stirring and Ax Grinding

(Ephesians 4:29-32; Philippians 4:8; James 5:9)

*Still another expression of ungodliness occurs when some people keep "stirring the pot" of controversy even after the church has clearly expressed its will on a matter.* Unless an issue is truly over some fundamental doctrine, believers must have the maturity and good judgment to live in peace though the church decision may not best suit them. After all, the majority could be right and we should have the humility to submit to the greater good. While it takes genuine humility and maturity to embrace this pattern, it is certainly God's will that we do so.

If a church member's disagreement is truly over fundamental doctrine, he or she should probably pray about going to a church that agrees with their conviction (rather than staying and angrily disrupting fellowship). Yet in far too many cases, certain individuals just keep grinding the axe of controversy. Worse yet, they often do everything possible to make the church decision fail. Sadly, we often see this when those who didn't vote to call a particular pastor actually work directly or indirectly to undermine his ministry. They will tend to minimize his positives and maximize any weaknesses. Very little could be more devilish, immature or damaging to God's work. While "love covers a multitude of sins," evil points out and magnifies every flaw! (James 5:20)

## The "Abomination" of Sowing Division in Church
### (Proverbs 6:16)

An even more serious form of this evil is witnessed in those who consistently seek to stir up controversies and divisions where none even exist. In Proverbs 6:16, God says one who sows division is literally an *abomination*! Yet some people have gotten trapped in such negative mind-sets they just aren't content unless they are complaining or pointing out some "problem." These individuals have very little positive to say no matter how well things may be going in most areas.

People caught in this pattern are continually complaining or unhappy about something. Even if eight out of ten things are going well, negative-minded people will invariably harp on the two that aren't. Not only is this extremely damaging to the spirit of a church, it is spiritually dangerous and blatantly disobedient to God (Philippians 4:8). Such attitudes are the exact opposite of a heart guided by the Holy Spirit. Thank God, there is hope in His grace!

In Philippians 4:8, we are clearly commanded to keep our focus on things that are good and positive. "Finally, brothers, whatever is noble, whatever is right, whatever is pure, whatever is lovely, whatever is admirable — if anything is excellent or praiseworthy — **think about such things**" (Philippians 4:8). In other words, we are commanded to barely glance at one another's weaknesses (which we all have) and gaze at the positives. Thank God, very negative people can learn to be positive and up-building to others. Furthermore, when negative people become more positive, the entire church is blessed and so are they. By God's grace, even the most complaining heart can become faith-filled, positive and encouraging to others.

## Experiencing "Across the Aisle" Revivals

The turning point in many great revivals is not only when people go "down" the aisle, but "across the aisle" to get right with others. When angry, divided believers take the first steps and go to one another, God often sends a flood of His Spirit! Dear believer, God is so ready to help you turn from your anger, criticism and judgment. His grace is more than sufficient to help you change. When you take that first step toward getting right with God and others, He will take ten toward you! *The hallowing of God's holy name is reason enough to immediately obey God's voice.*

Countless thousands long carry issues they have never truly surrendered to God. With some, the grievances are severe while others only represent a difference of opinion. Yet nonetheless, the inner walls remain. These believers have never come to the place of releasing the bitterness and committing to love and pray for the offender. While we are not required to ignore or minimize a difference, we are required to release the anger and show love. My friend, the time has come to once and for all "let it go." No more ax grinding or pot stirring! It is time to "bury the hatchet." (And not in someone's head.) Remember, harboring anger and bitterness is like "you drinking poison and expecting the other person to die." Yet instead of that, you are the one that gets sick, yours are the prayers that are blocked and they don't die!

## Putting On Christ — Putting Off the Flesh
### Steps for Repentance and Victory

Carefully consider the prayer below. If God has spoken to you and you are willing to pray a similar prayer, please pause and do it now. Ask God to grant you sincerity and take whatever steps of repentance His will requires. And remember, God's mercy is higher than the heavens for those who repent.

*A Prayer of Cleansing and Transformation* — "Father, I humbly confess the ways I have fanned controversy and division in my church. Please forgive me for focusing far too much on what is wrong and too little on what is good. By Your grace, I resolve to think on that which is good and show patience with the imperfections of others. Please fill me with Your Spirit and grace."

> *As study or prayer groups work through the questions on each pattern, remember to stay very focused on God's grace and hope for change. No church or person should forget God convicts to change us, not discourage. In discussing areas for change, do not call peoples' names and stay positive. Let God's revelations lead you straight to prayer and faith for change, not criticism or gossip.

## *Pattern Ten*
## *Questions for Prayer and Study Groups*

(for individuals, small groups or churchwide studies)

(1) Prayerfully read Philippians 4:8. What does it say about someone who tends to be negative and critical or often points out the flaws of other? Can those with constantly negative attitudes truly be speaking from the Holy Spirit?

(2) Since no believer or church is anywhere near perfect, why is James 5:20 such an important principle?

(3) Why will a negative complaining attitude be so damaging to the faith and health of a congregation?

(4) Carefully read Philippians 4:4 and 1 Thessalonians 5:18. Can anyone with a consistently negative or complaining attitude be right with God? Why or why not?

# Pattern Eleven
# Robbing God to Protest People

(Malachi 3:8-10; Luke 6:38; Galatians 6:7-9)

*A serious form of hindrance is when some members withhold tithes because of a particular church decision or circumstance.* In essence, this is blatant disobedience to the God who commands us to bring all the tithes into the storehouse. Furthermore, God did not command the tithe *unless* you don't happen to like some church decision. Failure to tithe is plain robbery and a direct affront to God (Malachi 3:8-10).

Dear reader, if you think terms like "robbery" are a bit strong, please understand they are not my terms — they are God's. We must come to realize that disagreement with a particular church decision, give us no right to rob God. If a situation is truly doctrinal and serious, believers should find a church they can support. On the other hand, if it really isn't a vital issue and they leave simply because they're angry, God's Spirit is seriously grieved in their lives. And no matter where they may go, they go without the full blessing and favor of God.

## Robbing God Carries Consequences
### (Malachi 3:9)

For the most part, withholding the tithe is a sinful way some try to punish others for not doing things their way. The tithe must be viewed as holy and not a tool for opposing people or policies we do not like. Robbing God is no way to protest our disagreement with the decisions or shortcomings of people! In fact, God warns of severe consequences to those who rob Him regardless of the reason. "You are cursed with a curse, for you have robbed Me, Even this whole nation" (Malachi 3:9).

Believers, we must return to the understanding that the tithe is a most holy part of our obedience and worship to God, *not* some bargaining chip to punish people. Neither is God's tithe a device for threatening others to get our way. According to Scripture, it is truly dangerous to play fleshly games with God's holy tithe. God indeed provides great blessing to those who tithe and chastisement to those who rob His work.

## Putting On Christ — Putting Off the Flesh
### Steps for Repentance and Victory

Carefully consider the prayer below. If God has revealed a need and you are willing to pray a similar prayer, please pause and do it now. Ask God to grant you godly sorrow that brings repentance. Take any steps of repentance His will requires. And remember, His grace is greater than your deepest need!

*A Prayer of Cleansing and Transformation* — "Father, I confess that I have treated Your holy tithe as an option or bargaining chip. Please forgive me for robbing You to punish others. By Your grace, I now resolve to reverence Your Presence and heed Your Spirit. Lord, please fill me with the Spirit of true reverence and genuine worship."

## *Pattern Eleven*
## *Questions for Prayer and Study Groups*

(for individuals, small groups or churchwide studies)

(1)  Carefully read Malachi 3:8-10. What does God call withholding regular tithes and offerings for His storehouse?

(2)  Do you think robbing God is the appropriate way to register displeasure with a person or policy? Why or why no?

(3)  What would be better ways to express disagreement with a church direction or policy?

(4)  Based on Malachi 3:8-10, what are the promised blessings of faithful giving? What are the promised consequences for robbing God?

(5)  Do you think God is serious about the promises and curses of Malachi 3:8-10? Should we then show Him the fear and reverence due His name?

# Pattern Twelve
# The "We've Never Done It That Way" Syndrome

## The Ungodly Automatic Resistance Response
(Numbers 14:8-10; 1 Corinthians 1:10; Hebrews 13:17)

*One of the most common spiritual hindrances could be summed up as the "automatic resistance response."* Without question, we all have at least some natural resistance to change. Yet with some, virtually any change is met with angry resistance. It is a fleshly, "knee-jerk reaction" of automatically opposing anything different. Even when there is absolutely no biblical basis for opposition, problem personalities will attempt to frame their objections in scriptural terms (though the objections are not really scripturally based). This is especially sad because change is often a vital part of spiritual growth. Without change, we get stuck in the past and see little progress either corporately or personally. Perhaps this is why the phrase *"we've never done it that way before"* is often called the seven last words of a dying church!

The truth is significant growth almost always occurs outside our "comfort zones." When we are determined to stay in our comfort zones and "keep everything the same," spiritual stagnation is virtually assured! Actually, the automatic resistance to change is among the most serious barriers to God's activity in modern churches. Until churches are willing to embrace the challenges of spiritual change, they are almost certain to decline and eventually die. If you doubt this, consider a sobering fact. At present, some where between seventy to eighty percent of American churches are either plateaued or rapidly declining. Clearly something needs to change!

## The Exhausting "Drain Effect" on Church Leaders

The "we've never done it that way" syndrome causes enormous grief and hindrance to God's Kingdom and to His leaders. Such constant resistance simply "wears out" God's servants and tragically draws their attention from far more crucial kingdom issues. Furthermore, those who automatically resist change often find themselves opposing the work of God Himself. (Yet they are usually fairly oblivious to how much they are profoundly hindering God's Spirit.) At its heart, this attitude is one of enormous selfishness and insensitivity. When we adamantly insist on having everything just like we want it, we're basically saying we don't care what others want or need. In essence, we are saying "we don't care about growth or reaching more people, we just want everything to stay in our comfort zone." Little is more damaging to the Church or the Kingdom of God!

Dear saint, have you been guilty of selfishly resisting change? Have you made your personal preferences equal to scriptural laws (when they really aren't)? Do you view those with different tastes as automatically evil and fleshly? Have you allowed your personal preferences to create anger, division and tension in the church? In truth, little could be more wrong than to split a church over changes that are less than fundamental. Let us determine to embrace the maturity to keep relatively minor issues from become major battles.

## Putting On Christ — Putting Off the Flesh
### Steps for Repentance and Victory

This particular issue causes enormous damage in today's Church. If God has spoken to your heart, you must indeed take it serious. Carefully consider the prayer below. If you are willing to pray a similar prayer, please pause and do it now. Ask God to grant you sincerity and take all the steps of repentance His will requires. And remember, God can give positive faith to the most doubtful heart.

*A Prayer of Cleansing and Transformation* — "Father, I confess the ways I have resisted change mostly because it was new and different. Please forgive me for reacting without deep prayer and careful consideration. Forgive me for being a burden and drain on those who lead Your church. By Your grace, I resolve to prayerfully consider all issues before I resist new directions. Please fill me with Your Spirit of loving maturity and wisdom."

## *Pattern Twelve*
## *Questions for Prayer and Study Groups*

(for individuals, small groups or churchwide studies)

(1)  Carefully read Numbers 14:32-33. What was the reaction of most Israelites when they looked at the new challenges of the Promised Land? How did God feel about their doubt and resistance to the changes and challenges ahead?

(2)  Do you think selfishness often plays a role in wanting things to stay just like they are? Why or why not?

(3)  In your own words, describe how constant complaining and resistance to change would create a "drain effect" on church leaders. How would discouragement and weariness tend to effect the leaders of a church? Why do you think discouraging and distracting church leaders would be a major tactic of Satan?

# Pattern Thirteen
# The Church Hopping
# "Jump and Run" Side-Step

(John 13:34-35; 17:21; 1 Corinthians 12-14; 1 John 2:19)

*Another tragically common condition is the "jump and run" attitude of more and more church members.* I call this pattern the church hopping "sidestep" because it enables some believers to sidestep the responsibility and spiritual challenge of developing meaningful fellowship with other believers. This pattern also allows people to avoid any real service or responsibility that go with healthy church membership. Through this method, *believers* can come to "enjoy" the music, programs or preaching yet carefully avoid most or all responsibility. In essence, such members embody the attitude of taking much and giving little. This shamefully betrays our responsibility to Christ.

*A related pattern is with those who retire from work and immediately retire from serving God.* Now that they have more time to serve God than ever, they decide to serve Him less. Instead of profound gratefulness for the ability to retire in reasonable health, we thank God by promptly dropping His work. Rather than gladly serving God with the extra time and resources He has so graciously provided, Christ's Church becomes a low priority. Everything and everyone now comes ahead of God. In essence, recreation and family now become our gods!

How it must break God's heart when people thank Him for a life of blessing by retiring from most meaningful service to His kingdom. Any of these patterns are the very opposite of the biblical picture for mature, responsible church membership (1 Corinthians 12-14; Ephesians 4:10-12). Let us return to the understanding that retirement from work in no way justifies retirement from Christ and His Church.

A similar unbiblical pattern is the *"let's just move on syndrome."* While there are certainly times God leads believers to change churches, many must later confess it was more from human reasoning than true spiritual guidance. Rather than making deep commitments to a local church, modern believers often play the unbiblical game of musical chairs with their membership. To God, church membership is a solemn commitment to deep, lasting relationships with a certain body of believers. Yet instead of embracing mature fellowship and service, for many believers it is all about *them*, not the body of Christ.

## The "Me" Generation

Church hopping has become an enormous problem in today's congregations. So many have the "picky shopper" mentality in deciding on a church. Rather than asking, "How can I serve this church," it is all about how can *I* be served. Unfortunately, so many modern saints look for a church exactly the way they would a health club — they want one with the least cost and most benefits! Often when the least thing becomes disagreeable, people immediately shop for another church. These patterns reflect little concept of a long-term commitment to meaningful relationships or selfless service. Unfortunately, it also suggests little concept of biblical fellowship or mature commitment to Christ. Such attitudes are the direct *opposite* of the deep biblical fellowship to which God calls all believers.

A major sign of Christian maturity is when believers learn to work and grow *through* their times of relationship challenges. Sooner or later we all face relationship challenges in virtually any church. Especially at these times, God offer us grace to learn to love, forgive and grow, not quickly cut and run. Without question, it is God's will that believers learn how to love and unite in spite of differences. Yet with so many, the attitude is "If you don't do everything I want, I'll just take my marbles and leave." Many even use the *threat* of leaving to try and force their will on others. Needless to say, such attitudes bear no resemblance to Christian love and maturity.

# When You "Move On" and the Holy Spirit Doesn't!

When believers quickly attempt to cut ties and "move on" without thoroughly addressing damaged relationships, *they* may move on but the Holy Spirit doesn't! While we may sever relationships or change churches, we can never again know God's rich fullness and blessing until we give and receive true forgiveness (Matthew 5:23; 6:14). In term of anger, bitterness and division, what is in the past is *not* in the past if it remains unresolved in our hearts. Dear saints, we may run but we cannot hide from buried bitterness.

Again let us acknowledge that God definitely leads some people to change churches. It is by no means our place to judge what is in the hearts of others. For each of us, the goal is to be utterly honest with ourselves and with God. Yet, it is vital that modern saints again come to view church membership the way God views it — *a sacred, generally lasting commitment to mature fellowship and responsible service with a particular body of believers.* Church membership is not a revolving door!

# The "We Don't Want to be Involved" Mindset

To truly follow Christ, we all must step up to the plate of mature service and giving to our church. Only by so doing can we glorify God and experience sweeping revival in our day. It is a major red flag when people say things like, "We've been looking for a church where we can just attend and *enjoy* ourselves but not really be involved." That pattern bears absolutely no resemblance to the call God gives to all true followers of Christ. With rare exceptions, those with such attitudes are utterly out of God's will. In essence, they want to selfishly *use* God for blessing but have no desire to serve Him or His Church.

Without question, we are all saved to serve, not sit. (Of course, this does not apply to those with severe health problems or other circumstances that make service impossible.) A popular phrase once used for our country would surely apply to our Savior's church. "Ask not what your church can do for you but what you can do for your church." After all, is the Son of God not worthy of our loving obedience and joyful service? If we view serving God as an unpleasant chore and imposition, something is desperately wrong in our souls. Serving God is a labor of love, not a duty or drudgery.

Let us now resolve to become givers and servers far more than sitters and takers. May we all commit to serve our Lord with the diligence and gladness of heart He deserves. To do anything less is profound ingratitude and disobedience. May God help us truly believe the clear and powerful words of our Savior, "It is more blessed to give than receive" (Acts 20:35).

## Putting On Christ — Putting Off the Flesh
### Steps for Repentance and Victory

Carefully consider the prayer below. If God has spoken and you are willing to pray a similar prayer, please pause and do it now. Ask God to grant you sincerity and take all the steps of repentance His will requires. And remember, you can be changed for His glory!

*A Prayer of Cleansing and Transformation* — "Father, I confess the ways I have treated Christ's Church as a secondary issue. Please forgive me for my lack of dedicated service and loyalty. Forgive me for repaying Your kindness by putting Your Church as a last priority. By Your grace, I commit to faithfully serve and love. Please fill me with Your Spirit of loving commitment, true maturity and godly wisdom."

## Pattern Thirteen
## Questions for Prayer and Study Groups

(for individuals, small groups or churchwide studies)

(1) Please read John 13:34-35 and 17:20-23. Based on Scripture, what importance should believers attach to being a faithful, loyal member of a local church?

(2) Carefully read chapters twelve and through fourteen of 1 Corinthians. Does an attitude of frequently moving from one church to another bear any resemblance to the love and oneness God commands for His Church? Why or why not?

(3) How would a mature attitude of love and forgiveness enable believers to either overlook or actually grow through areas of disagreement with other believers (rather than jump and run)?

(4) In your own words, tell why the "me-focused" mentality about church membership is contrary to the loving servant attitude that God requires?

(5) What does it suggest about the spiritual maturity of people who avoid commitment and always want to stay on the fringe of their church?

(6) In what way is joining a church similar to making a covenant in marriage? (Though of course, local church membership is not necessarily permanent.)

(7) Carefully read Luke 14:26-33. In what way could recreation and family actually become a form of idolatry? How do some allow retirement from work to become retirement from God?

(8) Carefully read Matthew 5:23-24 and 6:14-15. If people leave a church without seeking to reconcile wrongs or fully forgive offenses, can the Holy Spirit's fullness go with them? Why or why not?

# Pattern Fourteen
## Disrespect of Committees and Lay-leaders

(Romans 12:9-10; Ephesians 4:1-3; 5:19-21;
Colossians 3:8; 12-15)

*While not directly against pastor and staff, another common attack is toward church committees who are assigned challenging tasks.* Some of the more common targets of attack are building, finance, nominating and pastor search committees. Without question, these tasks are especially complex and require extensive deliberation and study. In many cases, committees are required to make decisions that cannot possibly please everyone. Unless there are extreme and obvious reasons to do otherwise, churches must respect the committee process and allow them to do their work. Especially when hard decisions must be made, everyone should make a strong effort to guard the bond of peace and refrain from demanding their own way.

A related attack occurs when some want pastor search or personnel committees to move faster or in a certain direction. As a general rule, patience and prayerfulness are God's directives. Mature believers will not badger or pressure committees toward a certain end or time frame. Without prayer and maturity, churches can easily divide in times of decision or change. Yet with prayer, patience and maturity, almost any decision can be traversed effectively. May God teach us the maturity and patience to respect one another and resist demanding selfish attitudes.

One unalterable fact of group life is that no decision perfectly pleases everyone. Being in biblical unity does not mean we all think and feel exactly alike. For this reason, true Christian maturity is often revealed when committees must make difficult decisions. May God grant us the commitment to pray and encourage much and criticize little. While this doesn't mean simply rolling over and rubber-stamping all recommendations, it does mean loving respect and cooperation. When we minister in that spirit, we can work through even the most challenging issues.

## Putting On Christ — Putting Off the Flesh
### Steps for Repentance and Victory

Carefully consider the prayer below. If God has spoken and you are willing to sincerely pray a similar prayer, please pause and do it now. Ask God to grant you deep sincerity and take whatever steps of repentance His will requires. You may well need to ask forgiveness of those you have criticized and maligned. But remember, His grace is sufficient for glorious change!

*A Prayer of Cleansing and Transformation* — "Father, I confess the ways I have been quickly critical and disrespectful of those who lead and work in my church. Please forgive me for a lack of prayer and a critical attitude. By Your grace, I resolve to pray more and criticize less. Please fill me now with Your powerful Spirit of loving, encouragement and wisdom."

## *Pattern Fourteen*
## *Questions for Prayer and Study Groups*

(for individuals, small groups or churchwide studies)

(1)  Please read Roans 12:9-10; Ephesians 4:1-3 and 5:19-21. What is to be believers' attitudes toward following other believers who are in leadership?

(2)  Why is it so important to pray for and encourage those in leadership rather than constantly grumbling or second guessing their directions?

(3)  What does it say about the spiritual maturity of those who are always ready to criticize but seldom ready to step up to the plate of genuine ministry themselves?

(4)  Why do key groups like pastor search teams, teachers' nominating committees and finance or building committees especially need our prayers?

# Pattern Fifteen
# Personalities and Politics
# Over God and Kingdom

(Luke 14:26-33; Acts 5:29; 1 Corinthians 1:10; 3:1-3;
1 Thessalonians 5:12-13)

*Closely related is the tendency for some members to be against calling new staff or other decisions simply because they oppose the pastor or committee that recommended them.* Though they may not have a thing against the particular person or position, they perceive key church leadership is for it so they are automatically against it. The same thing often occurs with church decisions or new programs. In essence, people with an angry, bitter spirit are opposed simply because the pastor or certain committees are for it. In most cases, they have not seriously sought God's face — they are just blindly against whatever the leadership wants. While they may "say" they have reasons for opposition, the truth is they just don't like who proposed the course of action. If someone they supported had proposed the action, they would have been all for it.

This condition is especially harmful because it often brings people into direct opposition to the vital purposes of God Himself. The Lord will not forever tolerate such serious and willful hindrances to His work. Yet for balance, let me clearly state that pastor and committees *should* be opposed if they are clearly wrong biblically. (And sometimes, they are indeed wrong!) However, when opposition to church leadership is mostly from anger or stubbornness, we find ourselves literally resisting God Himself. Concerning resisting God, we should all remember a simple but vital truth — *God loses no battles!*

## The Idolatry of Placing People Before God and Truth

Another real but subtle form of this condition occurs when believers do not stand for what is clearly right because it would mean disagreeing with friends or family. Yet when something or someone is obviously wrong, believers will then make a choice as to who is really first in their life. If they choose friends or family over God, it could only be termed idolatry.

Make no mistake — if we place anything (or anyone) ahead of obeying Christ, it is a most blatant form of denying Christ. (If anyone thinks this is in any way over-stated, all they need do is read the clear words of Jesus in Luke 14:26-33.) Some churches and people completely lose God's blessing because key members place the "approval of people" over standing for something or someone that is obviously right. While it is certainly difficult to stand against people we love, the alternative is to deny and disobey Christ. When we follow that path, no one wins and everyone loses. Worse yet, we utterly betray our Savior and His Church!

## "I Never Knew Him"
### When Silence is Betrayal!

A related form is when believers try to simply remain neutral and take no stance at all. Yet, almost no one can truly remain neutral! To refuse to stand for God's will is to allow evil to triumph. Many a church has lost God's blessing because believers chose to remain silent when they should have taken a stand. Countless pastors and church leaders have made difficult stands for truth only to suddenly find themselves standing alone. When they looked around for expected help, key leaders were conspicuously and *shamefully* silent. These abandoned leaders understand a little fraction of what our Lord felt at those stinging and cowardly words of Peter. "I don't know the man" (Mark 14:71). Let every reader be fully aware of one thing — to abandon Christ's faithful servants is to abandon Christ (Matthew 25:45)!

In many cases, simply remaining silent is among the most harmful ways we betray Jesus and His Church. Many a divisive church battle has occurred because more mature members took the easy way and "just didn't want to get involved." It is tempting for kind, godly people to remain quiet because trouble-makers are typically so loud and unpleasant to deal with. Yet, we cannot truly walk with Christ and take the easy way out. And thank God, when we stand in humility, wisdom and truth, we stand in the power of Christ! Dear saints, we are to *reprove* and *resist* evil, not cower and flee from it (Ephesians 5:11; James 4:7)!

Countless believers and churches can never know revival or full blessing until they seek forgiveness for abandoning Christ or His servants! May God grant us the courage to stand for Jesus and truth no matter the cost. Above all, if you know you have failed God or His servants, *do not* gloss over it. By all means, seek forgiveness and reconciliation. When we get honest about our wrongs toward Christ and others, God fully forgives and restores our power in prayer.

## The Power of "Reconciliation Services"

One of the most encouraging trends is for believers and churches to conduct some form of reconciliation meeting to lay aside past offenses. While the various groups are not required to dredge up or resurface old arguments, they are required to fully forgive from the heart. The goal is not necessarily to try and assess who is right or wrong but for all to acknowledge and repent of wrong attitudes or words. While split churches do not have to physically reunite, past bitterness must be forgiven. (However in some cases, churches have actually reunited!)

Whether such reconciliations are done in official services or believers just meeting privately, the results are often phenomenal! The fact is, many believers and churches will never fully heal or go forward without such meetings. Let no reader be discouraged — God will surely give you the guidance and grace to obey!

## Putting On Christ — Putting Off the Flesh
### Steps for Repentance and Victory

Carefully consider the prayer below. If God has spoken and you are willing to pray a similar prayer, please pause and do it now. Ask God to help you mean it and take the steps of repentance His will requires. Remember, God loves you and you can find forgiveness!

*A Prayer of Cleansing and Transformation* — "Father, I confess the ways I have placed the desire of people over standing for what is right. Please forgive me for making decisions more to please certain people or to get my own way. By Your grace, I resolve to seek Your face and follow Your will. I also resolve to ask forgiveness of those I have hurt and offended. Please fill me with Your Spirit of loving maturity and wisdom."

## *Pattern Fifteen*
## *Questions for Prayer and Study Groups*

(for individuals, small groups or churchwide studies)

(1) Carefully reflect on Luke 14:26-33 and Acts 5:29. What is God's attitude toward believers allowing personalities or personal preferences to come ahead of Christ and seeking God's will?

(2) Read 1 Corinthians 1:10 and 3:1-3. How could your feelings toward certain people cloud decisions in a church?

(3) How common do you think it is for people to either embrace or oppose a church direction simply because of who proposed it?

(4) Based on Luke 14:26-33, how could siding with people who are wrong be tantamount to betraying Christ?

(5) If we abandon God's servant who is standing for truth, is it a similar sin to being ashamed of Christ and His words before men? Why or why not?

(6) Do you agree or disagree with the following statement? "The only thing needed for evil to triumph is for the righteous to remain silent." How does this pattern occur in churches?

(7) Because people with loud critical attitudes are often unpleasant to deal with, is it acceptable to just give in to keep peace? If we have abandoned a servant of God standing for truth or given in to the loud and brash, is there a need to ask forgiveness of God and those we have abandoned?

# Pattern Sixteen
## Unfair Comparisons and "Good Old Days" Fixations

(1 Corinthians 3:3-7; 1 Thessalonians 5:12-13; 1 Timothy 5:17)

*Still another damaging pattern is against pastors, staff or lay-leaders who follow a long-term or well loved former leader.* As believers, we simply must understand that every leader is unique and we should avoid negative comparisons. Since all leaders have their own strengths and weaknesses, we must accept that reality. In fact, God usually guides us to a new leader because there *are* changes we need to make. We should be prepared to change and resist the temptation of over-comparison and unrealistic expectations. Changes and growth are seldom easy and we must not complicate the process by immaturity or over-comparisons.

An especially unfair attack comes from overly nostalgic attitudes and "good old days" fixations. In today's fast-changing society, circumstances both in and around churches are always in transition. When the area around a church is rapidly growing, that church is infinitely more likely to grow and have an atmosphere of excitement. The truth is plain physical circumstances and locations have far more to do with most modern church growth than we might like to admit. Churches in these settings often have higher percentages of children and youth which understandably mean far higher baptisms. These favorable demographic conditions also help create a natural sense of excitement, progress and quick easy success.

Naturally when the area surrounding a church plateaus or declines, congregational dynamics become very different. While churches in such areas can certainly still grow, it becomes much harder and requires far more human effort with greater power from God. No one is "to blame" for this, it is imply a reality of the circumstances. Yet church members often fail to fully recognize these realities. Consequently, they begin to blame their staff and treat them with less respect because things are "just not like they were when old so and so was here." For balance, let me also say ministers can sometimes blame congregations without considering factors churches really cannot help.

## Fairly Assessing the Past and Present

Without a full and honest assessment of current church factors, it is easy to give far too much credit to past leaders and way too much blame to those in the present. In many cases, such attitudes are utterly unfair and just plain wrong. In fact, if a church setting is not an "easy grow" expanding area, you should especially appreciate leaders who are willing to serve in your harder setting. In many ways, these leaders certainly need (and often deserve) your appreciation, encouragement and support far more than those in much easier, fast-grow areas.

A similar pattern is impatience with young or inexperienced ministers who simply need time to develop and grow. The horrific damage some churches cause to young or inexperienced ministers is beyond words to describe. Because of the unkindness of some, countless young ministers and staff have been permanently wounded or even left the ministry entirely. Today's shocking statistics of ministerial burnout suggest serious mistreatment on the part of many churches. The damage is even worse in leaders' wives and children.

## Ministers' Families
## The Saddest "Casualties" of Negativism

Today there is even a disturbingly high incidence of minister's children dropping out of church when they reach adulthood. One of the main reasons stated is the fact they have seen such outrageous pettiness and critical, loveless behavior from "church members," they want no part of such an organization! It is truly heart-wrenching to witness the lasting damage visited upon many a minister's wife and children. Make no mistake — unless they fully repent, those responsible for such pain will be held to fearsome accountability before God (Psalms 105:15; Hebrews 13:17).

Dear reader, do you sense any unfair criticism in your own heart or church? Have you been guilty of overly praising past leaders while unfairly condemning those who currently serve? Very little discourages God's servants or hinders Christ's kingdom like a critical atmosphere at church. Without question, we all need encouragement and we all need to encourage others. Certainly none of us are perfect and there are always things for which we could pick each other apart. But such attitudes are the exact opposite of Christ's heart. May God teach us the vital importance of tender-hearted love and patience with fellow believers.

Even now, increasing numbers are going to present and former staff to ask forgiveness and seek reconciliation. Though they still may not agree on all issues, they are at least laying aside the bitterness. The resulting healing in both parties is nothing short of miraculous! My friend, is God now speaking to you? If He is, I have no doubt that deep in your heart *you know it*! Please understand that you cannot be fully right with God until you humbly go to those you have hurt (especially now that He has spoken to your heart).

Before closing this pattern, I would be remiss if I did not state we must be equally vigilant to avoid allowing a "difficult community" to become an *excuse* for laziness, mediocrity and lack of spiritual power. The early Church certainly faced a setting with difficulties like we cannot even image. Yet, the New Testament saints shook the world! Dear saints, let us trust God for the balance of being encouraging and loyal when things are tough, yet avoiding the trap of justifying failure. If we ask, our Lord will surely give us wisdom to find the balance (James 1:5).

## Putting On Christ — Putting Off the Flesh
### Steps for Repentance and Victory

If God has revealed a need, you must take this seriously. Carefully consider the prayer listed below. If you are prepared to pray a similar prayer, please pause and do it now. Ask God to grant you sincerity and take whatever steps of repentance His will requires. And remember, His grace is greater than your deepest need!

*A Prayer of Cleansing and Transformation* — "Father, I confess the ways I have unfairly compared current staff with some in the past. Please forgive me for being negative, critical and unsupportive. Forgive me for blaming staff for things mostly caused by changing circumstances beyond their control. By Your grace, I resolve to honor You by honoring Your servants. Please fill me with Your Spirit of loving encouragement and grace."

## *Pattern Sixteen*
## *Questions for Prayer and Study Groups*

(for individuals, small groups or churchwide studies)

(1) Please read 1 Corinthians 3:3-7. What is God's attitude toward the practice of overly comparing one Christian leader to another?

(2) Carefully reflect on 1 Thessalonians 5:12-13. Is honor and support for our Christian leaders to be based on their personalities and our personal preferences or because of the God-ordained position in which they serve?

(3) When the communities and circumstances of churches change, do you think many church members fully take that into account when evaluating their staff?

(4) Do you think it is much easier to stay motivated and positive in a high growth community when expansion is easy as opposed to one which is plateaued or declining? How should these factors affect the way leaders and laypeople encourage one another?

(5) Is it fairly easy for people to blame one another when growth and progress is not quick or easy? How should Philippians 4:8 guide our treatment of one another?

(6) Could a difficult setting become an "excuse" for mediocre ministry and low expectations? Read Acts 2-4. What was their primary strategy for explosive growth in a terribly difficult setting?

# Pattern Seventeen
# The Congregational Cold War

(Matthew 5:23-24; 6:14-15; John 13:34-35; 17:21;
Acts 2:1, 42-47; *Romans 15:5-7; Colossians 3:12-15; 1 Peter 1:22*)

*By most indications, the modern Church is in the midst of unprecedented bickering, division and tension.* In fact, one estimate suggests over seventy percent of our churches are either in a major fight right now, just concluding one or about to head into another! Little could more displeasing to our Lord or damaging to the spread of the gospel. Virtually nothing grieves God's Spirit or blocks evangelistic power like anger and unresolved tension among believers.

In the face of so many congregational battles, a uniquely damaging condition has developed in epidemic numbers. Countless thousands of churches have now settled into what I call the "*congregational cold war.*" This condition exists when believers have mostly ceased outward battles, but neglected to deal with strained relationships.

A similar condition occurs in churches that may have never fought outwardly but still have serious unresolved issues between members. Unfortunately, they try to bury their grievances and just "move on." Yet, when real relational damage has occurred, it is both ineffective and unbiblical to simply ignore it (Matthew 5:23-6:14). While "let's just move on" may sound good, to move on without forgiveness and at least attempted reconciliation is utterly contrary to God's commands and principles.

When church members attempt to bury or ignore damaged relationships, at least five distinct patterns become evident. Any one of the five profoundly grieves God's Spirit. It is incredible how unaddressed walls between members create an atmosphere of tension and coldness in a whole church. Prayerfully assess whether there are significant patterns of any of these five in your church. And even if you sense several negative patterns in your church, do not be discouraged. *Over the years, I can tell of apparently hopeless divided churches who came to truly miraculous healing!* My friend, our God is the God of the impossible. Nothing is too hard for Him (Jeremiah 32:17, 27)!

## Five Telltale Signs of a Church in "Cold War"

(1) *Church members basically retreat to common corners and mostly associate with a little clique that shares their feelings.* While still members of the same church, the various groups purposely have little to do with the other. This is seen from the makeup of home fellowships to who sits with who at church events.

(2) *Some members barely speak to certain other members and actually plan their movements in church so as not to encounter them.* They will literally go out of their way to avoid a particular part of the building where certain people tend to gather. Such behavior reveals serious breaks in fellowship and severely grieves God's Spirit. We must *never* ignore or justify these sinful patterns. One thing is certain — God doesn't ignore these issues. It is vital that we fully admit and deal with them now!

(3) *Some members give the pastor, staff or other members the "cold shoulder" treatment.* When they get in a setting where they have to speak or shake hands, they are cool and make little or no eye contact. As visitors come to the church, they instantly detect a sense of coldness and tension. Though they may not know what is wrong, they sense that something is definitely amiss.

(4) *Certain members find it difficult to say anything positive about some people or church programs (no matter how well some things may be going.)* Because they are miffed in one area, they tend to be aloof and uncomplimentary about all areas. In other words, they are more or less "sulled up" or in a "spiritual pout."

(5) *Members become withdrawn and cease to share personal burdens or prayer needs with fellow believers.* When a church body becomes somewhat "formal and stiff," God's Spirit is grieved and His power seriously quenched. Obviously, such patterns virtually

destroy the koinonia fellowship that is so crucial to functioning as the people of God. One thing is certain — Christ's Church is to be a unified body of warmth and openness, *not* a collection of "cliques" nervously co-existing in an uneasy tension.

## Cold Wars Profoundly Grieve God's Spirit and Profane His Name

Clearly these five patterns of "congregational cold wars" are the exact opposite of warm, koinonia fellowship so vital to God's activity in a church. Yet today, many believers totally misunderstand both the nature and importance of loving biblical fellowship. Many others seem to think the mere absence of outward fighting is all God requires. They think it is more or less acceptable to be aloof and distant to fellow believers as long as they do not show overt anger or attack. Nothing could be further from the truth! *Koinonia fellowship is not simply the "absence" of outward fighting, it is the "presence" of loving warmth, outgoing kindness and relational closeness.*

Dear saints, it is truly important that we frequently eat together and gather in the homes of other believers (Acts 2:42-47; 4:31-32). For this reason, healthy churches have many fellowship activities and continually work at doing things together. They treat love, unity and togetherness with enormous seriousness. These mature believers would far rather lose an argument or not get their way than lose a brother or sister. Especially in today's individualistic, self-focused society, believers must be *intentional* about developing and nurturing *koinonia* fellowship. In our conflict-ridden transient world, deep fellowship and unity will not happen by accident. We must determine to take serious, consistent steps to deepen our fellowship and loving oneness.

## Relational Coldness is not an Option!

As followers of Christ, we simply do not have the option of withdrawing warmth and fellowship from other believers. (Except in extreme cases like 1 Corinthians 5:11 where we are *commanded* to withdraw fellowship.) To ignore relational damage is to grieve God's Spirit and destroy the power of your own prayers (Matthew 6:14; Mark 11:25)! Jesus even said we are to do good to those who persecute us (Matthew 5:44). As believers, God further commands us to love and forgive people "from the heart" (Matthew 18:35). In other words, we must genuinely forgive people, not just "say" we do while remaining aloof and distant.

Believer, please be completely honest with yourself and with God. If you sense any of these patterns in yourself or your church, immediately confess these sins. Whatever you do, please do not justify or rationalize these conditions! Do not justify your attitude by the fact, "They did it first." Another false justification is, "They're not friendly to me." Remember, you are responsible for *you* no matter what *they* do. Above all, do not be discouraged about your situation. Every believer should know that God will honor even small first steps to address church or family tension. *My friend, please do not think your church is hopeless or too far gone*! After all, no church is perfect and God still works with very imperfect people.

## Learning to Love "In Spite" of Differences
### (1 Corinthians 14)

While believers certainly do not agree on everything and there will be times of offense, we must learn to love anyway! (James 5:20) We must resolve to love our way *through* times of conflict, offenses or tension. After all, the Christ who lives within us said, "Father forgive them" while He literally hung on the cross. By His indwelling grace, we *can* learn to love and forgive those who offend us. As believers, we cannot just "sull up" or give people the cold shoulder. When we embrace this pattern, we hurt ourselves (spiritually) far more than we hurt the objects of our displeasure.

When we allow any anger or bitterness to remain in our heart, *we* are the spiritual prisoners and *ours* are the prayers that are hindered

(Matthew 18:32-35; Mark 11:25-26). Furthermore, it is *we* who end up having the heart attacks and strokes from internalized bitterness. Indeed, *we* are the ones who become most depressed and miserable. Someone said it well, "Choosing to harbor bitterness is like you drinking the poison and expecting the other person to die!" Untold thousands are caught in this damaging spiritual syndrome.

## Take the Initiative in Restoring Relationships!

My friend, if there are believers with whom you have been cold or distant, immediately confess and forsake this most damaging sin. If the matter is a serious offense, then closely follow the instructions of Matthew 18:15 and *go to them in love!* If it is a matter you just need to forgive and let go, then do it. Make it a point to spend some quality time with those who have been distant. Go out of your way to pay friendly visits or do something to bless and serve their needs. Only in this manner do we live as sons and daughters of God (Matthew 5:45). To do anything less is to play a religious game.

It is astounding to see what often happens when you take the initiative to show kindness to those with whom you have been distant. Again, the greatest revivals do not occur by people merely going "down" the aisle but also "across" the aisle. When you take the first steps to reconcile and restore closeness with the alienated, God will flood your life with Himself. Until you do, He cannot.

## Putting On Christ — Putting Off the Flesh
### Steps for Repentance and Victory

Carefully consider the prayer below. If God has spoken and you are willing to pray a similar prayer, please pause and do it now. Ask God to help you mean it and take the steps of repentance His will requires. And remember, you can do all things through Christ!

*A Prayer of Cleansing and Transformation* — "Father, I confess my broken, strained and cold relationships with fellow believers or family members. Please forgive me for denying, excusing and ignoring my need to seek reconciliation. By Your grace, I resolve to forgive and show kindness to those with whom I disagree. I commit to develop more loving relationships of unity and warmth. Please fill me with miraculous forgiveness, love and kindness."

## Pattern Seventeen
## Questions for Prayer and Study Groups

(for individuals, small groups or churchwide studies)

(1)  Please read Matthew 5:23-24 and 6:14-15. What effect will it have if churches try to ignore significant broken and damaged relationships within the membership?

(2)  Why is "let's just move on" not a biblical solution to damaged relationships between believers?

(3)  Carefully reflect on Ephesians 4:29-32. What might be some effects of "grieving the Holy Spirit" in a congregation?

(4)  Why is *koinonia* fellowship more than just the absence of actual fighting in a congregation? Is it acceptable to wait for others to make the first move in restoring love and unity in relationships? Why or why not?

(5)  Based on Acts 2:42-47 and 4:31-32, what were some of the primary marks of genuine fellowship between believers? Why do you think strong loving fellowship is so crucial to God powerfully flowing through His people? How does this affect evangelism?

(6)  What do you think Jesus meant by *"love and do good to your enemies?"* (Matthew 5:44)

(7)  Carefully re-read the *Five Telltale Signs of a Church in "Cold War."* Do you sense any of these operating in your congregation? How should we pray for change to correct it?

# Pattern Eighteen
# Hypersensitive Critics, Hot Tempers
# and Holier than Thou Judges

(Proverbs 29:11, 20:22; Ephesians 4:31-32;
Philippians 4:8; James 4:11-12)

*In many churches, there is a small minority of members whose hyper-critical, judgmental attitudes put everyone else on edge.* Rather than exhibiting the loving, positive attitudes commanded in Philippians 4:8, they have a negative mind-set of criticism and judgment. Instead of saying a glass is half-filled, they will invariably say it is half-empty! If a discouraging word is to be heard, rest assured it will come from them. Whereas periodic constructive criticism is both necessary and positive, their criticisms tend to be chronic, destructive and negative.

Perhaps even more damaging are individuals who are quick-tempered and prone to spout angry, critical words. God's Word reserves some of its strongest language for those who have short fuses and little self-control. "A fool gives full vent to his anger; but a wise man keeps himself under control... Do you see a man who speaks in haste? There is more hope for a fool than for him... An angry man stirs up dissension, and a hot-tempered one commits many sins" (Proverbs 29:11,20,22). God's Word leaves absolutely no doubt that control of one's temper and tongue is among the very first steps of following Christ. Without question, angry spirits and sharp tongues are ugly expressions of carnality and spiritual immaturity. No one walking in the Spirit consistently exhibits such tendencies.

## Anger and Negativism
## Profoundly Grieve God's Spirit!
(Ephesians 4:29-32)

Angry unloving speech does *enormous* damage to people and seriously quenches God's activity in a church. Absolutely nothing more

139

hinders God's Spirit, dishonors His name or releases the activity of the devil. It is crucial that believers see this pattern for what it is — a serious grieving of the Holy Spirit.

No believer should *ever* excuse a short fuse or say "that's just my personality." Yet the truth is, these people often tend to take a secret pride in the fact others treat them with kid gloves or are somewhat intimidated by their bluster. What they may think is respect is in actuality the simple fact most believers have enough maturity to try to avoid ugly scenes and guard the bond of loving peace. One thing is for certain — a loud mouth and high temper is nothing to be proud of and everything for which to be ashamed!

Since God is love, little could be worse than to be known as one who is often prone to blow up at others. Those who have little control over their tempers do untold damage to Christ's Church. Perhaps this is why Jesus was often merciful to prostitutes and thieves yet spoke extremely strong words to the critical, mean-spirited and religiously self-righteous (Matthew 23:13-27). Make no mistake — there is virtually nothing worse than to be known as someone who is unkind, high-tempered and mean-spirited. The Bible is absolutely clear that little is more offensive to God.

## The Devastating, Long-Term Effects of Unloving Behavior

Countless thousands have dropped entirely out of church because they witnessed so-called "Christians" behave with obvious anger and malice. Imagine the tragedy of some desperately seeking soul going to church only to see anger, division and ugliness among believers. According to Scripture, this all too common occurrence is nothing less than an *abomination* (Proverbs 6:16)! Only eternity will reveal how many people end up entirely rejecting Christ because of the unkind attitudes and actions of carnal church members. Their blood shall surely be required of those who so seriously damaged their faith (Matthew 18:6).

But of all the horrible damage done by unkind church members, by far the worst is visited upon the most precious and vulnerable among us. Without question, unloving attitudes and actions are especially devastating to children, youth and new believers! When they see adults act in anger and harshness, they are often permanently affected in their view of Christ and His Church.

## Avoiding the "Millstone Principle"
### (Matthew 18:6)

Before anyone expresses an ungodly attitude around a child or young believer, they should long reflect on Jesus' stern warning in Matthew 18:6, "But if anyone causes one of these little ones who believes in me to sin, it would be better for him to have a large millstone hung around his neck and to be drowned in the depth of the sea." Believers, it is vital that we come to view sin the way God views it. God sees sins of attitude and spirit just as vile as outward sins of the flesh. In many cases, He actually views attitude sins as far worse than sins of the flesh.

When we hear of the critical, nitpicky attitudes of some we must wonder if they ever read such passages as Ephesians 4:31-32. "Get rid of all bitterness, rage and anger, brawling and slander, along with every form of malice. Be kind and compassionate to one another, forgiving each other, just as in Christ God forgave you." Indeed, we would all do well to often read 1 Peter 4:8-9. "Above all, love each other deeply, because love covers over a multitude of sins. Offer hospitality to one another without grumbling."

The fact is none of us are anywhere near perfect. Yet true attitudes of godly love cause us to *overlook* one another's flaws. After all, there are certainly no perfect pastors or laypersons. We should all remember one great truth — one is never more like God than when kind and forgiving and never more like Satan than when critical and harsh.

# Judge Not Thy Brother!
### (James 4:11-12)

Closely related to the critical and high-tempered is the "holier than thou judge." These are people who tend to view others as "unspiritual" if they do not follow their exact patterns or practices. Prideful judgmental attitudes are subtle and infect all age groups and personality types. Condescension and harsh judgment seriously hinders God's Spirit in local churches. Prayerfully consider the patterns under the next heading.

## Five Subtle Patterns of Prideful Condescension Among Believers

(1) Those who raise their hands or show emotion in worship may criticize those who don't as spiritually dead or legalistic. Conversely, those who don't show much expression may harshly criticize those who do as overly emotional or doctrinally unsound.

(2) People who frequently attend prayer meetings or prayer groups may automatically view those who do not as unspiritual and immature.

(3) Those involved in evangelism or outreach may harshly judge those who are not as uncommitted and unspiritual.

(4) Those who attend Bible studies and discipleship groups may automatically view those who do not as unspiritual.

(5) Those who pridefully tout themselves as "Bible scholars" may become nit-picky and start seeing "doctrinal problems" where no significant issues really exist. In other words, they tend to make doctrinal mountains out of molehills. Worse yet, they get fixated on a particular doctrine or practice and lose all sense of balanced biblical focus. They become "one dimensional" and focus on one or two truths to the virtual exclusion or all others. Mature saints are able to recognize which issues are simply not

worth the risk of splitting a church or getting distracted (and most issues aren't!)

## We Can Actually Grow Through Disagreement

We must remember that good and godly people do not always agree and there is certainly room for variance on non-essential matters. Indeed a vital part of maturity is the ability to recognize the difference between the essential and the non-essential. Yet some lack the wisdom to keep from turning smaller, non-essential issues into major controversies and divisions that are wholly unnecessary. In other words, they develop some pet doctrine or issue and drive it into the ground. Such patterns badly distract us from the main issues of discipleship, fellowship, evangelism and missions. Obviously, angry internal arguments and distractions are exactly what Satan intends!

In 1 Corinthians 12-14, God pictures Christ's Church as having many members with very diverse gifts, needs and strengths. Yet, with all our diversity, we are to "endeavor" to live and work in loving unity (Ephesians 4:2-3). The Greek word for endeavor is *spoudadzo,* which actually means zealously making every effort to preserve unity. God clearly commands us to go to great lengths to guard the bond of peace in church.

Indeed, we do not all worship, pray, witness or serve God in exactly the same ways (*and neither are we required too!*) Christian love and maturity demands that we accept and even value our diversity, not divide and fight over it!

It is wonderful to report a growing remnant of churches are working toward greater unity *in spite* of many differing likes and dislikes. Though some of these believers in churches have fought for years, they are now learning to disagree agreeably. No matter how long you or your church has lived in anger and negativism, it is *not* too late to change! God can turn the most tension-filled churches and families into glorious pictures of grace and love.

## Putting On Christ — Putting Off the Flesh
### Steps for Repentance and Victory

Dear reader, this pattern is particularly offensive to God. If God has spoken to you and you are willing to pray a similar prayer, it is *urgent* that you pause and do it now. This is one area we ignore at great risk! Ask God to grant you sincerity and take all the steps of repentance His will requires. And remember, God always receives the broken and contrite heart (Psalms 51:17)!

*A Prayer of Cleansing and Transformation* — "Father, I fully confess my tendency to be high-tempered, critical and unkind. Please forgive me for being angry and harsh toward those with whom I disagree. By Your grace, I repent of my angry and critical patterns. Please fill me with Your forgiveness and kindness toward others."

## *Pattern Eighteen*
## *Questions for Prayer and Study Groups*

(for individuals, small groups or churchwide studies)

(1) Prayerfully read Proverbs 29:11, 20, 22. How strongly does God feel about the importance of controlling our tempers and tongues?

(2) Please read Proverbs 6:16. What role do you think pride and anger play in dividing congregations? Is it significant that God lists the proud (condescending) look and a spirit of divisiveness among sins that are called abominations?

(3) Reflect on 1 Peter 4:8-9 and Matthew 18:6. What is the "Millstone Principle"? How could obvious anger and harshness in church deeply damage children or new believers?

(4) Based on Matthew 18:6, how serious is it to damage the faith of children or new believers? Could displaying anger and harshness fit this scenario?

(5) Carefully re-read the *Five Subtle Patterns of Prideful Condescension Among Believers*. Do you sense any of these operating in your own heart? What is God's solution?

(6) Is it automatically wrong for believers to disagree on issues? How can we actually *grow* close through times of disagreement?

# Pattern Nineteen
# Decision-Time Free-for-Alls

(Matthew 5:9; 1 Corinthians 1:10;
James 1:5; 3:14-18, 4:1-4; 1 Peter 4:8-9)

Where do wars and fights come from among you? Do they not come from your desires for pleasure that war in your members? (James 4:1) Times of major church decisions are often opportunities for disgusting displays of fleshly anger and petty bickering. In fact, many pastors, staff and lay-leaders feel a wave of pure dread when it comes to proposing major projects or calling new staff. From painful experience, they realize how quickly people can become angry and divided. When churches come to times of decision, Satan immediately starts probing for possible ways to bring anger, division and distraction to the church. Worse yet, this is another shameful way we *profane* God's holy name before a watching world!

Make no mistake — our enemy is always searching for ways to *disrupt* unity, *damage* the bond of peace and *distract* believers from evangelism and missions. Unfortunately, he usually knows exactly where to go to find a willing instigator. In many churches, there are certain people always ready to quickly (and quite loudly) voice an opinion without careful prayer and thorough deliberation. No doubt the primary question to address is *why* major church decisions so easily move into bickering and division. Though certainly there are a variety of reasons, I believe six are most preeminent.

## Six Reasons for Decision-Time Church Battles

(1) *Angry divisive bickering is clear indication people are walking in the flesh, not the Spirit.* According to dozens of passages, angry division and bitter strife are the distinct, telltale fruits of immaturity and carnality (1 Corinthians 3:1-3; Galatians 5:19-21; James 3:14-16). When the Holy Spirit is in charge, believers can make decisions and discuss significant differences with

love, maturity and respect. Yet, when people are not yielded to God, selfish attitudes and angry divisions are the order of the day. Fleshly people can and do fight over even the smallest of issues. If several people are exhibiting fleshly attitudes, the church should strongly consider postponing any decisions and go through a period of spiritual cleansing.

(2) *Believers forget the vital kingdom principle of guarding unity and hallowing the name of God through Christian love* (John 13:34-35; 17:21 Ephesians 4:3). How quickly some saints forget the incredible importance of love and unity as a glory to God and testimony to all peoples the earth. When personal preferences get stretched, some quickly forget everything but "getting their way." Little could be more profaning to God's name or devastating to our evangelistic witness. Believers, we must strenuously resist the tendency to dishonor God by attacking one another! Indeed, the world can only know we are His by the way we love and work together in holiness.

(3) *Divisive bickering occurs when believers fail to carefully and prayerfully examine all facts before they form opinions and start promoting them to anyone who will listen.* In today's Church, it is astounding how many people start spouting opinions before they ever even hear the whole project or its reasons. So often, they have not practiced even a modicum of prayer and fasting, yet start loudly proclaiming their opinions. In truth, God's opinion is only one that matters and we find His will only by deep prayer and meditation, not fleshly reasonings. Yet some people are so arrogant, they think they don't need special time in deep prayer to fully discern God's mind. Obviously, individuals with such attitudes often have little real connection with the heart and mind of God (1 Corinthians 2:10-16).

(4) *Leaders or committees may indeed be proposing something that is ill-advised, wrongly-timed or improperly researched.* In other words, they may be proposing something that is simply wrong.

A related problem is the fact their presentations may be unclear and incomplete. Leaders or committees may also present a matter at the *wrong time* or in an *improper manner!* Wise leaders know it is often as important to know the *how* and *when* of God's leadership as the *what*.

(5) *Some people so love controversy and politics, they turn decisions into a "contest" of who can get their way.* By politicking and manipulations, they may attempt to swing the vote. They often do not even realize the real source of their objection. For many, times of decision also become key opportunities to settle old scores. If someone has anger toward a pastor or other leader, they may be opposing their proposal as a subconscious way to get even. Though they may not even realize it, some people oppose a project simply because they don't like those who proposed it!

Dear reader, if you find yourself often opposing your church, you should do a thorough examination of the source of your resistance. If it is truly of God, then well and good. However, if your opposition is more about personal feeling, you will often be opposing God Himself. One thing is certain — no one ever wins a contest with God!

(6) *Satanic opposition is a major causative factor in the anger and bickering surrounding many decisions in church.* In most major church decisions, Satan has a definite stake in how it turns out. Especially if a proposed step has great potential to expand God's kingdom, it would frankly be surprising if Satan didn't oppose it. Make no mistake — his primary means of hindering and opposing God's purpose is to stir up those who will listen to his voice and spread his suggestions and whispers.

We find a prime biblical example in Matthew 16:23. In speaking to Jesus, Peter undoubtedly thought he was giving sound advice. Yet Jesus responded with the words, *"Get thee behind me Satan!"* Jesus instantly knew the source of Peter's words. Like Peter, those being used by Satan usually have no idea they are tools in his hands. In most cases, they are following human reasoning instead of direction from God's Spirit. While they may sincerely believe they are fighting for the right thing, the enemy has deceived them into opposing the very purposes of God.

## Do Not Judge the Inner Motives of Others

Though satanic influence can certainly be a factor, we must be careful not to quick judge people who disagree as "speaking from Satan." We should always remember that God alone can fully see into hearts and godly people can honestly disagree without one being the voice of the devil. In great humility we must *all* ask God to guard our own hearts from deception and pride. Except in the most extreme or obvious of cases, we must also remain non-judgmental as to other people's motives for opposition.

Again, respectful discussion of varying viewpoints is good and entirely normal, not evil. In fact, such prayerful discussions and deliberations are usually how we come to a fuller understanding of the whole will of God. In other words, we *need* each other's reasonable impressions and thoughts. Dear saints, we must trust God for the grace to discuss differences and options without becoming angry or defensive.

## Four Simple Biblical Rules
## to Healthy Church Decisions

While the potential reasons for division may seem overwhelming, they are easily overcome by God's grace. *Four simple biblical guidelines will solve most problems in decisions.* (1) If leaders approach their tasks with thorough deliberation and fervent prayer, God will surely guide them to right proposals. (2) If lay-people are swift to hear, slow to speak and fervent in prayer, they will receive clear wisdom concerning God's will. (3) If everyone asks God's protection from deception and patiently awaits His timing, decision time will become glorious moments of united growth, not division. Both leaders and laypeople need to understand that *timing is everything!* (4) In those areas we still disagree, love teaches us to *disagree agreeably*. May God give us the determination to approach decisions in humility, prayer and thoroughness, not anger, fleshly reasoning or haste. Indeed, many a battle can be defused by simply putting a decision on hold to enter a period of intense prayer and further deliberation. (However, this must be a time of individual prayer and reflection, *not* further politicking and camp-building!)

## A Final Thought on Church Decisions

One of the most important rules to remember about times of decision is simply this — *most decisions are not worth dividing a church! They are certainly not worth dishonoring God's holy name.* Except in cases of fundamental doctrine or practice, we must carefully avoid dividing or fighting over smaller issues. In Scripture, we are commanded to "*diligently* keep the peace" (Ephesians 4:3). In other words, it is often better to keep peace than to cause an argument by angrily demanding our way on non-essential issues.

Another important principle is to simply "let it go" once a church decision is embraced. To continually complain or stir the pot is one of the most immature and spiritually damaging practices a believer can commit (see Pattern Ten). Again, we must realize that we cannot always get our way. We must humbly accept the church decision and move on.

## Putting On Christ — Putting Off the Flesh
### Steps for Repentance and Victory

Carefully consider the prayer below. If God has revealed a need and you are willing to pray a similar prayer, please pause and do it now. Ask God to help you mean it and take any steps of repentance His will requires. And remember, His mercy and power are without end to those who heed His voice!

*A Prayer of Cleansing and Transformation* — "Father, I confess the ways I acted in unkindness or rashness in a church decision. Please forgive me for treating as enemies those brothers or sisters with whom I disagree. By Your grace, I resolve to act in wisdom and love. Help me seek reconciliation with those I have alienated. Please fill me with the Spirit of love, wisdom and patience."

## Pattern Nineteen
## Questions for Prayer and Study Groups

(for individuals, small groups or churchwide studies)

(1) According to Galatians 5:19-21, what does anger, bickering, division and unkind behavior represent?

(2) Carefully reflect on Galatians 5:22. Why would walking in the Spirit and embracing simple spiritual maturity prevent angry divisive battles?

(3) Please read number 3 under *Six Reasons for Decision-Times Battles*. Why is it so vital to prayerfully consider all facts and angles before reaching and promoting a particular point of view?

(4) Is it common for Satan to use times of decision to bring division and distraction in a church? Why or why not?

(5) Carefully re-read the *Six Reasons for Decision-Time Battles*. Do you see areas about which you should be on guard?

(6) Carefully read *Four Simple Rules for Healthy Church Decisions*. Discuss how you could perhaps improve in some of these areas.

## Pattern Twenty
## Relational Brushfires and Molehill Mountains

(Matthew 5:9; John 17:21;
1 Corinthians 1:10; 3:1-3; James 4:1-4; 5:9)

*In today's Church, a common problem is the fact so many pastors and lay-leaders are exhausted from constantly dealing with relational brushfires in the congregation.* In many churches, there is also a tragic tendency for some to make "mountains out of molehills." Leaders can hardly focus on kingdom matters for having to referee constant controversies and disputes that should never even arise in the first place.

One of the most damaging effects of brushfires and molehills is what I call the "*drain effect.*" When leaders must constantly deal with "so-called" crises, they lose precious energy and vision for things that really matter. If Satan can thus get leaders distracted, disillusioned and emotionally drained, the work of God is enormously hindered. His predominate method of achieving this end is the willing complicity of certain people in the church. And quite often, these believers may not even realize they are being used. With many, their harm to God's work is truly not intentional. However, there are some with whom these damaging patterns are both consistent and willful. These individuals do enormous harm to the kingdom of God.

## Unattended Brushfires Can Become Raging Infernos!

Some readers may wonder why we shouldn't just ignore brushfires and molehills. The reason is something seasoned church leaders know all too well. *They know that left unchecked, brushfires and molehills can evolve into raging infernos and major mountains.* When conditions are right, just a small spark can race through a whole forest. Thus, it is incumbent upon every believer to be sure of one thing — he or she is neither the spark nor the kindling wood!

Unfortunately, issues for potential brushfires and molehills are virtually endless. If people are so inclined, there are innumerable issues about which to fight or grumble. We must also realize that one man's molehill is another man's mountain. Thus, a huge part of maturity is the ability to recognize the difference between the *essential* and *nonessential*. While it is certainly appropriate to occasionally share our concerns, feelings or preferences with fellow believers, we must do so with love and proper perspective. With nonessential issues, love demands that we all show much flexibility and consideration for the feelings of others (not angrily demanding our own way).

The next section outlines some of the most frequent points for petty, unnecessary bickering. Yet, these issues are urgent because they quickly become roaring fires. And even if they don't become raging fires, the constant smoldering creates enormous "distraction" and general "resistance" to the working of the Holy Spirit. Frankly, some believers should be deeply ashamed of the petty issues with which they continually monopolize the attention and energies of their spiritual leaders. Whether it's a raging fire or several persistent brush fires, God's name is shamed and His work tragically hindered!

At this point, every reader should pause and ask God if any of these patterns are in his or her life. *Above all, we must avoid becoming angry or defensive at God's conviction!* If God speaks through this section, simply admit the pattern and trust God's grace to help you change. Humble confession and full repentance is the only proper response to God's Spirit. Any other response is to invite God's chastisement for things that profoundly grieve His heart. Dear friends, we must never make light of things that offend God and dishonor His holy name.

# Common Examples
## of Potential Brushfires and Molehills

*(1) Hymns or choruses, traditional or contemporary* — It is actually possible for some believers to become so demanding for their own music preference, they strongly criticize leaders simply for

including a variety of other styles. Rather than considering the worship leaders' direction or preferences of other believers, they refuse to give an inch. They have no interest in allowing a mix of styles, they want it all their way. We should note this selfishness and intolerance occurs as much (or more) with the young as with seniors. When attitudes of immaturity are present, the stage is set for continual brushfires on a variety of issues.

(2) *To clap or not to clap in church* — Some people create problems by turning personal preferences like clapping or not clapping into serious biblical injunctions. Yet it is a great mistake to make a big deal about something when the Bible does not. Generally speaking, where the Bible issues no prohibitions neither should we. After all, who are we to judge the inner motivation of "why" someone claps in approval or agreement?

(3) *Music or no music* — Believe it or not, some have actually fought over whether or not to have soft instrumental music during a Lord's Supper observance. Again, we should never make an issue of something that is clearly not an issue in Scripture.

(4) *We shall not be moved* — Some people would literally rather fight than give up their favorite classroom to groups that need it more. Such attitudes are tragically different from the humble, sacrificial patterns of New Testament Christians. These attitudes reveal an incredible degree of self-centeredness.

(5) *We shall not be divided* — When classes need to be divided for growth or fairness to other age groups, some will actually threaten to leave the church. We can only wonder what Paul would have said to people with such smallness of spirit.

(6) *Possessiveness and territorialism* — Some become instantly angry when simply asked to alter their ministry assignments. Others are hyper-sensitive about overlapping responsibilities with other committees. Rather than working together in love and maturity, they become territorial and competitive. Some people are hyper-sensitive about anyone's work that crosses into

"their" area. Such attitudes reveal a disturbing level of pride.

*(7) Feelings on sleeves* — In far too many cases, people become angry if others seem to receive more appreciation or attention. Wrongly-motivated, immature people are quickly upset at the smallest perceived criticism or slight. Again this reveals a serious root of pride. If they are asked to alter or improve something, they are immediately defensive and offended. At the drop of a hat, they are ready to attack others, quit their position or leave the church.

*(8) Self-appointed overseers and unsolicited supervisors* — Some people seem to think it is their life calling to provide a running commentary on the way everyone else does their work in church. They are always telling anyone who will listen how *they* would do it different. If such comments should ever be made at all, they should be made only after much prayer and only to the appropriate leaders. Self-appointed critics and unbidden supervisors do enormous damage to the spiritual atmosphere of a church. That also reveal a disturbing degree of prideful arrogance.

*(9) Hyper-legalists and modern-day Pharisees* — While effective church policies and rules are certainly important, some churches have by-laws that make IRS forms look simple. And rather than applying rules with a spirit of love and grace, some become harsh and condescending. When churches become overly knit-picky and legalistic, hurt feelings and disunity are bound to flourish. It was to harsh legalistic people Jesus directed the descriptive phrase, *"they strain at a gnat but swallow a camel."* In other words, some people become so angry and rigid about every little rule, they completely lose sight of loving-kindness and grace (which is the rule of all rules!)

*(10) Rules are for others* — While some drift into hyper-legalism about rules, others want no rules at all. These individuals truly have a defiant, rebellious spirit and a real problem with au-

thority. To them, rules are "meant to be broken." Their inner attitudes toward other believers are, "Who are you to tell me what to do?" People with this fleshly attitude consistently ignore church policies and cause enormous problems in churches. Obviously, such attitudes are utterly inappropriate and create fertile ground for relational brushfires and tension.

*This sin is especially damaging when committed by staff or church leaders.* Even a little division among staff has far-reaching effects. When staff fail to follow church guidelines or set good examples, major problems quickly ensue. This pattern becomes especially serious when staff or leaders consistently undermine the pastor's authority. Of course, it is equally damaging for pastors to undermine staff. In either case, brushfires explode into raging infernos of churchwide division. Before you know it, church members are "taking sides" and tension fills the air. Genuine worship is replaced by fleshly distractions and tension.

*(11) You're in My Pew* — We often hear people jokingly refer to a certain pew as being "theirs." Yet with some there is only one problem—they are not joking! Though it sounds unbelievable, there have been more than a few cases of visitors being given a very hard look when they unknowingly sit in someone's favorite spot. In some instances, guests are even somewhat sternly told to get up and move. Imagine the utter absurdity of someone coming to church seeking God, only to be treated rudely because they sat in someone's favorite "spot." Even as I worked on this section, I was told firsthand of an unchurched visitor leaving a particular church in tears after twice being abruptly told to move from different church members' favorite sitting places. It is truly hard to conceive of anything more petty, immature or out of touch with God's heart!

*(12) Temperature Tantrums* — Still another occasion for pettiness on display are angry battles over temperature preferences. While

there is certainly nothing wrong with people letting leaders know if they are seriously cold or hot, there is everything wrong with being excessively demanding or unkind. Yet some seem utterly unaware we all have different preferences and a church has to avoid extremes in either direction. In other words, we all may at times have to dress warmer or cooler if our preferences are out of the middle range. But sadly enough, some refuse and actually threaten to stop attending church if their exact demands are not met. We must wonder what God thinks of those so quick to abandon church when believers in some countries risk their very lives to attend in places having no heat, air-conditioning or even furniture. If the early Church had taken the attitude of some modern believers, it would never have survived the first century. May God help us keep an eternal perspective!

*(13) Well, He Didn't Come to Visit Me* — While ministers and leaders must certainly avoid favoritism, many unavoidable factors prevent all illness or problems from being treated exactly the same. For any number of legitimate reasons, not every hospital visit or call can be in exactly the same frequency. Yet, some members become overly-sensitive and start meticulously counting number of visits. The Holy Spirit has little or nothing to do with such pettiness! Not only is this often a sign of deep immaturity, it can easily place pastors under a strain that is wholly unbiblical (see Pattern Twenty-one). While serious neglect by a pastor is *utterly unacceptable*, hypersensitivity and unreasonable expectations are enormous hindrances to church health.

*(14) But She Doesn't Even Play the Piano* — In some churches, unfair comparisons between current and former pastors' families lead to serious division and criticism. Churches must come to understand every pastor's wife is different with her own unique gifts and calling for church ministry. If churches expect one pastor's wife (or family) to be like previous ones, unfair criticism

and division are the inevitable result. What begins with mild criticism quickly becomes serious division and hindrance to God's Spirit. The families of pastors and staff must be allowed to follow their own unique gifts and callings. They must also be extended the understanding that a pastor's family is human too. Because of their strategic positions, ministers and their families are under far greater spiritual attack than the average lay person. For this reason, the last thing they need is church members adding to the devil's arsenal!

As you can see from this list, potential issues for brushfires and molehills are almost endless. When people are selfish and overly sensitive, almost anything quickly becomes a major issue. Yet in most cases, one simple principle prevents these damaging distractions — *basic spiritual maturity and placing the needs of others above our own* (1 Corinthians 3:3; Philippians 2:4).

For balance, let me again say this section is *not* intended to suggest believers shouldn't ever share their concerns, feelings or preferences to other believers. When done in love and humility, we can certainly share concerns and problems without creating brushfires or mountains out of molehills. In fact, we *should* share significant concerns and needs. Yet, when non-essential issues start becoming angry chronic battles, believers must step back, pray up and ask God to grow us into loving maturity.

When the same individuals are always the squeaky wheels of complaint, you can know they have a major problem. The Bible gives sobering warnings about consistent complaining and grumbling (1 Corinthians 10:10). Dear saints, it is essential that we stop brushfires and molehills *before* they become infernos and mountains. It is vital that we "grow up" in spiritual matters.

## Putting On Christ — Putting Off the Flesh
### Steps for Repentance and Victory

Believers, it is crucial to understand these matters are not minor with God! If God has spoken to your heart, you must take this with great seriousness. Carefully consider the prayer below. If you are willing to pray a similar prayer, please pause and do it now. Ask God to help you mean it and take the serious steps of repentance His will requires.

God may well lead you to ask forgiveness of your church. My friend, you will be amazed how your repentance will release God's Sprit in your congregation! Please let God make you a great blessing to others. And remember, His grace is greater than your deepest need!

*A Prayer of Cleansing and Transformation* — "Father, I confess the ways I have turned smaller issues into major offenses. Please forgive me for reacting without deep prayer and careful consideration. Lord, forgive me for selfish attitudes that have hindered Your Spirit in my church. By Your grace, I resolve to prayerfully consider all issues before I resist change and growth. I resolve to embrace a loving heart that places the needs of others above my own. Please fill me with Your Spirit of loving maturity, patience and wisdom."

*As study or prayer groups work through the questions on each pattern, remember to stay very focused on God's grace and hope for change. No church or person should forget God convicts to change us, not discourage. In discussing areas for change, do not call peoples' names and stay positive. Let God's revelations lead you straight to prayer and faith for change, not criticism or gossip.

## *Pattern Twenty*
## *Questions for Prayer and Study Groups*

(for individuals, small groups or churchwide studies)

(1) Carefully re-read the *Fourteen Most Common Molehill Mountains.* What role do you think immaturity and selfishness plays in most molehill mountains?

(2) How do you think brush-fires and molehills can distract a church from the main things of discipleship, evangelism, missions and loving one another?

(3) Please read Ephesians 4:29-32 and 1 Peter 4:8-9. How would brush-fires and molehills grieve the Holy Spirit and block His power in a congregation?

(4) Reflect on Philippians 2:3-4. How would the attitude of simply "placing others first" solve most brush-fires and molehills?

(5) While some of the patterns in this section have humorous titles, do you really think God finds any of these patterns amusing? On a scale of 1-10, how seriously do you think these attitudes quench and grieve God's Spirit?

(6) The Corinthian church had many relationship problems and yet God used them for His name's sake. How does that grace of God give us great hope though none of our churches are anywhere near perfect? Thank God, there is grace for our failures!

# Pattern Twenty-One
## Over-Extended Pastors and Unbiblical Expectations

(Acts 6:2-4; 1 Corinthians 12-14; Ephesians 4:11-12;
1 Thessalonians 5:12-13; 1 Timothy 5:17; Hebrews 13:17)

*Unscriptural and unrealistic job expectations have become enormous hindrances to the effectiveness of many modern pastors.* While this pattern is largely unintentional, the damage is nonetheless profound. When pastors and lay leaders are expected to assume so many non-essential roles, they have little time to focus on the "main" things. In Acts 6:2-4, we find the clear biblical pattern for the essential focus of preachers. "So the Twelve gathered all the disciples together and said, It would not be right for us to neglect the ministry of the word of God in order to wait on tables. Brothers, choose seven men from among you who are known to be full of the Spirit and wisdom. We will turn this responsibility over to them and *will give ourselves to prayer and the ministry of the Word."*

In today's Church, most congregations have expectations of pastors that are very different from the clear patterns of Scripture. Unrealistic job expectations cause enormous diversion of pastors' energies. If the pastor is expected to be present for every tiny illness, attend all meetings and guide every committee, when can he spend the major time in prayer and Scripture study so necessary for highly anointed preaching and teaching of Scripture? If he is consumed by far too many roles (that others really should be doing) when does he pray, win souls or hear God's full vision for the church? *The answer is he doesn't!*

When a pastor is divided by so many roles, he often cannot preach in dynamic power, hear God's vision or win large numbers to Christ. Because of excessive, unbiblical expectations, huge portions of his time are consumed on issues of lesser eternal impact. When this occurs, pastors are seldom able to lead churches into powerful revival and kingdom growth. It is a classic example of the "good" becoming the deadliest enemy of the "best."

# We Will Give Ourselves
## to the "Word of God and Prayer"
### (Acts 6:4)

While pastors must certainly perform effective administration, visitation and ministry to the sick, they cannot be expected to do it all (especially when illness and needs are relatively minor). In reality, mature church members would not really want their pastors to take precious time from critical eternal matters to give them unnecessary attention. Furthermore, God's Word clearly shows the "whole church body" as ministering one to another (Romans 12:3-8; 1 Corinthians 12-14). It plainly shows the minister's role as primarily giving himself to the "Word of God and prayer for the equipping of the saints" (Acts 6:2-4; Ephesians 4:12).

When the pastor's role becomes excessive and overextended, essential kingdom work invariably suffers. In this unbiblical pattern, church members are deprived of developing their gifts and pastors have little time for the most crucial kingdom issues. Pastors become exhausted from overwork and church members spiritually stale and weak from inaction. This pattern is a perfect prescription for weak churches, exhausted ministers and idle, immature church members who seldom use their spiritual gifts.

# A Satanic Strategy for
## Weak Churches and Burned-Out Pastors
### A Perfect Prescription for Defeat

In Ephesians 6:11, Paul describes the devil as an evil adversary with elaborate schemes to harm believers and hinder Christ's work. Indeed, a master plan of Satan is to get churches (and pastors) structured in ways that are unbiblical and inefficient. Without question, unbiblical and excessive expectations of pastors are among Satan's most effective tools. Studies show more and more pastors are exhausted, burned out and dying early from stress-related illnesses.

Today, shocking numbers of pastors are leaving the ministry from sheer exhaustion, discouragement and burnout. Unprecedented numbers of seminary graduates leave the ministry within their first-three years! For a variety of reasons, many churches are becoming increasingly difficult to pastor. What is happening to modern pastors and staff is utterly unprecedented and devastating to kingdom work. In today's church practices and philosophies, something is clearly wrong!

For balance, let me stress that few churches purposely abandoned biblical patterns of leadership. Subtle changes slowly evolved over several decades until churches finally reached today's patterns. Yet concerning these patterns, there is at last indication of positive change! More and more churches desire a pastor who is truly an anointed prophet, shepherd and spiritual leader. These churches do not expect their pastor to visit everyone who has a slight illness, lead every committee or attend every meeting. While he certainly attends to those in real need, he is expected to spend much time in prayer and study to lead the church into revival and powerful evangelism. Dear saints, this attitude is the only one that is truly biblical.

## It's Time for a Biblical Attitude Adjustment!

Before some churches even call a new pastor, they are asking their members to step up to the plate of ministry. They are thus freeing their pastor for greater focus on issues of higher kingdom impact. Members are asked to stop expecting the pastor to attend to every tiny ache or pain. These churches are not only freeing him for greater kingdom focus, they *expect* it. It should come as no surprise these are the churches seeing dynamic growth and health.

I wish I could report that most churches have moved more toward leadership patterns of the New Testament (Acts 6:2-4; Ephesians 4:12). Tragically, the vast majority still expect pastors to try and be all things to all members. Self-centered members continue to attack pastors for the pettiest of so-called slights. When members unnecessarily demand the pastor's time, he has little or no time for the more essential kingdom issues of discipleship, soul winning, missions and revival. No doubt, such immaturity is a huge reason many churches never see revival, vibrant health or explosive evangelism.

Yet to God's praise, there is at last some good news to report! Growing numbers are returning to more biblical ministry expectations for pastors and lay leaders. More and more church members are not expecting attention over very small matters and encourage their pastors toward greater kingdom activities. May this trend continue until revival again sweeps our land! For help on biblical ministry philosophies, check out three related resources: *Vital Spiritual Principles for Pastors Search Committees: Seeking God before Seeking a Pastor; Restoring the Missing Elements of Revived Churches;* and *Seven Essentials of Holiness and Power in Christian Leaders.* All these books by Gregory Frizzell are available through the Baptist General Convention of Oklahoma at very nominal costs.

## Putting On Christ — Putting Off the Flesh
### Steps for Repentance and Victory

Dear reader, please carefully consider the prayer below. If God has spoken and you are willing to pray a similar prayer, pause and do it now. Ask God to help you mean it and take all the steps of repentance His will requires. And remember, we can all continue to change and grow!

*A Prayer of Cleansing and Transformation* — "Father, I confess the ways I have placed unbiblical burdens and expectations upon Your servants and leaders. Please forgive me for placing my own smaller needs above bigger priorities of Your kingdom. Forgive me for wanting more than my share of attention. By Your grace, I resolve to place bigger kingdom issues above my smaller personal comforts. Please fill me with Your Spirit and help me seek first Your kingdom and righteousness."

## *Pattern Twenty-One*
## *Questions for Prayer and Study Groups*

(for individuals, small groups or churchwide studies)

(1)  Carefully reflect on Acts 6:1-4. What pattern does God give for the primary use of time and priority focus for God's pastors and ministers?

(2)  What affect does it have if pastors are so busy with various ministries that they have little time for intense prayer, sermon preparation or soul-winning?

(3)  It is likely any church can see revival or New Testament power if their minister is not following the priority patterns from the Acts model?

(4)  What adjustments must ministers make to embrace the patterns of the New Testament leaders?

(5)  What adjustments must church members make to encourage their pastor to embrace the priority patterns of the New Testament and Great Awakening?

# Pattern Twenty-Two
# Prayerless Programs and
# Change for the Sake of Change

(Joshua 9:14; Proverbs 14:12; Jeremiah 10:23;
1 Corinthians 12-14; James 1:5)

*While change is an important part of growth, certain members may become overly restless and start pushing toward "change for the sake of change."* Because some other church did something, they may become insistent on immediately embracing that exact plan. Some groups may put excessive pressure on leaders to quickly make major changes in certain patterns or practices.

We also live in a day of unprecedented proliferation of new formulas, programs and theories on how to "do church." While some are clearly biblical and blessed of God, not all that is new or popular is right for every church. Unfortunately, some programs have in their structure very little prayer and virtually *no* spiritual cleansing of participants. No program or formula should be allowed to become a substitute for either fervent prayer or seeking God's unique direction and timing for each church. While proposed changes can often be God-led and positive, churches must resist four common mistakes that can cause enormous damage.

## Four Common Mistakes
## When Making Changes in Churches

(1) *We must resist the pressure to make changes without carefully seeking God's specific leading for our particular congregation.* It is important to realize that every church and community is unique. God is generally not into "cookie cutter patterns" which suggest all churches are supposed to be nearly identical. Some may read the latest approach and start pressuring leaders to immediately embrace those exact changes or programs. Because some church down the road did something they assume it must be God's

will for us. Yet because every church has unique-nesses in age makeup, history, setting and vision, each must find and follow God's specific guidance, not just grab the latest program.

While we can certainly use modern books and strategies, each church must always seek God for any unique applications or timing for their setting. In some cases, it is a real mistake to take someone else's formula and arbitrarily plug it into a church without seeking God's unique method, timing or adjustments in application. Churches must get their primary direction from *God*, not just men or pre-programmed strategies (Joshua 9:14; Proverbs 14:22). While God may well use programs and strategies, we must not let these replace the practice of continually seeking His unique directions for each congregation.

(2) *We must resist the pressure to make changes that may be right in content or theory but wrong in method and timing.* In some churches, dramatic change can happen quickly and smoothly while in others, the very same approach would create a shipwreck. Following God's will includes the *how* and *when* as much as the *what*. In other words, it would be far better to take two years to process a change (and guard healthy unity) than force it in six months and split the church (John 17:21; Ephesians 4:2-3)! Many churches experience unnecessary damage and division because of simple haste. While it is important not to fall *behind* when following God's direction, it is equally important not to get *ahead* of His leading.

(3) *We must resist the unbiblical idea that bloody "transition wars" are simply inevitable and normal.* While some conflict is to be expected in major changes, following God's direction and timing usually brings minimal damage and maximum growth. When it comes to needed change, our Lord is certainly concerned that transitions occur with the greatest possible love and unity. The belief it is acceptable for groups to run roughshod over one another is simply not biblical. With God, it is all about

relationships— loving Him and loving each other (Matthew 22:37-38; John 13:34-35; 1 Corinthians 12-14)!

(4) *We must resist the false idea that certain music styles, growth formulas, programs or organizational structures are the primary keys to revival and growth.* Throughout history, God has sent sweeping revival and explosive evangelism in a vast array of differing worship, preaching and organizational styles. Sweeping revival and kingdom growth are *never* mostly about particular methods or styles! However, in every historic move of God there are four unchanging principles. Revival and New Testament power are always centered around (a) fervent personal and corporate prayer, (b) strong biblical preaching, (c) relational unity and (d) deep repentance! These are God's non-negotiable, essential principles. In other words, God has plan A and there is no plan B. Methods or styles will come and go but principles are eternal — they never change! (Malachi 3:6; James 1:17)

While methodological changes are certainly important and positive, they must *never* supercede fervent prayer, repentance, unity, discipleship and biblical evangelism (not shallow, man-centered substitutes.) When it comes to empowering His Church, God has always had only one principle! The changeless, eternal principle for empowerment is intense united prayer, deep repentance and biblical fellowship (2 Chronicles 7:14; Matthew 21:13; John 13:34-35; 17:21; Acts 2:1).

If church growth emphases get out of balance, we may well find ourselves with bigger crowds but lower commitment, shallow discipleship and declining baptism ratios. Contrary to some philosophies, the goal is *not* simply bigger — *it is growth with healthy biblical balance!* God's primary goals are always revival and balanced New Testament Christianity, *not* just bigger crowds and better entertainment. While some of today's church growth philosophies have helpful elements, some are just plain biblically unbalanced. And while numeric growth may indeed occur, the long-term fruit will be a crop of lost church members and shallow Christians who never grow to maturity or Christian service.

## The Seven Biblical Tests for Healthy Church Changes

As we observe rapid changes in today's Church, it is evident some are good and biblical while others simply are not. We must carefully evaluate all changes by the doctrines and principles of Scripture, *not* by what is merely popular. While some claim "success" from certain changes, the efficacy of any change should always be tested by seven questions.

(1) Are the changes thoroughly biblical in *doctrine, balance* and *principle?*

(2) Do we see Christian commitment, discipleship, Bible-focus and spiritual growth moving to a deeper level?

(3) Are the changes moving the church toward far deeper levels of kingdom-focused prayer, repentance, holiness and worship?

(4) Are significantly more people being reached through true conversion, biblical evangelism and focus on missions? (Do our "conversions" yield deep repentance, changed lifestyles, and committed service to Christ?)

(5) Does the church more resemble the New Testament pattern of reaching a diverse culture?

(6) After the initial challenging period of adjustment, will the church become stronger in the bond of peace and loving unity? (In other words, the changes are being approached in a manner and timing that brings the least division and maximum blessing.)

(7) Do these changes make us more or less like the actual doctrines and practices of the New Testament Church?

We should be very wary of any changes that keep us from sharing the "whole council of God" or "watering down" the message? All philosophies must be judged by the clear teachings and patterns of the New Testament Church *not* the latest popular fad. If something sounds different from the practices and teachings of the early Church, we had better take a long hard look at what we are doing. We need to become very aware that "all that glitters is not gold' in current philosophies of church growth and health.

*In concluding this point, let me again stress that change is a real part of growth!* Churches definitely need to adapt and evolve to better reach an ever-changing culture. Toward that end, many of today's changes in worship and approach are very positive and much used of God. Several modern books and strategies are well worth reading and have indeed helped millions. We must all further realize that transition is seldom easy and churches should be thankful for leaders willing to help them adjust to better reach our world.

Believers, in all changes we are to remember three vital principles. (1) We must ensure that all changes are absolutely Bible-centered, theologically correct and spiritually balanced (2 Timothy 3:16). (2) Let everything be done decently and in order (1 Corinthians 14:40). (3) Let all things be done with the laws of love and unity preeminent (Matthew 22:38; 1 Corinthians 1:10; Ephesians 4:3). Thank God, His grace is sufficient to help us change and grow without World War III!

## Putting On Christ — Putting Off the Flesh
### Steps for Repentance and Victory

Carefully consider the prayer below. If God has revealed a need and you are willing to pray a similar prayer, please pause and do it now. Ask God to grant you sincerity and take whatever steps of repentance His will requires. And remember, His grace is sufficient for all the growth and change we could ever require!

*A Prayer of Cleansing and Transformation* — "Father, I confess the ways I have ignored Your ways when making or adjusting to changes in my church. Please forgive me for reacting without deep prayer and careful consideration. Forgive me for impatience and insensitivity.

By Your grace, I resolve to prayerfully consider all issues before I either resist or embrace changes in Your kingdom work. Please fill me with Your Spirit of wisdom."

## *Pattern Twenty-Two*
## *Questions for Prayer and Study Groups*

(for individuals, small groups or churchwide studies)

(1)  Carefully re-read the *Four Common Mistakes When Making Church Changes*. Are there ways you could help your church grow in any of these areas? Name them and take the needs to God in prayer.

(2)  Please re-read the *Seven Biblical Tests of Health Church Changes*. Are there areas we need to pray about for wisdom and improvement? Spend time praying for God's power and touch.

# Pattern Twenty-Three
# Organizational Maintenance Over
# Kingdom-Focused Expansion

(Matthew 6:33; 9:37-38; 28:16-18;
Mark 11:17; Luke 6:38; 14:23)

*A most tragic development in today's Church is the strong tendency toward "inward organizational maintenance" over "outward kingdom expansion."* This pattern exists when the vast majority of church energy, focus and resources are centered inward rather than outward. So what happens when the majority of church activities and focus are upon believers' enjoyment rather than serious discipleship, evangelism and missions? Two conditions become pronounced.

First, the Holy Spirit is seriously quenched and grieved because the focus is totally different than that of Christ. Second, the predominantly inward focus produces a sense of lukewarmness and spiritual deadness. I call this condition the "Dead Sea effect." The Dead Sea effect is when churches or people have little or no outlet for significant kingdom-ministry and service. When there is little or no outlet for kingdom service, we inevitably become stale, lifeless and self-absorbed. Sadly enough, inward-focused churches exhibit all too familiar characteristics.

## Seven Characteristics of Inward-Focused Churches

Churches or people caught in an inward focus exhibit very distinct characteristics. As you read these characteristics, prayerfully consider whether they reflect your church. If they do, don't despair! Remember, our God can bring glorious floods to the driest ground.

(1) If a church is inward focused, baptisms tend to be very low and worship service decisions infrequent. In these churches, there is a general lack of God's anointing and power.

(2) Planning meetings are mostly about setting calendar and activities, not seeking God's unique strategic vision for ever-expand-

ing ministries through that congregation. At such meetings, prayer is mostly just a perfunctory formality at the beginning and end of the session.

(3) Church ministries see very little change or development from year to year. Any changes tend to be declines and reductions.

(4) Finances tend to be plateaued or declining. In most cases, there are ever-shrinking resources.

(5) Conflict and tension over smaller issues is disturbingly common. Inward-focused churches tend to bicker over a wide range of non-essential matters. In general, their focus is more on the temporal than the eternal.

(6) Pastor and staff spend far more time on minor needs and organizational maintenance than activities of vital kingdom expansion. In many ways, they are more "organizational managers" than kingdom ministers and leaders.

(7) Pastor and staff often feel somewhat smothered by a general church attitude of smallness and self-focus. They may often feel more like "caretakers" of a dying Christian social club than bold leaders of Christ's victorious Church on mission (see author's note).

> **Author's Note:** In reviewing the *Seven Characteristics of Inward-Focused Churches*, readers should note that a balance of inward-focused ministry is also desirable and God-ordained. Obviously, not all kingdom ministry is focused *outside* the body of Christ. The Church is also commanded to maintain a strong ministry to the physical and spiritual needs of Christ's flock. The common problem today is one of balance. Sadly, most modern churches are profoundly over-balanced toward an excessive inward focus on temporal issues.

## "Majoring on Minors" Breeds Bickering and Conflict

When churches turn inward, it is far more common for members to battle over a wide array of lesser issues. In fact, if some believers exhibited half the passion for evangelism they show for small non-essentials, church baptisms would explode through the roof! Conversely churches that are heavily focused on kingdom expansion and ministry tend to have phenomenal unity and vision. Never forget this critical principle and truth — *when we focus on the "main things" we have little time (or inclination) to fight over smaller issues.* Being kingdom-minded has a glorious way of putting things in eternal perspective. People that are Spirit-filled and kingdom-minded simply don't have time to battle over such things as music styles, classroom arrangements or personal preferences.

Concerning this issue, there is at last good news to report. There is a small but growing trend toward churches seeking to become "kingdom" rather than "inward" focused! Though admittedly, it is still a small minority, kingdom-focused churches are increasing. It is also encouraging to report that *any* small church can embrace kingdom principles. Even churches that are predominately senior adults are finding creative new ways to embrace significant-kingdom focus. And when they do, the resulting change is astounding!

In God-focused, kingdom-centered congregations, God's Spirit becomes far more active and bickering much less prevalent. As focus and ministry becomes more outward, the river of God's Presence brings glorious new life and newness. Best of all, I stress that *any* church can learn to be more God-focused and kingdom-centered! No matter what our challenges, God will meet us where we are and graciously lead us to a whole new level of life and ministry. Most of all, God leads us to greater closeness with Himself. The results are absolutely miraculous!

## Seven Tests for God-Focused, Kingdom-Centered Churches
### Embracing Strategic Visions that Truly Come from God!

In researching history's great awakenings, I have identified seven factors that generally characterize churches in full New Testament power. Indeed, the churches that actually experienced sweeping revival and awakening, typically embraced *seven* key elements, *not* just the four or five common today. Thus, it is indeed possible for a church to evaluate its purpose and vision to determine whether it is in a full revival and kingdom-focus pattern. Any church that is truly kingdom-focused and revival seeking can generally answer yes to seven specific questions. Please prayerfully evaluate your church's practices, priorities and strategic vision based on seven key points.

(1) *Have you sought a God-revealed strategy to move your church into Spirit-initiated times of thorough biblical cleansing and repentance periodically?* (i.e. solemn assemblies, church-focused revival meetings, special periods of relational cleansing, etc.) Though essential, we practice this principle as God leads and not in some rigid, periodic program. In other words, we let *God* tell us when to schedule revivals and solemn assemblies, not a pre-set calendar. Yet let us be clear — churches serious about seeking God are utterly committed to regular patterns of deep cleansing and repentance (at the Spirit's leading).

(2) *Do you have a God-led strategy to greatly increase the personal and corporate prayers and holiness of the congregation?* (i.e. developing intense discipleship in prayer, embracing powerful corporate prayer meetings and corporate repentance, developing evange- listic prayer ministries, family prayer emphases, etc.) Churches serious about seeking God are utterly committed to developing fervent personal and corporate prayer.

(3) *Do you have a God-led strategy to greatly increase personal and group evangelism practices in your church?* (i.e. soul winning train- ing, Sunday School outreach emphases, evangelism projects, etc.) Churches serious about seeking God are utterly committed to evangelism.

(4) *Do you have a God-led strategy to greatly increase personal and corporate missions involvement in your congregation?* (i.e. empha- sizing sacrificial missions giving, missions praying, missions

trips and projects, adopting certain countries, etc.) Churches serious about revival are utterly committed to missions.

(5) *Do you have a God-led strategy to greatly increase personal and corporate discipleship patterns in your church?* (i.e. serious discipleship training, discipleship/prayer groups, discipling converts, marriage and family prayer development, etc.) Churches serious about seeking God and revival are utterly committed to ever-deepening discipleship.

(6) *Do you have a God-led strategy to greatly deepen church fellowship, guard unity, minister to the Body and quickly address strained relationships?* (i.e. strong ministries to sick and needy, effective koinonia fellowship and activities, relationship cleansing processes to deepen unity and heal damaged relationships, etc.) Churches serious about seeking God are utterly committed to deepening koinonia fellowship, internal ministry and loving relational oneness.

(7) *Do you have a God-led strategy to greatly deepen patterns of worship and balanced biblical preaching?* (i.e. prayerful planning to enhance and develop corporate worship, sending pastor on conferences for biblical preaching, etc.) Churches serious about seeking God are utterly committed to deepening their corporate worship with balanced preaching and teaching of the Word. God-centered churches will be Bible-centered! In other words, we will heavily center on preaching and teaching through the whole Bible, not just books written by men about selected parts of the Bible.

## How Any Church Can Become God-Guided and Kingdom-Centered!

I am thrilled to assure readers that any church can embrace a God-initiated, kingdom-focused vision! Obviously each church will certainly have its own God-guided uniqueness as to which of the seven priorities they devote focus at any given time. But one thing is certain — *all seven of these areas are vital to bringing a church into true revival and kingdom-focused health!* We cannot afford to be consistently lax or unfocused in *any one* of God's key priorities. For this reason, our strategic planning and vision must specifically address all seven key priorities of God. However, we must allow God to guide the details and timing in all we do! After all, it must be *His* vision we follow, not merely asking Him to bless *ours*.

Any church can use the seven steps to prayerfully seek God in strategic planning and vision that originates with His heart! These seven points enable churches to become highly *focused* and *specific* in obeying God's essential priorities. However, we must use the kingdom priorities to help us look to God, *not* just formulas or principles! Far too many are trying to work formulas and principles without seriously seeking God Himself. We are to let God Himself be our main focus. God alone must give us the exact particulars and timing of obeying His purposes.

## Staying "God-Focused"
## Not Just "Principle or Formula-Focused"

*It is vital that churches (and believers) not allow principles and purposes to replace close listening to God.* If we are not careful, following principles can become somewhat impersonal and program-ish. For some, these can become a subtle substitute for utter focus on God Himself. In other words, we may start following the principles and purposes without intimate closeness and detailed guidance from God. While embracing key principles is certainly vital, only consistent closeness with God enables us to apply His principles to our unique lives and settings.

Dear saints, the minute we think we can just "work the formula" without closely listening to God, we drift into man-guided programs. Above everything else, revival is all about the *relationship* of utter closeness and surrender to Christ. It is all about loving, knowing and walking with God Himself, *not* just following principles or pre-packaged programs. While various studies and emphases can certainly be mightily used of God, they must not become our steady diet. We must not let human books replace *the* Book. Neither must we allow programs and formulas to replace the need for leaders and people to personally seek God for their unique lives and setting.

While we can certainly benefit from various resources, every church is unique and is to receive a unique vision from God Himself, not men. While we can and should use helpful studies and emphases, we must remember the *balance* of never letting these substitute for closely seeking and following God Himself.

## Rediscovering the Essential "Relational Foundations" of Revival

Many churches are already to some degree focused on the basic four or five common purposes (though often inadequately). Indeed, we pretty well know to target evangelism, missions, discipleship, fellowship and worship. And yet, the elements that are the actual *"relational foundations"* to revival are almost wholly ignored. The actual relational foundations to revival and New Testament power are: (1) *Intense personal and corporate prayer.* (2) *Deep personal and corporate repentance.* (3) *A powerful focus on fellowship and relational unity.* If these three emphases are missing or only lightly emphasized, the power for the other five is greatly diminished. Only an intense focus on fervent prayer, profound cleansing and relational oneness can fully empower the other basic purposes! To marginalize these elements causes us to be "doing the purposes" without the intimate closeness, love and surrender to Christ.

If the three relational foundations are neglected, we are reduced to functioning without the full revival power of God. While we can certainly see some blessing, we do not see sweeping revival and spiritual awakening. If anyone doubts the truth of that statement, all one need to do is take an objective look at today's statistics and trends. Have we not been mostly focusing on the basic five purposes the past fifty years? Have we not seen one new strategy or formula after another? Indeed we have! So what has been the result? *We have witnessed by far the worst moral and spiritual collapse in our nation's history!*

When we look at today's patterns, it is clear something *is* missing. Without question, intense united prayer, deep cleansing and loving relational unity are the three missing elements! These elements cannot be treated as "side issues" and still maintain the intensity of focus so necessary for revival and New Testament power. Yet in truth, that is exactly what we have done. While the three relational foundations are not wholly absent, they are somewhat marginalized. It has killed our power and vibrancy!

So how about it dear reader? In your personal and church planning, do you prayerfully consider *all seven* priorities of kingdom-focus? More importantly, are you doing it in a way that keeps you truly "God-focused" over formula or principle-focused? By God's grace, we can all adjust to include the intense relational focus so often missing from our priorities and planning. It is truly amazing what happens as we become totally God-guided and kingdom centered in our planning and practice! *By so doing, we at last begin to seek the Reviver not just revival.* And guess what — when we seek the Reviver, we find all the revival we could ever imagine!

## Putting On Christ — Putting Off the Flesh
### Steps for Repentance and Victory

Carefully consider the prayer below. If God has opened your eyes and you are willing to pray a similar prayer, please pause and do it now. Ask God to help you mean it and take any steps of repentance His will requires. And remember, through Christ we can all become God-focused and Kingdom-Centered!

*A Prayer of Cleansing and Transformation* — "Father, I confess the ways I have been more focused on my needs and comforts than larger kingdom purposes. Please forgive me for being more self-focused than kingdom-centered. By Your grace, I resolve to embrace Your heart and burden for a lost world. Please fill me with the Spirit of love and kingdom focus."

## *Pattern Twenty-Three*
## *Questions for Prayer and Study Groups*

(for individuals, small groups or churchwide studies)

(1) Please read Matthew 6:33; 28:16-18 and Mark 11:17. What are to be the major priority emphases of a New Testament church?

(2) Carefully re-read the *Seven Characteristics of Inward-Focused Churches*. Are there certain areas we should pray for wisdom to improve our focus?

(3) Review the *Seven Tests for God-Focused, Kingdom-Centered Churches*. Are there certain areas we should pray for wisdom to improve?

(4) Is it possible to become so focused on working formulas and principles that we lose the closeness of intensely seeking God Himself? What are some ways to prevent this?

# Pattern Twenty-Four
# Naysaying and Perpetual Doubting

(Numbers 13:27-33; 32:7; Matthew 9:29; 13:58;
Hebrews 3:12-19)

Of all the vital spiritual principles, powerful expectant faith stands at the very top. In Matthew 9:29, Jesus summarized this principle of enormous eternal importance. "It shall be unto you according to your faith." In the gospels, Jesus repeatedly taught that God is at work in and through our lives to the degree we are specifically trusting Him. Make no mistake — powerful expectant faith is absolutely central to both revival and New Testament ministry. Yet, strong faith has implications even beyond spiritual power. It is the very heart of our love relationship with God!

Faith is not only crucial to spiritual power, it is essential to pleasing God. "But without faith it is impossible to please Him: for he that cometh to God must believe that He is and that He is a rewarder of them that diligently seek Him" (Hebrews 11:6). Throughout Scripture and history, God consistently tests His people to see if they genuinely trust Him. In fact, fulfilling a God-given vision nearly always requires genuine courage and faith. Furthermore, a true vision from God is always bigger than humans and requires both faith and patience to see fulfillment (Hebrews 6:12). If the enemy can persuade us to doubt and give up, the power and blessing of God is seriously blocked. Thus, it is little wonder that Satan's first line of attack is getting believers discouraged, doubting and self-focused.

> *For balanced perspective, let me point out that honest questions, hesitation or opposition to a proposed direction does not necessarily mean doubt. In some cases, a proposed direction is simply wrong and *should* be opposed. God indeed hold leaders to great accountability in what they propose. Furthermore, people can honestly disagree about issues or projects without one group being doubters and naysayers! As with the issue of decisions, we

should be very careful about judging people as "hindrances" simply because they do not agree on all points. After all, walking in faith does not mean we automatically embrace all projects.

Just as unbelief is a serious sin, so is presumption! To charge into a project without God's clear direction and promise is not faith, it is presumptive foolishness. We must clearly understand that God is not obligated to back plans and projects He did not originate. (God indeed holds leaders to great accountability in what they propose.) Yet, be aware that when a church has definite God-given kingdom-building direction, Satan's number one strategy is to create discouragement and doubt.

## Discouragement — An Inside Job!

So how does the enemy most often damage the faith of individuals and churches? For the most part, it is an "inside job." According to Scripture, his primary tools often involve fellow believers who sow subtle or overt seeds of discouragement and doubt. Make no mistake — persistently negative-minded believers are close spiritual relatives of the Israeli spies who brought a bad report of discouragement and fear. "And they spread among the Israelites a bad report about the land they had explored. They said, "The land we explored devours those living in it. All the people we saw there are of great size. We saw the Nephilim there (the descendants of Anak come from the Nephilim). We seemed like grasshoppers in our own eyes, and we looked the same to them" (Numbers 13:32-33).

It is significant that the doubters looked at the land God had promised and saw the size of the obstacles instead of the size of God. They foolishly focused on themselves and their enemies rather than the power and promise of God. Tragically the Israelites listened to the doubters and the result is an object lesson for all generations. And what is that lesson? *Generations, churches or people that consistently doubt, die in the spiritual wilderness!* Dear readers, this sad pattern is rampant in thousands of churches today. When we begin to doubt God, we immediately short-circuit the flow of His presence in our lives and churches. The sad phrase from Matthew 13:58 so aptly describes thousands of modern congregations. "And He did not many mighty works there because of their unbelief" (Matthew 13:58, KJV).

When people or churches grieve God's Spirit by unbelief, they are quickly reduced to living by fleshly abilities rather than God's enablement. As a result, countless thousands live dry, defeated lives with very little power or vision. Year after year, church baptisms remain low while conflict and tension seem even present. When people or churches fail to live by expectant faith, they live their lives in the spiritual desert! Since God has provided such glorious victory and power, little is sadder than believers and churches existing in the desert of doubt.

## Chronic Doubters and the Death of Church Vision!

An attitude of doubt is also a dead knell to any church vision. When people doubt God, they seldom receive His vision for their lives or churches. In Proverbs 29:18 (KJV), God leaves little doubt as to the importance of a powerful vision from Him. "Where there is no vision, the people perish." Today it is sad but true that most churches have no specific God-breathed vision for expanding their ministries.

Simply going through the latest study or program is *not* the same thing as receiving and following a unique vision from God (though some studies can certainly move us in that direction.) If a church is neither attempting nor accomplishing anything beyond human efforts and programs, that church likely has no real vision from God. His visions are usually far beyond the reach or anything but supernatural enablement.

Believers, when we consider the devastating results of unbelief, it is little wonder that Satan works feverishly towards causing churches to doubt God. The devil is indeed a master at creating discouragement, fear and negative thinking in congregations. And as with many of Satan's attacks, his most powerful weapon is willing accomplices within the church. While virtually no believer would intentionally become a voice to create doubt, it is nonetheless a very common occurrence. In fact, the Bible contains clear examples of doubt doing its deadly work among believers. In the next section, I briefly describe the primary ways the enemy uses people to foster doubt and defeat churches. Please pause and ask God if any of these sinful patterns are at work in your own life or church.

## Five Sources of Doubt Within Congregations

(1) *Doubt often comes through members who think and speak far more through human reasoning than faith in the all-powerful God.* These individuals measure potential much more by human abilities than by God and His promises. While there are many biblical examples of this condition, among the clearest is the ten spies who were assigned to assess the Promised Land for conquest (Numbers 13:17-20). Yet a tragic thing occurred. When they looked at the land and its challenges, they measured by their own abilities instead of God's omnipotence. Even though God had clearly promised to give them the land, they looked through human reasoning and doubted. They simply did not believe God's promise was also the assurance of His power and provision. Thus they committed the fatal error. They looked at their challenges, measured by their own abilities and said, "*We can't do it.*"

Absolutely nothing more displeases God or assures our defeat than doubt! God loves the "can do" spirit of faith and rejects those who often lean toward unbelief. Furthermore these patterns are especially deadly because doubt and fear are *terribly contagious!* It often only takes a few vocal naysayers to discourage and derail a whole church. Only eternity will reveal the glorious opportunities and visions that failed because people listened to voices of unbelief.

(2) *Doubt comes through the unbiblical idea that problems, challenges or setbacks automatically mean we are out of God's will.* Yet in God's Word, we see it is actually quite normal to run into serious problems and challenges in the very center of God's will. Throughout all of Scripture, God's people constantly faced challenges and crises as they followed His path. In fact, trials are the primary way God tests and grows our faith (Romans 5:1-3)! We are even commanded to "count it all joy when we fall into various trials" (James 1:1-4).

We must also remember we are in a raging spiritual war with an enemy who fires real bullets. How could we expect to be in a real war and not encounter great challenges and setbacks? No doubt, this is part of God's meaning when He inspired Peter to write these words. "Dear friends, do not be surprised at the painful trial you are suffering, as though something strange were happening to you" (1 Peter 4:12). Though battles, challenges and problems sometimes do indicate God's displeasure, often they are just a normal part of our journey of faith and spiritual warfare.

While mature saints understand the inevitability of battles, perpetual doubters are always ready to give up and quit. Again, we find a prime example in Israel's wilderness wanderings. Every time they faced a new crisis or need, they panicked and assumed the worst. Whether it was an urgent need for water, food, direction or protection, their reaction was always the same — *we should have stayed in Egypt* (Exodus 16:3)! Does this sound familiar? If churches (or people) are to walk in victory, they must view problems and needs as opportunities to trust and move forward, not doubt and give up! For this reason, those often prone to voice doubts are enormous hindrances to the progress of any church or family.

(3) *Doubt and discouragement frequently come through the "blame the leader syndrome."* When God's people encountered trials, the reaction of some was consistent and predictable — let's blame

Moses! To them, difficulties *must* be someone's fault and leaders were the easiest target. Since, most people will not come right out and attack or malign God, they target a human leader. Yet the Bible plainly teaches a much forgotten truth. "If a leader is sincerely following God's direction, to reject or malign the leader is to reject God!" (Exodus 16:7-8; 1 Samuel 8:7) Before believers attack God's servant, they should think long and hard about whom that servant represents.

Unfortunately, this pattern is all too common in the modern Church. The condition is especially damaging for two reasons. (a) Complaining and unbelief deeply offend and anger God. (b) Blaming and complaining causes people to get their eyes off God. However, for balance, let me clearly state that leaders are not to be afforded blind allegiance. If they are leading in a way that clearly contradicts Scripture or God's Spirit, we must address it by the patterns of Matthew 18:15. Yet, in general, God sends much of His direction and power through His appointed leaders. For this reason, Satan constantly seeks to inspire people to attack, belittle or discourage God's leaders. One thing is certain — if someone has a persistent habit of criticizing leaders, there is very little doubt who controls their tongue.

(4) *Doubts may come from a sense of condemnation or inadequate understanding of God's goodness and grace.* Without question, every shred of our faith and confidence is wholly dependent upon God's grace through the blood of Jesus Christ. One thing is certain — none of us *deserve* God's mercy, power or blessing. It is further evident that none of us have achieved perfect holiness in our daily walk. Yet our confidence still rests secure in one great truth — *we are accepted in the Beloved!* (Ephesians 1:6)

God is our Emmanuel who never leaves or forsakes His own. (Hebrews 13:5). While our loving God must certainly chastise those who persist in willful sin, He is not an angry

God meticulously searching for the slightest reason to judge His children. God's grace is incredible and His goodness higher than the heavens! Because of God's grace, we have every reason to pray and believe for glorious kingdom conquests.

Yet for believers with a mindset of doubt, their God is small, angry and stingy with His power. They tend to live in fear and condemnation, expecting little beyond average existence. We see such fear in the Israelites' doubt-filled statements, "He has brought us into the dessert to kill us" (Exodus 14:11-12). Doubting God's goodness, power and grace also gives believers a bad case of the *"grasshopper complex"* (Numbers 32). Such fearful attitudes stem either from serious unconfessed sin or a shallow understanding of our covenant of grace. Either way, churches must not let doubters or naysayers keep them from vibrant faith and vision. To do so is to "die in the spiritual wilderness."

(5) *Doubt comes from subtle unwillingness to embrace the necessary challenge and spiritual exertion of vibrant faith and vision.* In truth, many prefer the predictability of living in a rut to the challenge of following a God-size vision. It is also true that greater vision brings greater warfare and sacrifice. While the eternal results are well worth the sacrifices, doubters prefer the safety of the harbor to the open sea challenges of a God-size vision.

Indeed some people will discourage and oppose any aggressive project because it will surely mean hard work and financial sacrifice. In many cases, these brothers and sisters are not even aware the real source of their objection. May God grant us the insight and honesty to avoid this vision-killing mindset. Let us avoid the attitude so tragically expressed by Israel in the desert. Many actually preferred Egypt to the battles and challenges of glorious conquests in Canaan. Thousands of great ministries and dreams "die in the desert" because believers doubt God, love the status quo or are too apathetic to go forward.

In Daniel 11:32, God reminds us that people who know Him will "*be strong and do exploits.*" Chronic doubters and small thinkers reflect the very opposite of God's will for His people. Virtually nothing could be more displeasing to God!

## Leaders Even More Accountable!
(James 3:1)

Unfortunately, examples of attacks on churches and leaders are ever increasing. In light of today's disturbing patterns, one thing is certain — before some churches can experience true revival or blessing, they must seek forgiveness from pastors, staff or fellow believers they have mistreated. Many churches also have to ask forgiveness from a former pastor, staff person or lay-leader. *However, let me be clear that in many other cases, pastors, staff or committees must ask the forgiveness of churches or individuals they themselves have wronged.* Unity problems in churches are by no means always the fault of lay-people. In fact, many pastors and staff must pray about ways they may have worsened congregational problems by failing to seek God's full direction, method or timing in church decisions.

When it comes to leading churches, discerning God's *method* and *timing* are almost as important as discerning *what* He wants us to do. In many cases, we (leaders) may need to publicly apologize for careless leadership or immature attitudes toward our laymen. Sometimes we quickly blame laypeople for "not following" when the truth is our leadership timing and methods were simply wrong. Thank God when we humble ourselves and ask forgiveness, glorious healing comes to us and our churches! But until we get honest and admit our own failures, healing and revival will virtually never come. Dear leaders, honest humble confession and repentance must begin with us.

## Putting On Christ — Putting Off the Flesh
### Steps for Repentance and Victory

Carefully consider the prayer below. If God has spoken and you are willing to pray a similar prayer, please pause and do it now. Ask God to help you mean it and take whatever steps of repentance His will requires. And remember, His grace is greater than your greatest struggle!

*A Prayer of Cleansing and Transformation* — "Father, I confess the ways I have doubted and may well have caused others to doubt. Please forgive me for looking more at the obstacles than at Your mighty power and promises. Forgive me for being a discouragement to those around me. Help me to discern Your will and then stand strong in the faith to believe it. By Your grace, I resolve to embrace Your promises in determined faith. Please fill me with a heart of boldness, faith and hope."

## *Pattern Twenty-Four*
## *Questions for Prayer and Study Groups*

(for individuals, small groups or churchwide studies)

(1)  Prayerfully reflect on Numbers 13:27-33 and Hebrews 3:12-19. What effect would doubt and unbelief have upon an individual or church?

(2)  Please read Matthew 9:29 and 13:58. Why is strong faith and confidence so important to believers and churches?

(3)  How would church projects and vision be affected by those who have little faith?

(4)  Carefully read Numbers 13:32-33. What are the primary elements that discouraged the people of God? Has Satan's strategy changed today?

(5)  Please re-read the *Five Sources of Doubt Within Congregations.* Discuss how these factors could slip into any of our hearts. How do we avoid falling into patterns of naysayers and perpetual doubters?

## Growing Signs of Hunger to Exalt God's Name

After describing these patterns in today's Church, I am delighted to say there are some small but rapidly growing signs of hope! More and more believers are beginning to realize, *"It is impossible to truly love and hallow God without loving one another."* To God's praise, we are at last seeing maturity and unity increasing in some churches. Slowly but surely, some churches are finding the love and maturity to deal with cultural and generational differences in a Christian manner.

Through God's grace, love and unity are certainly possible (if we're ready to forsake childish and selfish behavior.) *Thank God, the most divided church can actually become the most united!* Friends, if we are to experience a modern day revival flood, intentional love and unity must again become our priority and practice (John 13:34-35; 17:21). We must again put the glory of God's name and furtherance of His kingdom above all else! Revival in our day totally depends on God's people embracing the kingdom perspective.

**Another glorious trend is the growing number of churches that are getting right with congregations that formed as "a split" from their own!** Again, this does not mean the churches have to physically reunite, but it *does* mean they must fully confess and forgive past offenses. Dear reader, until you attempt to reconcile with those you fought in the past, there *cannot* be full blessing on your church or your life! Remember, until you are prepared to get right with others, your very prayers and worship are seriously hindered before God (Psalms 66:18; Matthew 5:23; 6:14, Ephesians 4:30; 1 Peter 3:7). But let there be on doubt — you can change! Please do not let Satan give you any more excuses! Seek God and you will surely find His wonderful grace and deliverance.

# Conclusion

If you have been honest and thorough in confessing your sins, you are beginning to experience God's full cleansing power. Sins that are admitted and forsaken are fully cleansed. It is important to trust in God's promise of forgiveness, *not* your feelings (1 John 1:9).

Three basic guidelines are helpful in your confession:

(1)  If the sin is against God, confess it to God, and make things right with Him.

(2)  If the sin is against another person, confess it to God, and make things right with the other person.

(3)  If the sin is against a group, confess it to God, and make it right with the group. (Though you should use discretion not to hurt or slander other people in the process.)

To the degree there is full confession, you will experience full cleansing and glorious transformation. As you confess your sins, ask God to fill you with the Holy Spirit. Do not be discouraged if some sins at first seem difficult to overcome. Some will require a *process* of frequent confession and claiming Christ's fullness. Don't ever give up and don't feel condemned in the process of the battle. If you persist in daily confession and truly trust God for Christ's indwelling power, you *will* experience complete and total victory. Don't ever say you can't change when God's says you can! "I can do all things through Christ!" (Philippians 4:19, KJV)

Dear saint, it is vital that you believe Christ's death and resurrection provides your present victory over sin's *power* as well as its *penalty*. According to Romans 6:6, we are to claim Christ's victory over our sins. As we reject the patterns of sin and self, we then trust Christ to fill us with His own power and righteousness. We can then experience the glorious declaration of the apostle Paul in Galatians 2:20 (KJV): "I am crucified with Christ: nevertheless I live; yet not I but Christ lives in me."

As you experience this continuing process of cleansing and filling, you will move into a dynamic daily walk with God. Yet, the absolute key is your daily prayer life! Without question, God wants every believer to experience a dynamic prayer life. He wants you to walk in spiritual victory and experience miraculous answers to prayer. God wants you to be able to clearly hear His voice and learn how to be a powerful intercessor. He wants to teach you how to daily worship and walk in His continual guidance. But how do you move into such a balanced, biblical prayer life on a daily basis? What are the practical steps? Please carefully read **Appendix C** which provides a powerful biblical pattern for a dynamic daily prayer life. My friend, as you learn to abide in Christ through powerful prayer and Scripture, you will never be the same!

# Appendix A

## How to Be Absolutely Certain of Your Salvation

Without question, really knowing God and being certain of eternal life is by far the most important issue in any of our lives! Jesus makes this crystal clear in Matthew 16:26. "For what profit is it to a man if he gains the whole world, and loses his own soul? Or what will a man give in exchange for his soul?" In other words, if you are not right with the Judge of the Universe, nothing else matters regardless of how much you possess. Without Christ, you lose everything and everyone. With Christ, there is nothing to fear in this life or the next!

Absolutely nothing compares with truly knowing God and having complete assurance of eternal life. It brings a joy, peace and meaning in life that is too wonderful for words. When I experienced eternal assurance in my own walk with God, it was by far the greatest turning point of my life! Yet tragically, so many people do not have this glorious assurance. Today, there is also a widespread epidemic of many who have an assurance that is biblically unfounded. There is no question the Bible teaches that many are deceived into believing they have eternal life when they do not. But thank God, Scriptures also reveal how we *can* have absolute certainty and peace!

My friend, if you have any doubt about your salvation, I have great news for you. God wants to remove your doubts and give you glorious certainty! In a day when many have mistaken a "form of religion" for truly knowing God, this section is designed to help every reader experience absolute certainty in their relationship with Christ. In this tool, we will look deeply into what it truly means to be saved. In a day of thirty second gospel presentations, is it indeed vital that we carefully consider what it truly means to know God in "new birth" conversion.

While salvation is *gloriously simple*, the Bible teaches that many have unintentionally embraced nominal religion or some shallow prayer that simply did not produce the new birth. Based on the clear biblical indicators of salvation, millions of people either have little assurance of salvation or they have an assurance that is false. Yet, God intends *all* believers to have deep assurance in a genuine saving relationship to Him! The following Scriptures make this clear beyond any doubt.

# God's Word on Full Assurance

"These things have I written to you that believe on the name of the Son of God; that you may **know** that you have eternal life, and that you may believe on the name of the Son of God" (1 John 5:13, KJV).

"For God so loved the world that He gave His only begotten Son, that whoever believes in Him **should not perish** but have everlasting life" (John 3:15).

"All that the Father gives Me will come to Me, and the one who comes to Me **I will by no means cast out**" (John 6:37).

"And this is eternal life, that they may **know** You, the only true God, and Jesus Christ whom You have sent" (John 17:3).

"And it shall come to pass that whoever calls on the name of the LORD **shall** be saved" (Acts 2:21).

"The Spirit itself bears witness with our spirit, that we **are** the children of God" (Romans 8:16, KJV).

"The Lord is not slack concerning his promise, as some men count slackness; but is long-suffering to us-ward, not willing that any should perish but that all should come to repentance" (2 Peter 3:9, KJV).

What glorious assurance God gives through His Holy Word! It is clear God intends for your relationship with Him to be one of beautiful certainty, not some frightening guessing game. But since

Scripture leaves no doubt God wants His children to have peace and certainty, why do so many still have unsettling doubts? Does not the Word of God give crystal clear evidences by which we can *know* we have true salvation? Indeed it does! Then why must many answer "no" to the questions that indicate a genuine relationship with Christ? Why do so many have a "form" of religion, but lack the distinct biblical indicators of true salvation? Worse yet, why do such vast numbers have a false assurance that simply cannot get them into heaven?

## Just How Widespread Are Lost Church Members?
### Many will say to Me in that day

Though I would never claim to know the exact percentage, Jesus warns of a disturbingly common occurrence of people who are religious but lost. Worse yet, these dear people fully believe they will go to heaven. Carefully consider our Lord's sobering words concerning judgment day. "**Many** will say to me in that day, Lord, Lord, have we not prophesied in thy name? and in thy name have cast out devils? and in thy name done many wonderful works? And then will I profess unto them, **I never knew you**; depart from me, you that work iniquity" (Matthew 7:21-23).

In the Matthew passage, Jesus stated *many* very active in religion are going to be utterly shocked to find themselves barred from heaven. It is profoundly significant that Jesus didn't say this would happen to some or a few, He specifically said it would happen to *many!* Clearly, it is going to be frighteningly common for religious people to be excluded from entering heaven. Jesus leaves no doubt as to the shocking frequency of that occurrence. But how could this possibly happen? Is God trying to make salvation hard or play tricks with people's souls? Absolutely not!

The key to understanding deception is found in the phrase. "I never *knew* You" (Matthew 7:23). Mark this well — biblical salvation is a *personal relationship* of faith and surrender to Christ as Lord.

199

Salvation is *not* just a religious belief, church membership or "trying to be good." It is a personal relationship of surrender to Jesus Himself. Yet our adversary the devil, seeks to deceive people into embracing some kind of religion or human works system that stops short of full surrender, personal faith and relationship with Jesus. Unfortunately, the deceiver is very good at his job and people usually have no idea this has happened to them. And that is precisely the reason for this book — to make sure deception doesn't happen to you!

## Receiving a "Form of Religion" But No Saving Relationship

The Scriptures tell us many embrace a "form of religion" that fails to bring eternal life. Let me be utterly clear that in most cases, their inadequate decisions were wholly unintentional. And though they may hold some nominal religious beliefs or church membership, they definitely lack the biblical indicators of a saving relationship with God. In many instances, they even have a sense of assurance they will go to heaven. Yet tragically, the Bible leaves no doubt their assurance is unfounded (Matthew 7:21). The life patterns among many believers tell us millions are indeed caught in this dangerous trap of false assurance.

There is no question that Jesus teaches *many* will approach judgment day assured of salvation only to be totally rejected. The Matthew seven passage even goes so far as to say many of these will be religious *leaders!* Jesus states definitively that many highly active in church have missed receiving the new birth. But what is the cause of this disturbing reality? How could this happen with such alarming frequency?

After much prayer and research, I believe at least five church and societal factors most contribute to today's high incidence of lifeless religion. In writing this book I am in no way seeking to be negative or exaggerate a condition. I write from God's burning passion to guard precious souls from today's rampant spiritual deception.

Dear friend, as you read the following factors, simply ask God to reveal whether any of these conditions may have impacted you or your church. If you have a point of need, I am confident our Lord will quicken your heart.

## Five Factors Producing Inadequate Professions of Faith

(1) *Much modern preaching and evangelism has placed far less emphasis on God's holiness, judgment and full surrender to Christ's Lordship.*

Because of shallow evangelism and preaching, many have treated Christ as cheap "fire-insurance" to keep them out of hell. In such shallow man-centered preaching, God is almost portrayed as man's servant who primarily exists to make us happy and fulfill all our desires. The preaching of God's holy law and character alongside grace has become rare. For this reason, deep conviction and repentance is the exception rather than the rule. Thus, so many of today's "decisions for Christ" are dangerously lacking in depth, sincerity and perseverance.

Though largely unintentional, many preachers have so emphasized God's love that the message of His awesome holiness is virtually ignored. Many have failed to preach the full consequences of sin, righteousness and judgment. Such shallow, unbiblical preaching is very different from that of the New Testament church. It's also very different from the preaching in the generations of sweeping spiritual awakenings. Under such "man-centered" preaching, it is frighteningly easy for people to join a church without experiencing the strong conviction that produces genuine conversion (2 Corinthians 7:10). In many churches, there is little evidence of anything remotely resembling the deep conviction and godly sorrow that produce genuine repentance and salvation.

(2) *For much of the past century, church membership was the socially "popular" thing to do. (In so many cases, full surrender to Jesus as Lord and Savior is no longer the primary essence of "joining the church.")*

When casual church membership is the norm, it can be easy for people to join without a deep personal commitment to Christ. In many denominations, people can join churches with little or no thought about a serious relationship with Jesus. Far too often, people are not even asked about their relationship with Christ. Extreme elements of the seeker friendly movement has also caused many churches to present church membership as something utterly different from the strong patterns of the New Testament.

(3) *Churches often fail to give effective biblical counseling and instantly receive those desiring membership.*

In far too many cases, candidates are instantly received on the mere "assumption" they have been born again. For this reason, modern churches have many members who joined the church, but never joined Christ. Their names were put on a membership card, but no one ever counseled them toward a personal prayer of deep repentance and faith.

(4) *Some churches are not thorough in dealing with the very young or uninformed who inquire about being a Christian.*

In a disturbing number of cases, very young children are sped through a shallow process of membership counseling. Some churches also fail to consider how easy it is for children to make decisions from peer pressure and group dynamics. There is little question this is a factor in the alarming percentages of early converts who quickly leave the church or have later doubts about their salvation. Many who were subjected to inadequate and shallow counseling as children later realize their early decisions were not genuine. Thank God, some eventually come to Christ for true conversion.

(5) *Over the last forty years, America has experienced profound moral and spiritual decline.*

There is no doubt our society has experienced a shocking moral plunge. It is also true that many churches are increasingly affected by societal patterns. Historically, in times of such spiritual decline, strong conviction of sin and reverence for God tend to lessen. Evidence of deep repentance and godly sorrow are far less evident than in times of great spiritual awakening. During periods of moral decline, history reveals a rising number of church members who evidence no life-change whatsoever. (They don't hold true to their professions.)

In 1 John 2:19, we likely find a likely clue to the reason more than half of America's church members never attend! "They went out from us; for if they had been of us, they would no doubt have continued with us: but they went out, that they might be made manifest that they were not all of us" (KJV). Though such members may have raised their hand in some meeting or signed a membership card, they manifested no repentance and often cannot be found even six months later.

Considering these five societal factors, you can see how easily people could join many churches without being saved. As you have read these factors, you may suspect it describes some of your own experience. In the following section, I list common statements of church members who later came to realize they were lost. At the time of their original decision, most of these dear people had no idea they were making a false profession. Only in retrospect did they realize why they had made an inadequate decision. Pause now and ask God to reveal whether any of the following statements apply to you.

## But How Do Inadequate Professions Happen to Us?
### Understanding the Spiritual Mechanisms of Deception

In this section, we examine the issue of *how* and *why* people who make professions of faith fail to produce genuine salvation. In 2

Corinthians 10:5, Paul said it was "imaginations" that keep people from truly knowing God. In that text, the Greek word (*dialogismos*) means "thought patterns, reasonings or philosophies." In other words, people have "wrong ideas" or selfish motivations about what it means to truly come to Christ. So what are some of these "imaginations" or "wrong ideas" that deceive precious souls?

To describe how deceptions usually happen to people, I list twenty of the most common statements from church members and the unchurched who later came to realize they were not born again. It is important to note that at the time of their original decision, most of these dear people had *no idea* they were making a false profession! Only later did they realize why they had made an inadequate decision. Once they realized their earlier profession was inadequate and shallow, they were then able to come to Christ in genuine salvation. The change in their lives is incredible!

Dear friend, if any of these deceptions have happened to you, God will quicken your heart as you carefully read the statements. However, let me also state these descriptions are not intended to cause people unnecessary concern about their earlier decisions for Christ. No doubt, many truly saved people had more than one reason in their minds when they came to Christ. *Neither* am I suggesting that someone must be a theologian or have perfectly selfless motives in order to come to Christ. Again, salvation is wonderfully simple! The danger comes when our *primary reason* was among those listed below. If the primary reason for coming to Christ was mostly shallow, selfish or inadequate, there is grave reason for concern!

There is no question that a person's sincerity, understanding and motive can profoundly affect whether their profession of faith produces true conversion. The parable of the sower clearly highlights this reality (Matthew 13:7-9). Dear reader, if inferior reasons were *primary* in your profession of faith God will help you to see that. Above all, do not be afraid to honestly evaluate your conversion. After all, God commands us to "examine ourselves as to whether we be in the faith" (2 Corinthians 13:5).

If God does convict you, it is certainly not to hurt or shame but rather to save your soul! Furthermore, if you determine you need to make a deeper decision for Christ, there is absolutely no reason to be afraid or ashamed. If you joined the church or hold beliefs that are inadequate, I am sure you certainly didn't mean to do so. In fact if God opens your eyes to a spiritual need, it is the greatest reason in the world to rejoice! All other true believers will rejoice with you! And now you must look to God to help you see your true spiritual condition. Since we cannot understand spiritual truth with mere human reasoning, pause now and ask God to reveal whether any of the following testimonies describe your *primary* experience. And be assured, He will give you clear wisdom as to your current spiritual condition (James 1:5-7).

## Twenty Most Commonly Stated Reasons for False Professions of Faith

(1) **No Genuine Conviction of Sin or Lostness** – "I mostly heard sermons about God's love and never truly understood my utter lostness and separation from God. For this reason, my former decision was shallow. It involved neither repentance nor total dependence on Christ alone."

(2) **Carelessness with Childhood Inquiries** – "When I made a decision for Christ I was so young and impressionable, I had no idea what I was doing. Those who dealt with me did so rather hurriedly and carelessly. Only later did I make a decision of depth and meaning."

(3) **Peer Pressure** – "Many of my friends were getting saved, so I joined mainly to be part of the group. Looking back, that decision did not bring me into a personal saving relationship with Christ. "

(4) **Expectations of Others** – "My family and friends wanted me to get saved, so I joined the church mainly to please them. I

now realize you do not become a Christian trying to impress or please others."

(5) **Social Reasons** – "Many of my friends were members of the church, so I joined in order to be socially acceptable. To be a responsible member of the community, I felt I needed to be a church member."

(6) **Inadequate Understanding** – "When I made my decision, I really didn't understand the gospel of grace. I didn't comprehend my total dependence on Christ's blood and His gift of salvation." (In retrospect, I realize I was still trying to "earn" God's acceptance.)

(7) **Shallow Motives** – "When I first made a decision, I only came to Jesus seeking happiness, success and getting problems solved. That was how Christ was presented. Only later did I realize my total separation and need for forgiveness. It was then I came to Jesus as my Lord."

(8) **Insincere Commitment** – "When I made a decision, I experienced no real conviction or repentance. Though I made a surface decision, there was no change of ownership in my life. Consequently, I did not experience the new birth and neither did I become a new creature in Christ. Later when I experience the real thing, God made an enormous difference in my life."

(9) **Shallow, Man-centered Preaching** – "For the most part, I heard preaching that was shallow and un-evangelistic. I mainly heard devotions and social lessons. The full gospel of Christ was not made clear to me and I basically joined because I thought it was expected."

(10) **Inadequate Decision Counseling** – "I simply did not receive clear biblical counseling when I joined the church. No one asked me to personally pray and seek God for a life-changing encounter with Christ. Though I joined the church, I was never led to seek Christ through a personal prayer of surrender and faith."

(11) **Wrong Beliefs About God** – "For years I had no concept of the awesome holiness and law of God. I couldn't believe God would send any but the most outwardly wicked to hell. Until I realized what the Bible teaches about God's law and holiness, I didn't understand why I must be forgiven and born-again. Only when I later came to see God's holiness, did I realize my utter separation from Holy God. At that point I trusted Christ and truly surrendered my life to Him. Oh what a difference to truly know the power and certainty of new-birth in Christ!"

(12) **Dependence on Baptism and Church Membership** – "I falsely assumed because I was baptized (or christened) as a child that I was automatically a Christian. I believed church membership and baptism were enough to get me into heaven. Later, God helped me understand that salvation is a deep personal relationship and commitment to Christ, *not* merely an outward ritual.

(13) **Intellectual Belief Without Heart Transformation** – "For years I thought the fact I believed in God and occasionally prayed meant I was a Christian. I now realize just believing there is a God is *not* the same as turning from sn and truly surrendering your heart to Him (James 2:19). Before I was saved, I knew *about* God intellectually — now I *know* Him from a heart transformed."

(14) **Reliance on Church or Community Works** – "I told myself I was a Christian because I had done church work. Because I had been quite involved in church and community activities, I believed I must be saved. When God later opened my eyes to the truth, I realized no amount of religious service could earn my salvation. I soon came to the deep faith and confidence of truly knowing God — I was born again by His Spirit."

(15) **Personal Goodness** – "For years I assumed I was a Christian because people told me that I was a good person. Only later, did I realize human goodness is "filthy rags" compared to God's

perfection (Isaiah 64:6). When I understood "**all** have sinned and are utterly separated from God," I realized that I must be born again to became a Christian. I finally saw my utter lost-ness and knew my human goodness could never save me. When I saw these truths, I truly came to Christ."

(16) **High Pressure Witness Tactics** – "People led me through a quick gospel presentation and were so high pressure I said the prayer mainly to please them (or to get them to leave.) I now realize that prayer did not at all come from my heart. When later I truly sought Christ, He changed my life completely."

(17) **Shallow Witnessing Presentation** – "I was led through a quick presentation and told if I want to go to heaven just repeat a prayer. Little or nothing was said about seriously surrendering my life to Christ. Looking back, I realize I prayed a meaningless prayer with no real depth. Though I repeated their little prayer, I wasn't convicted or sincere and nothing changed in my life."

(18) **False Assurance From People** – "Over the years, when I periodically expressed doubts about my salvation, people assured me I was saved because I had previously "said a prayer" or been baptized (*even though my life did not change*). Others told me I was a good person and had nothing to worry about. When I later experienced true conversion, I had no difficulty sensing the awesome difference of really knowing God. At last, I found deep assurance and power"

(19) **Satanic Deception** – "Because I was a good person or went to church, I falsely reasoned that I indeed was born again. I reasoned if the church accepted me as a member then I must be saved. I now know Satan deceived me into believing I was a Christian. Looking back, I realize Satan was feeding me lies to keep me from true salvation."

(20) **Pleasant Life and Material Blessings** – "My life had usually been quite pleasant with strong financial blessing. Because

things seemed to go fairly well in my life, I reasoned that God must be pleased with me. I thought my earthly blessings meant I surely must be saved. It even seemed as if God had answered some of my prayers. Only when God revealed my lostness did I realize that earthly success is no real indication of salvation."

## So How Can I Really Be Sure I Am Saved?

From the above statements, it is clear people can join churches for many reasons besides being genuinely born again. In fact, after reading the various ways people have been deceived into making false decisions, you may wonder how anyone could ever really know if their profession of faith is true. Make no mistake — you definitely can know! So how can you tell for sure if *your* decision was genuine? My friend, you *can* know full assurance because the Bible gives very clear indicators of true salvation! When you look at all the signs *together*, it truly isn't very difficult to tell whether you have experienced the new birth in Christ.

Under the next heading, we will carefully examine the key biblical indicators of true salvation. However, for sake of balance, let me clearly state that true Christians will certainly have days when all the signs are not so evident. Truly saved people definitely experience periods when God can seem somewhat distant. *It is certainly not my purpose to try to scare Christians into believing they are lost.* Yet at the same time if your faith is so weak it can easily be shaken, it probably needs to be strengthen. Dear reader, you must take these biblical indicators of salvation very seriously! The stakes are far too high and millions of well-meaning people have been deceived.

## Take Your Time and be Completely Honest

Above all, ask God to help you evaluate yourself with *complete honesty*! Do not read these indicators and try to convince yourself you fit them when you really do not. Do not let fear or pride keep you from acknowledging if God reveals an urgent need. Plain old pride and fearing what people might think has no doubt kept countless people lost and condemned to eternal separation from God. Indeed, there is nothing wrong and everything right with finding out whether you need to experience a deeper surrender to Christ. And remember, if God convicts, He does it for one reason — to give you true knowledge of Himself!

Again, do not be afraid to be both honest and thorough as you read the salvation indicators. *Nothing bad and everything good will come from letting God clearly speak to your heart right now.* You will either add deeper assurance to the confidence you already have or you will receive it for the first time. Either way, you cannot lose and there is nothing to fear!

According to God's Word, the following factors are generally real and present in the lives of all who are truly saved. If the indicators are not clearly present, we should assume we have not received the new birth. It is infinitely better to err on the side of safety and seek God than to falsely assume we are saved and lose everything! Also bear in mind, these indicators are not just some author's opinion and neither are they exaggerated or overstated. They are not trick questions as they come straight from the Word of God. Please ask God to give you discernment as you prayerfully examine your life in light of the Biblical Indications of True Salvation.

## The Essential Biblical Indicators of True Salvation
How to Accurately Evaluate Your Spiritual Condition

1.  **Saved people have experienced genuine conviction of sin and trust Christ alone for eternal life.** "No one can come to Me unless the Father who sent Me draws him; and I will raise him up at the last day" (John 6:44). "And when he is come, he will reprove the world of sin and of righteousness, and of judgment" (John 16:8). "Now when they heard this, they were pricked in their heart, and said unto Peter and to the rest of the apostles,

men and brethren, what shall we do?" (Acts 2:37). "For by grace are you saved through faith; and that not of yourselves: it is the gift of God" (Ephesians 2:8). No one is saved by merely knowing intellectual facts about God. Neither can anyone be saved by just being in church or around Christian people. No one is saved by being a good person.

Before anyone can be saved, he or she must receive God's revelation that they are lost (John 16:8). You must be personally convicted of sin and drawn to Christ by the Holy Spirit (John 6:44). By God's conviction and revelation, you come to see you are totally separated from Him and cannot save yourself. For true Christians, there came a point when you fully realized your sin utterly separated you from God. That awareness moved you to personally pray and trust Christ as your own Lord and Savior. As a rule, saved persons can readily testify to such a process in their lives. For some this process may have been a slow dawning of spiritual truth. For others, the revelation was rather dramatic and fast. Whether the process is fast or slow, saved people came to a point of deep conviction and trusted Christ alone.

2.  **Most saved people can describe a sense of "before and after" in terms of their salvation. In other words, a true believer came to a point of true repentance and a personal covenant to seek to live under Christ's Lordship.** "If any man be in Christ, he is a new creature: old things are passed away; behold, all things are become new" (2 Corinthians 5:17). "I tell you, no; but unless you repent you will all likewise perish" (Luke 13:3). In the case of younger children, the sense of life transformation is generally not as pronounced (though some changes are apparent even in children.) To be born again is the most powerful transformation in all of human experience. The term "born again" is a strong term describing a dynamic change in one's life. In describing salvation, God uses other strong terms such

as "all things new" and "new creation." While no Christian is any where near perfect, there is nonetheless a definite heart change and a far deeper desire to live for God.

Put simply, it is extremely doubtful that old things could pass away and all things become new and you not experience some observable differences in your life! Think about it — how could anyone become a *totally new creature* yet notice no real change? I do need to qualify and say that some saved people will not be able to give the exact day or moment it happened. However, they should be able to describe a general process that led up to their life-altering relationship with Christ. Knowing some exact past moment is not nearly as important as seeing the genuine fruit of a changing life today. "You shall know them by their fruits" (Matthew 7:16).

3. **Because God's Spirit indwells them, Christians possess supernatural assurance they are saved and forgiven of their sins.** "The Spirit itself bears witness with our spirit, that we are the children of God" (Romans 8:16). "These things have I written unto you that believe on the name of the Son of God; that you may know that you have eternal life, and that you may believe on the name of the Son of God" (1 John 5:13). While the above passages do not mean Christians can never have times of doubt, it does mean their inner peace ultimately overshadows the doubts. In general, saved people have a supernatural inner assurance they are God's child. By God's indwelling presence they simply *know* in their spirits they are saved (1 John 5:13).

While many genuinely saved persons may go through periods of struggle or doubts, God gives an assurance that is ultimately deeper than their doubts. Yet for reasons of personality type, illness, lack of understanding, personal failure, suffering or abusive backgrounds, some believers naturally struggle more to sense assurance than might others. Periodic struggling with assurance does not automatically mean someone is lost. (See page 232 for factors that can certainly cause believers to struggle with doubt.)

*Yet related to assurance, I need to again share a word of biblical perspective and warning.* Just as Christians can at times struggle with doubt, lost people can have a type of assurance that is false and unfounded. In fact, Scriptures tell us it is not at all uncommon for lost people to have a false sense of assurance. According to the clear teaching of Jesus, *many* people think they are going to heaven when in truth they have never been saved (Matthew 7:14, 23; 13:26).

So how can we really tell if our assurance is genuine or false? I find the following principle a reasonable guideline. If someone has an assurance they are saved yet clearly lacks most of the other indicators, the assurance is likely false and unreliable. On the other hand, if someone struggles with periodic doubts, but clearly evidences most of the other salvation indicators, they are very likely born again. But of course, only God and that person can be the final judge.

Naturally in every believer's life, some salvation indicators will be stronger than others. We are all unique and struggle with some things more than others. It is the "whole picture" that tells the real story, not just one or two elements. Yet when examining the whole of these biblical indicators, saved people should have a *genuine confidence* in their standing with God. In general, saved people have a supernatural assurance and peace they know God.

4.  **Genuine Christians can testify to a real and personal relationship with Christ.** "My sheep hear My voice, and I know them, and they follow Me" (John 10:27). "And this is life eternal that they might know thee the only true God, and Jesus Christ whom thou hast sent" (John 17:3). In this context, the Greek word for "know" is a spiritually intimate form of close personal relationship. True salvation is far more than mentally believ-

ing certain facts "about" God. It is actually "knowing" God in a supernatural life-changing personal relationship. In other words, Jesus Christ is quite real and personal to saved people. To them, He is far more than a doctrine or mental belief.

To true believers, Jesus is a living Being who is spiritually real to them. While this certainly doesn't mean Christians walk around hearing voices or physically seeing Christ, it does mean they generally sense God's real presence in their lives. Neither does it mean they constantly experience glorious emotions or always hear direct daily words from God. However, it does mean Christ is more than a mere doctrine or mental belief — He is a personal relationship! If to you it sounds a bit strange to hear someone say, "The Lord spoke to me," that is a major real flag of concern about your spiritual condition. It is indeed *normal* for God's children to sense Him speaking to their hearts (John 10:27; 17:3). If sensing God's voice is *never* your experience, something is seriously wrong.

For balance we should state there are certainly times when God speaks to our hearts far more than at others. There are also times of relative silence. But friend, if you almost *never* sense God speaking to your heart, you have reason for deep concern. If you have no desire for prayer and the Bible makes little sense to you, it is very likely you do not know the Savior. "The natural (unsaved) man does not receive the things of God" (1 Corinthians 2:14). Tragically, many people will miss heaven by about eighteen inches. (The distance between intellectual *head knowledge* and personal *heart experience*.)

5.  **Because they have a new heart, children of God have a "spiritual mind-set" that hungers for growth and exhibits a real desire to turn from sin.** "And every man that hath this hope in him purifies himself, even as he is pure" (1 John 3:3). "Whosoever is born of God does not commit sin; for his seed remains in him; and he cannot sin, because he is born of God" (1 John

3:9). "For to be carnally minded is death, but to be spiritually minded is life and peace" (Romans 8:6). While Christians can certainly experience times of spiritual dryness, true believers exhibit a general desire for growth and holiness. The Bible describes salvation as a powerful life-changing experience. Thus, if someone has little or no desire for Bible reading, prayer or worship, there is great concern for their salvation.

Make no mistake — saved people simply think differently than before they were converted. The new birth produces more of "spiritual mindset" (Romans 8:6). While they may not think of God and spiritual things constantly, He is never far from their minds. God has put His own laws into the very hearts of those who know Him (Hebrews 8:10). This new mindset produces a desire for spiritual growth, service and closeness with God. Spiritual insights just make sense and they truly sense God speaking through the Bible and sermons.

Closely related is the distinct desire to turn from sin and please God. Put simply, if someone can consistently live in known sin without deep sorrow and God's chastisement, they are simply not saved. While saved people are certainly still tempted and at times fail, there is a distinct inner desire toward God and holiness. When truly saved people commit sin, they are convicted and quite miserable. If they persist in sin, they will definitely experience God's chastisement (Hebrews 12:6). Dear reader, if persistent willful sin is no big deal, you are almost certainly unsaved.

6. **True Christians have a loving heart and genuine love for the Church and people of God.** "We know that we have passed from death unto life, because we love the brethren. He that loves not his brother abides in death" (1 John 3:14). "They went out from us, but they were not of us: for if they had been of us, they would no doubt have continued with us: but they went out, that they might be made manifest that they were not all of us"

(1 John 2:19). One of the most important marks of salvation is a loving compassionate spirit. This love is especially evident toward other believers. Conversely, if someone is predominately critical, mean-spirited and unloving, he or she is almost surely unsaved (1 John 4:7-8).

A distinct hunger for Christian fellowship, service and worship also characterizes saved people. If you consistently lack the desire to worship and be with God's people, there is strong reason to question your salvation (1 John 2:19). In a general sense, saved people desire to be in worship and around other believers. However, in cases where someone has been badly hurt by church people, they may go through a period of fear or withdrawal. But the desire for worship and fellowship will soon move us back to meaningful involvement with other believers. True Christians have a hunger for the things of God and seek spiritual fellowship. Based on Scripture, it is highly doubtful that a saved person could drop entirely out of church and stay out permanently.

## So What Do the Indicators Say to Your Heart?

My friend, if you have prayerfully and honestly read through the biblical indicators of salvation, you should have some real sense of whether or not you are truly saved. While virtually no one dramatically exhibits all the salvation indicators all the time, saved people should be able to answer a confident yes to most if not all the indicators. And now we come to what is by far the most critical question in any of our lives. *Are you absolutely confident you are genuinely "born again" by the Spirit of God?*

Your answer will be one of four. Based on the biblical indicators of salvation, you are now either; (1) Fairly convinced you are not born again, (2) Simply not sure, (3) Fairly confident you are saved but still struggle with occasional doubts or (4) You are absolutely confident you are born again and are hungering for spiritual growth.

In the next section, we will see exactly how God will surely meet the needs of those in each group.

## What to Do If You Think You May be Unsaved or Still Have Doubts

If you are either fairly convinced you are not saved or simply not sure, then first of all *thank* God for the fact He has opened your eyes to that crucial awareness. According to Scripture, you could not have come to that awareness without God opening your eyes and speaking to your heart (John 6:44; 16:13). Please further understand it is no "accident" you are reading this book at this exact moment. I want you to realize God has gone to great lengths to place this unique book in your hands at this precise moment in time. Furthermore, He has clearly spoken to you for one reason — *so you can know Him and be certain about it!*

God has certainly not convicted merely to hurt or frighten you. He has revealed your need for one purpose — to draw you to Jesus for forgiveness, grace and eternal life! By His powerful grace and love, He will replace your doubts with certainty and peace. Furthermore, Jesus said there is *no way* He will turn you aside if you sincerely come to Him. "All that the Father gives Me will come to Me, and the one who comes to Me I will by no means cast out" (John 6:37).

So how can you come to Christ right now? We must look straight to His Word for God's perfect answer and the perfect peace He provides. It is very vital that you take your time and prayerfully read through the section entitled *How to Know Christ in Full Assurance*. Please skip past the next couple of paragraphs and go straight to *How to Know Christ in Full Assurance*. As you work through this section, pay special attention to carefully reading the *Essential Truths of Salvation*. Ask God to open your heart to the truths of genuine salvation.

## For Those Who Believe They Are Saved But Still Struggle with Doubt

If after reading the previous biblical indicators of salvation you are confident you are saved but at times still struggle with doubt, be assured there is an answer for your needs! Appendix B is designed to provide clear answers for periodic doubts. It is indeed possible for saved people to struggle with occasional doubts for a variety of reasons. In most cases when people finally see the source of their doubts, they are able to put their fears aside and find victory. In saved people, doubts usually stem from one of three sources: (a) a lack of biblical understanding concerning grace, (b) lies of the enemy, or (c) unrealistic expectations of themselves as human beings. In any case, God's truth will set you free! (John 8:32)

For insight into sources of doubt, prayerfully read through Appendix B. Pause and claim God's clear promise from James 1:5, "If any of you lacks wisdom, let him ask of God, who gives to all liberally and without reproach, and it will be given to him." God's wisdom and truth will set you free!

## How to Know Christ in Full Assurance

I ask you to set aside the next several moments and get utterly quiet before God. Claim God's wonderful promise from James 4:8. "Draw near to God, and he will draw near to you" (KJV). Ask God to draw near and clearly speak to your heart. Trust God to help you fully surrender to Christ's Lordship.

As you now draw near, purposely center your thoughts on God. Be assured, He is indeed with you this very moment. *Reflect on the glorious fact that God wants you to be saved and certain even more than you do!* Be assured, God is not playing hide and seek with you. He wants you to know Him! Meditate on the glorious fact that Almighty God is very near to you this very moment (Matthew 28:18; James 4:8).

You now need God's revelation and wisdom in the truths of salvation. You need to *know* for certain where you stand with Him. Pause in prayer and claim the following promise for wisdom. "If any of you lack wisdom, let him ask of God, that giveth to all men liberally, and upbraideth not; and it **shall** be given him" (James 1:5, KJV). God wants to give you wisdom concerning the true source of your doubts.

My friend, you will find peace when you learn trust God's infallible Word, *not your own feelings*. Your salvation does not depend on your feelings, but on Christ's unfailing grace and power. Because your salvation is based on God's own Word and faithfulness, it is vital to fully understand the central truths of God and salvation. Prayerfully read the following essential Scripture truths of salvation.

## Understanding the Essential Truths of Salvation
"Faith comes by hearing and hearing by the Word of God"
(Romans 10:17)

1. **We have all sinned and stand utterly guilty before the Holy God who must judge sin. The consequence of our sin is eternal death, hell and total separation from God.** Isaiah 64:6 – "But we are all like an unclean thing, And all our righteousness are like filthy rags; We all fade as a leaf, And our iniquities, like the wind, Have taken us away." Romans 3:23 - For all have sinned and fall short of the glory of God." James 2:10 - "For whoever shall keep the whole law, and yet stumble in one point, he is guilty of all." Hebrews 9:27- "And as it is appointed for men to die once, but after this the judgment." As the Scripture clearly demonstrates, God's standard for heaven is absolute perfection. Yet according to James 2:10, we have all repeatedly broken His holy laws. Since we cannot possibly save ourselves by our own righteousness (because we have none) in God's eyes, God made a way of forgiveness through the substitutionary death of His own sinless Son.

2. **God loves you and wants to forgive and grant you eternal life. He gave His own Son to secure your eternal salvation.** John 3:16 - "For God so loved the world, He gave his only begotten son, that whosoever believeth in Him should not perish but have eternal life" (KJV). Dear reader, place your name in that verse. Put your name in the place of the words *world* and *whosoever*. Now I want you to read that verse with your name in it. Read it slowly with your name in it. Read it out loud at least three times.

3. **Jesus took all your guilt and paid your penalty for sin.** Isaiah 53:6 – "All we like sheep have gone astray: we have turned every one to his own way; and the Lord has laid on him the iniquity of us all" and Romans 5:8 – "But God commendeth his love toward us, in that, while we were yet sinners, Christ died for us" (both verses KJV). My friend, God took **all** your sins and placed them on Jesus. He then took the full penalty and death for all your sins (past, present and future). If you now receive Christ's forgiveness, there is absolutely nothing left for which God could condemn you! Jesus has already paid your *entire* debt. On the basis of what He has done in your behalf, Jesus is fully ready to forgive all your sins and grant you eternal life right now!

4. **God Himself is giving you the genuine desire to come to Jesus.** John 6:44(a) – "No man can come to Me, except the Father which hath sent Me draw him" (KJV). The very fact you are reading this book and have a deep desire to know Christ is strong indication God is drawing you to Jesus. Friend, if you truly desire to give your life to Jesus, rest assured God gave you that desire. Remember, God wants to save you even more than you want to be saved!

5. **You must by simple faith receive eternal life as a free gift of God's grace.** Romans 6:23 (KJV) – "For the wages of sin is death; but the gift of God is eternal life through Jesus Christ

our Lord." Ephesians 2:8 (KJV) - "For by grace are you saved through faith; and that not of yourselves: it is the gift of God, not of works, lest any man should boast." Salvation is a **gift** that we could never earn or deserve. We receive eternal life by simple child-like faith, not through human efforts to be good. "All our righteousness are as filthy rags" (Isaiah 64:6, KJV). There is absolutely nothing you could ever do to "deserve" God's forgiveness and salvation. "For by the works of the law no flesh shall be justified" (Galatians 2:16d).

6. **Jesus definitely promises to receive all who sincerely come to Him in faith and repentance. God covenants to forgive and grant eternal life to those who truly believe on Jesus.** John 6:37 - "All that the Father gives me shall come to me; and him that comes to me I will in no wise cast out" (KJV). Please hear the certainty in Jesus' promise to receive you. In essence, He is saying "There is no way I will turn away those who sincerely come to me." By His own infallible promise, Jesus covenants to answer your prayer for salvation. God cannot lie! He is not playing cosmic hide and seek with those who come to Him. God makes a "covenant" with all who come to Jesus. If by His grace, you sincerely come to Him, He promised to receive you! (Romans 10:13, KJV "For whosoever shall call upon the name of the Lord shall be saved.")

7. **You must be willing to repent of sin and seek to follow Jesus as your Lord.** Luke 13:3 (KJV) – "I tell you, no; but, except you repent, you shall all likewise perish." I want to stress that repentance is not some human effort that *earns* salvation; for we are saved by grace through faith alone (Ephesians 2:8; Titus 3:5). Salvation is all of grace and none of works (Romans 9:11). However, when you have saving faith, it means you recognize the Lordship of Jesus and are willing to surrender to His direction. You are willing (in reliance on His help) to transfer your life to His ownership. In true salvation you are making a

*covenant* (by His grace) to love and live for Christ. A covenant is a solemn agreement from one to another. Perhaps best of all, God will even give you the strength to keep your covenant to Him (John 1:12; Philippians 2:13)!

8. **God will give you a new heart and the grace to change.** 2 Corinthians 5:17 (KJV) – "Therefore if any man be in Christ, he is a new creature: old things are passed away; behold, all things are become new." Dear reader, you don't have to wonder, "Can I change?" Remember, it is God that changes you, not you that changes yourself. There is no one so bad that God cannot grant a brand new heart when they sincerely turn to Him. Do not make the tragic mistake of waiting until you think you can "fix" your own life before coming to Jesus. (That is a clever lie of Satan to keep you lost.) While some changes come quickly, others will be progressive over time. But nonetheless, God will surely continue His work to conform His own to the image of Christ (Romans 8:29). "He who has begun a good work in us will bring it to completion" (Philippians 1:6)!

Dear reader, salvation doesn't mean you must somehow become perfect and never sin again, but it does mean a deep willingness to turn from known sin and follow Christ. Salvation is a deep commitment of your life to Jesus, not some cheap ticket to heaven and a license to continue in sin. But, no matter how weak you may feel, if you come to Jesus you will receive the grace to change! (John 1:12 KJV - "But as many as received Him, to them gave He power to become the sons of God, even to them that believe on His name.") When by God's grace, you choose to receive Jesus, you also receive the power to change!

Please carefully read the following sentences and place a check beside each statement you truly believe.

❏ I believe my sins totally separate me from God and that my own goodness can never save me.

❏ I believe Jesus Christ is the only begotten Son of God and died for the sins of the world.

❏ I believe God loves me and gave His Son to secure my salvation.

❏ I believe Jesus took my sins on Himself, paid sin's penalty, died a sacrificial death to remove my guilt and is resurrected at the right hand of God.

❏ I am deeply sorry for my sins that cost the death of God's own Son.

❏ I believe Jesus is King of Kings and worthy of my full surrender and life-long obedience.

❏ I believe God's Spirit has opened my eyes and is drawing me to true salvation.

❏ I believe if I sincerely ask Jesus to forgive and save me, He will answer my prayer.

❏ I realize surrendering to Jesus means I covenant to embrace a life of repenting from sinful habits or wrong relationships in my life.

❏ By depending on God's enabling grace and strength, I am truly willing to turn from my sins and surrender to Christ's Lordship.

❏ I desire to trust Jesus as my personal Lord and Savior right now.

Dear friend, if you could sincerely check off all the above statements, then according to God's promise, nothing in heaven and earth can keep you from being saved! "For whosoever **shall** call upon the name of the Lord **shall** be saved!" (Romans 10:13) As we now come to the crucial part of your journey, I prayed much over whether to even include a sample prayer. After considerable deliberation, I believe God has led me to do so along with some basic cautions and explanation. In a day of "twenty second" sinner's prayers, I fear some may have little more depth than ordering a pizza. While coming to Christ is simple, it is neither shallow nor casual.

I ask you to very carefully read the words of the prayer below. While you certainly do not have to say all the words in the prayer, it does capture the key elements of coming to Christ. Does this prayer truly represent what you desire to do? If so, simply talk to God in your own words and tell Him your heart. Please understand this sample prayer is not some rote formula or plan you must dutifully repeat verbatim.

As you pray, ask God to help you truly surrender your life and trust in Christ. Ask Him to help you turn from your sins and live for His glory. If you do use any of the sample prayer as a guide, I encourage you to *pause* after each sentence and let it sink in. You may even want to *repeat* some of your words until you truly sense they come from your heart. Take your time and genuinely encounter God.

Salvation is not just "saying some formula," it is the "relationship" of truly surrendering your heart and trusting Christ. In other words, just *talk* to God. He is not going to reject you because you didn't say some exact wording. He is looking at your *heart*, not your exact phrases. Never forget, He wants you to be saved even far more than you do! And remember the glorious promise of Jesus, "Whosoever comes to me, I will in no wise cast out!" (John 6:37, KJV) Now go to Him, precious friend, He is waiting to receive you.

*"Dear Lord, I believe You are Holy and worthy of all obedience and praise. God, I know I am a sinner and deserve eternal death. I understand my sins totally separate me from You and place me under Your judgment. I realize I can do nothing to save myself. Dear Lord, I believe You gave Your Son to forgive and save me. I am truly sorry for my sins (prayerfully name some of your major sins). By Your grace and help, I now turn from my sins (pledge specific points of repentance). Jesus, please forgive me and grant me Your Spirit and life right now. I trust You to be the Lord and Savior of my life. Both now and forever, I surrender myself to obey You. God, please enable me to love You with all my heart.. Help me fully live for You and serve You from this day forward. Dear Lord, thank You for the grace and strength to turn from my sins. Thank You for Your promise of eternal life. In Jesus mighty name, I pray — Amen"*

Friend, if you sincerely believe and give your life to Jesus, you will begin to sense the fruit of a changed life (Romans 10:13). Do not overly concern yourself with what you feel or don't feel immediately. We are saved by faith in *Him*, not faith in our feelings. Remember, faith is a choice not a feeling.

If you meant your prayer and truly believe the Lord has given you eternal life, it is very important for you to tell key people you have received Christ. The Bible says we are to "confess Him before men." If you believe God has touched your heart, I encourage you to sign in the blanks below. Your written signature can become a powerful point of faith should Satan whisper doubts in the future. The illustration of *Standing on the Word and Character of God* will further prove a powerful strategy for overcoming any future accusations or doubts. (Illustration is included at the conclusion of this section.)

Date and Time Prayed: _____

Signed:_____

## So Where Do I Go From Here?
### Embracing Christian Growth and Service

As you truly meant the prayer you prayed, your life will begin to change. If you are truly saved, you must now act on the first steps of obedience to Jesus. Indeed, no one should believe they are saved if they refuse to obey even the first and most basic commands of following Jesus. Think about it — how serious could anyone be if they won't even obey Jesus' first simple command? That kind of non-committal prayer saves no one. So what are our first steps of obedience?

Jesus clearly said we are to *confess* Him before men (Mark 8:38). For this reason, it is vital to let others know of the decision you just made. What just happened is the *beginning* of your walk with God. You now have the power to grow and develop into a mature child of God. However, growth will not occur by accident and it is crucial for you to get in a discipleship group. **To be crystal clear, the first four steps in following Jesus are as follows.** *(1) Seek believer's baptism and (2) confess Christ before people (usually in a local church.)* Also be sure to tell key people in your life that you have become a Christian. *(3) Become an active member of a local church (if you're not already).* *(4) Establish a daily time of reading God's Word and spending time in prayer.* This is called "abiding in Christ" (John 15:4-8). Your pastor will provide materials to aid in your growth as a new Christian. *(5) Tell others about Jesus and embrace useful service to God through your local church. Again your pastor will give you guidance.*

## What about Being Re-baptized

At this point many ask, "*What about being re-baptized?*" Concerning this, your pastor should give you the primary guidance. However, I find the following simple principle to be helpful. *If you have a strong sense you were not saved when you were previously baptized, then baptism is definitely in order.* It is vital that you not allow pride to keep you from confessing and being baptized! (I have often seen one person's public profession cause many other lost church members to come under conviction and be saved!)

If however, you believe you really were saved and you just prayed to "drive down the stake of assurance," you and your pastor will decide the best course. You should definitely share your decision of new assurance with the congregation. In any case, I strongly urge you to get the counsel of your pastor. Now go forth and live your life in the peace of God's glorious grace and endless love! Romans 8:1, KJV "There is therefore now no condemnation to them which are in Christ Jesus, who walk not after the flesh, but after the Spirit." For a biblical strategy to walk in full assurance, prayerfully work through the following illustration.

# Standing on the Word and Character of God
## An Illustration and Strategy for Gaining Full Assurance

The following illustration comes from my own experience and thousands who have walked a similar journey. When I was a boy of ten, I came under conviction and was born again by God's grace. For a time, I grew spiritually and sensed wonderful assurance in my salvation. Yet upon reaching the teenage years, I faced the struggles and temptations most experience as we move toward adulthood. The closeness, joy and confidence I once had in the Lord, lessened and at times seemed to disappear entirely.

Though I remained in church and basically lived a moral life, struggles and temptations were strong. And then it happened — I began to doubt my salvation and God seemed distant. As struggles with doubt kept resurfacing, I would often pray to try and make sure I was saved. Yet sadly, the doubts persisted and my spiritual life was dry. Temptations were increasingly hard to deal with and God seemed ever more distant. It was at this point God mercifully revealed the biblical pattern for victory over doubt and defeat. Dear reader, I soon found complete victory and you can too!

# God's Word
## The Perfect Answer to Doubt and Defeat

*In essence, we find victory over doubt by learning to fully trust in God's character and His word.* In my own life, I prayerfully read a list of the biblical indicators of true salvation. Though I was certainly far from perfect, I knew I had experienced the basic fruits of having been saved. It then dawned on me that Jesus' own pattern for victory was to quote God's Word and stand on His truth (Matthew 4:4). That is what I was *not* doing when it came to my assurance of salvation!

It was around this time that God led me to stand on His Word regarding my periodic doubts of salvation. While at the time I didn't fully understand the process, looking back it is now crystal clear how God removed my doubts. Victory over doubts centers in *choosing* to believe God's truth! I stress the word "choose" because emotions alone are ever-changing and unreliable as ultimate indicators of salvation.

Complete victory came as God led me to seven simple Scriptures to help anchor my faith and assurance in Christ. In essence I became familiar with these Scriptures and began to pray them anytime I had doubts. In the next paragraphs, I describe how these Scriptures truths can become powerful anchors for victory over doubt.

The first Scripture God used was 1 John 5:13. "These things I have written to you who believe in the name of the Son of God, that you may **know** that you have eternal life, and that you may continue to believe in the name of the Son of God" (1 John 5:13). The simplicity of this truth is incredibly beautiful. God tells us we can know we are saved by the certainty of His promises! In other words, we can utterly count on the word and character of God. He is not trying to deceive us and only asks our simple faith. This passage also tells us God *truly wants us to know* we have eternal life. When I had struggles with doubt, I simply began to claim the certainty of His promises.

Two other verses God used were Ephesians 1:6 and 2:8-9. "to the praise of the glory of His grace, by which He made us **accepted** in the Beloved" (Ephesians 1:6). "For by grace you have been saved through faith, and that not of yourselves; it is the gift of God, not of works, lest anyone should boast" (Ephesians 2:8-9). When you fully grasp these truths, it forever delivers from the bondage of trying to "earn or deserve" salvation. Every time I sensed doubt about my unworthiness and doubted my salvation, I simply reflected on these verses and thanked God that I was saved by His grace. Over time, the truths of His glorious grace became more and more real to my heart. As I prayed these truths back to God, my assurance grew ever stronger.

To address certainty, two other verses became powerful tools of the Holy Spirit. John 6:44 and 37 had especially great significance. "No one can come to Me unless the Father who sent Me draws him; and I will raise him up at the last day" (John 6:44). "All that the Father gives Me will come to Me, and the one who comes to Me I will by no means cast out" (John 6:37). These two verses reveal a particularly comforting reality. *First* of all, no one will come to Jesus unless the Father draws them and *second*, Jesus will never reject those who truly come to Him.

When I had doubts, I would simply reflect on these two great truths. In prayer I would thank God He had drawn me to desire Jesus. I then thanked Jesus for His promise to receive me. The more I reflected and prayed these truths, the less I sensed doubt and fear!

Two final Scriptures were John 3:16 and Romans 10:13. "For God so loved the world that He gave His only begotten Son, that whoever believes in Him should not perish but have everlasting life" (John 3:16). "For whoever calls on the name of the LORD shall be saved" (Romans 10:13). These two passages tell of the awesome simplicity and certain result of calling on the name of the Lord. How glorious to know our God did not make salvation complicated or tricky! When I would doubt, I began to thank God for the certainty of His promises to all who come to Christ.

Dear reader, I am in no way suggesting these particular seven passages are somehow above any others. In fact, God may lead you to other verses with greater meaning to you. Yet the point is simple — our assurance of salvation is anchored to the word and faithful character of God Himself! Now *there* is someone you can rely upon!

## A Summary of the Biblical Assurance Strategy

For absolute clarity, let's summarize this basic pattern for applying God's Words to our doubts. (1) First, prayerfully read through the *Biblical Indicators of True Salvation* and *Essential Truths of*

*Salvation* (listed in the early part of this section.) It is important to first make sure we have indeed surrendered our hearts to Christ. Regarding this whole illustration, I do give one caution. This pattern is not for those who have not truly come to Christ or lack the indicators of the new birth. Claiming God's promises for salvation is not for those who have never sought the Lord. The Bible is not some legalistic code by which we can "trap God" into having to save someone with an insincere heart. (2) For those who have come to Christ, write out the seven Scriptures in this illustration (or some passages more meaningful to you.) Make it your habit to frequently pray these Scriptures back to God in your own words. (3) Every time doubt knocks at the door of your mind and heart, answer it by quoting and praying these glorious promises of God. (4) Do not over rely on your feelings — stand on the Word and character of God. (5) Do not let your imperfections and temptations destroy your confidence. Our confidence is in His righteousness, not ours. (6) Understand this is a life-long process of standing on His Word. Over time, your assurance and confidence will grow strong. Do not panic if you don't feel great assurance quickly. It may indeed take time. (7) Periodically pray and re-read the truths of salvation and reflect on God's wonderful promises. Little by little, your mind will be renewed in Him!

# The Crucial Importance
## of Regular Prayer and Scripture Reading
### Abiding in Christ Brings Assurance

I would be remiss if I did not remind of the crucial importance of regularly spending time in prayer and Scriptures. For me and others, this is a *vital* part of gaining full assurance. One thing is certain, if you allow unconfessed sin to remain in your life, you will *never* have full assurance no matter how many Scriptures you quote! Developing a simple but effective quiet time is crucial to the daily fullness and power of the Holy Spirit.

It is vital for every reader to work through **Appendix C** to insure you are on a solid path of daily cleansing and prayer. You will be delighted to discover daily cleansing and prayer is not complicated or out of reach. My friend, daily abiding in Christ will change your life like you cannot even imagine! Establishing this pattern will not only give you assurance, but the very closeness and power of Christ Himself! But understand one thing — this is not an *option* if you are to walk in full assurance and power. Yet be encouraged, dear saint. By God's grace, you cannot fail!

# Appendix B

## How to Gain Full Victory
## Over Doubting Your Salvation

In this appendix, we address an issue that prevents countless believers from experiencing full confidence and victory in their Christian walk. I am referring to nagging, periodic doubts about one's salvation. However, let me be very clear that I am referring to people who otherwise evidence the indicators of genuine salvation. I am not talking about those who exhibit few indicators of the new birth. People with few or no indicators of salvation should seek God for salvation and not casually assume they are saved but simply lack assurance.

While occasional doubts are not unusual for saved people, chronic severe doubts are not typical of those genuinely saved. Except in cases where someone has some level of clinical depression or anxiety disorder, chronic, severe doubt suggests a need to seek salvation and serious counsel. I strongly urge those with deep persistent doubts to get the wise counsel of a pastor, counselor and perhaps also a medical doctor. God certainly has an answer but you may well need personal counsel to gain full victory. Pease don't be discouraged. If you seek Him, God will surely meet your need.

## God's Word Can Answer Periodic Doubts

For saved people who need greater assurance, it is my joy to share how you can experience a glorious new peace. In this appendix, we examine seven of the more common reasons saved people can struggle with unfounded doubt. One thing is certain, until you understand the *source* of your doubt, you are unlikely to experience full victory and growth. This issue is crucial because people who struggle with doubt are robbed of joy, stunted in their growth and hindered in service to Christ. God certainly does not desire such an existence for any of His children!

So what is God's answer for lack of full assurance? In essence His answer is the *truth* of Scripture. Once you fully understand the truths of God's grace and His acceptance, the devil's condemning lies lose their power. Make no mistake — the shield of faith and breastplate of righteousness will quench all the fiery darts of the enemy! (Ephesians 6:10-18) Though it certainly may take a process of greater understanding and growth, you will come to assurance and peace.

Dear saint, your victory can begin when you gain insight into the true sources of your doubts. Pause now and ask God to give you supernatural wisdom concerning your fears. Remember, God has *promised* wisdom to all who ask (James 1:5). Prayerfully read the next section and carefully follow the leading you receive from God. And be assured — God will lead you to full assurance. "These things I have written to you who believe in the name of the Son of God, that you may **know** that you have eternal life and that you may continue to believe in the name of the Son of God" (1 John 5:13).

## Seven Possible Sources of Doubt

(1) *You may lack the biblical understanding that salvation is completely God's gift by grace through faith.* Dear reader, if you do not understand God's salvation is a gift of grace, you will always be looking to yourself to see if you deserve God's salvation and love. Of course, the honest answer to that question will always be no. The fact is *none* of us deserve salvation! Friend, it is vital for you to read (and believe) Ephesians 2:8-10, Romans 6:23 and Romans 10:13. Salvation is God's *gift* by grace through faith. God wants you to have rest in Him, not doubt in yourself!

It is also critical to understand that Christians certainly still struggle with sin and weaknesses. (If you doubt this, read of Paul's struggles and growth in Romans 7 and Philippians 3:12-

16.) While God certainly gives us new strength and grace, we will all be a "work in progress" until the day we die. Do not let periodic struggles or weaknesses cause you to think you are not saved. Stand on the confidence of God's glorious grace and forgiveness. As you learn to stand on God's Word and faithfulness, your doubts will disappear like the morning dew.

(2) *You may have grown spiritually cold and backslidden through unconfessed sin or lack of abiding in Christ* (John 15:4-8). It is entirely possible you were never discipled or taught how to walk daily in the fullness of God's Spirit. As a result, you may have experienced little spiritual growth and are living in a near perpetual state of quenching God's Spirit. If God's Spirit is quenched and grieved in your life, you will certainly lack the fullness of His power and may often lack the feeling of His presence. It is possible you are saved, but in serious need of the daily cleansing and filling work of the Holy Spirit. If that is your case, go to page 248 and embrace the clear pattern described in **The Critical Importance of Daily Cleansing and Surrender**. As you learn to daily abide in Christ, your doubts will melt away.

(3) *You may be unaware of how to resist the accusing, doubt-inspiring tactics of the devil.* One of the main titles (and tactics) of the devil is the "accuser of the brethren" (Revelation 12:10). If Satan can keep you in doubt, your spiritual growth will be stunted and service to Christ limited. You may indeed be saved, but simply need to learn to stand on God's promises and effectively resist the enemy. Make no mistake — our security is in God's Promise and He cannot lie! So how do we overcome the enemy's wide arsenal of fiery darts of doubts? By standing on the truth of God's grace and acceptance because of the blood of Christ! Thank God our confidence is in *His* righteousness, not ours.

When Jesus encountered the attack and lies of the devil, how did He respond (Matthew 4:4)? He resisted and overcame Satan by quoting the truth of God's Word. My friend, you can learn to do exactly the same thing. When you learn to "Submit to God and resist the devil," he will flee from you (James 4:7)! On page 227, I outline a powerful Scripture-based pattern for getting rid of doubts and fears about salvation. Please carefully read the illustration of *Standing on the Word and Character of God*. By God's grace, you can and will find peace!

I should note another of Satan's favorite ploys is to tell struggling saints that they have committed the "unpardonable sin." Dear reader, if someone has committed the unpardonable sin, they would likely not be reading this book and certainly would not be deeply concerned over whether or not they were saved. My friend, if you truly desire to know and walk with Christ, you have *not* committed the unpardonable sin. You can put that out of your mind!

(4) *You may have experienced intense pain and suffering which causes you to doubt God's acceptance, faithfulness and love.* Even though persons are saved, they are certainly still human and vulnerable to the normal emotions that come from prolonged or severe suffering. Especially with today's unbalanced "health and wealth" emphasis, suffering believers may think God is rejecting them because their lives are not filled with miracles. Of course, this teaching is unbalanced and can cause struggling saints to feel they are somehow abandoned and rejected by God. We certainly do not see constant comfort and ease in most of history's greatest servants of Christ.

Believers, it is vital to understand that many of history's most godly believers experienced incredible suffering and long-term pain. God by no means answers "yes" to all prayers and He certainly didn't promise an easy ride on earth! While God often greatly blesses and protects His children, there are also times of *severe* suffering. In fact, He clearly states we should *expect* great persecution, suffering and trials (John 16:33; 2 Corinthians 12:9; 2 Timothy 3:12).

Because of the nature of living in a fallen body and evil world, most of us will encounter significant trials. Some will experience much more than others. However, this *by no means* indicates they are less accepted or unloved by God! In fact, those who have suffered most (and borne it well) will very likely have far greater rewards in heaven. It is vital for saints to base their assurance of salvation upon God's Word and character, *not* pleasant circumstances.

Dear reader, if you have known a lot of pain, don't think it strange that you may struggle with doubt and fear more than some other people. To be clear, you can certainly experience peace and you should seek it in faith! However, do not be surprised or hard on yourself if you have some struggles with doubt. Remember, true faith is not the absence of all questions; it is the *choice* to believe anyway (whether you feel like it or not)! Please do not base your confidence on feelings or circumstances — they are unreliable indicators. Base your confidence in the unchanging Word and faithfulness of God!

(5) *Especially today, many people have been badly hurt by authority figures and thus have enormous difficulty trusting anyone.* In a day of rampant, child abuse, disintegrating families and marital unfaithfulness, millions have experienced horrible abuse, betrayal and rejection from their earliest memories. It is understandable these dear people might have increased difficulty with trust and security. Without question, such issues can also affect our emotions in many ways.

While the new birth certainly changes our hearts, God generally does not take us over like a robot and instantly erase all experiences and memories. Though we are fully forgiven and changed at salvation, part of our transformation will be progressive and on-going. Those who have been abandoned, betrayed or badly hurt may indeed have greater struggles with issues of security, peace and trust. Let's face it — for many today the word "father" brings only painful images of an abusive, unloving figure who abandoned them. Such experience can definitely affect the ease with which we trust our heavenly Father.

Again, please do not misunderstand the point. People who have suffered betrayal and rejection *can certainly* still experience full assurance and peace concerning their salvation! They simply may take a bit longer to sense the full emotions of deep assurance and peace. We can take great comfort in the fact we are saved by God's grace and unfailing character, *not* our feelings. My friend, do not be too hard on yourself about difficult emotions — our loving Father certainly understands your struggles and wounds. Indeed, our Savior is "touched by the feeling of our infirmities" (Hebrews 4:15). Do not let emotional feelings cloud your trust in God. He is a faithful and gracious Father in every way!

(6) *Some people have a basic temperament or physiological conditions that predispose them toward feelings of doubt and fear.* While in seminary, I did a clinical internship in a professional Christian counseling center. Believe me, people came though our doors with some of the severest problems known to man. Many of these precious people also struggled deeply with doubts about their salvation. There is no question that certain personalities and temperaments are naturally more prone to over-analysis and fear than are others.

Each temperament type has its own unique strengths and weaknesses. For some, their weakness is a tendency toward insecurity and doubt. In fact, certain temperaments tend to worry, question and over-analyze virtually everything! About a quarter of the population has a temperament that somewhat leans toward hypochondria and worry.

With certain temperaments, if they hear of a disease, they soon find themselves imagining some of the same symptoms and think they probably have it. People with this temperament often do the same thing with salvation which creates unnecessary bouts with uncertainty. While these temperaments can certainly still learn to experience God's full peace, they may find it a bit more of a struggle. However, this by no means indicates they are not saved.

I also want to stress such struggles do not mean someone is weak nor has anything for which to be ashamed. In fact, studies show that people most prone to over-analysis and worry often have high IQ's and are gifted, sensitive people. Some people just have a tendency to be more analytical and anxiety-prone than others. If you have that personality, it may well explain some of your struggles with doubt.

Remember the Bible says it is the "truth that sets us free." Understanding the truth about your personality pattern can help you largely ignore those unfounded thoughts and feelings. But let me be clear, temperament is not an excuse for continuing in doubt and fear. *Any* temperament type can learn to trust God and overcome doubt.

Let me also say that some people have physical and emotional conditions that definitely affect their brain chemistry and thus their feelings. Clinical depression and anxiety disorders are more than just being a little tense or blue. These conditions are as real as a broken leg and are nothing for which to be ashamed. If a person has any degree of these conditions, their emotional and spiritual feelings are bound to be affected. People with these problems need to realize they cannot believe their emotions when it comes to determining assurance of salvation. They must learn to stand entirely on God's promises regardless of how they "feel." People with these struggles should prayerfully work through the illustration, *Standing on the Character and Word of God* (page 248). They should also seek the ministry of a pastor, counselor or godly doctor. Above all, do not be discouraged — you *can* learn to trust God's Word, nor your feelings. And when you learn to fully rely on God's promises, it is amazing how your feelings start changing as well!

(7)  *You may indeed be among thousands of lost church members (or the religious unchurched) who unwittingly made a profession that simply wasn't real* (Matthew 7:21-24). In most cases, this was wholly unintentional. You certainly didn't mean to make a false profession but for a variety of reasons, you suspect you have. For whatever reason, you find you are a church member with no peace about your salvation. Over my ministry, I have seen several deacons, teachers and even pastors come to this realization and receive true salvation. In every case, they came to a glorious new assurance and changed life. My friend, you will too! At this point I must caution readers against too quickly deciding their problem is that they are saved but just struggling with doubts. When it come to deciding the source of doubts, if there is any question in your mind, err on the side of seeking God in total surrender now. It is infinitely better to be a bit over-cautious and make sure you truly come to Christ than to wrongly assume you have and miss eternal life.

# Appendix C

## How to Experience Powerful
## Daily Prayer and Bible Reading
### Learn to Abide in Christ and Walk in Spiritual Fullness

In this section, we examine a simple but powerful biblical pattern for daily abiding in Christ. Without question, a dynamic daily prayer life is God's will for every believer. Furthermore, it isn't complicated and God's grace is more than sufficient to help us experience closeness with Christ.

For your convenience, I am dividing this section into two parts. First, I will give a simple outline getting started in a basic pattern for powerful daily abiding. Second, I include an expanded, more detailed explanation of powerful daily prayer and time in God's Word. Let's begin with a simple outline by which anyone can experience powerful daily abiding in Christ.

## Part One

### A Basic Pattern for Powerful
### Daily Prayer and Abiding in Christ

I.  *Set aside anywhere from twenty minutes to one hour for daily (or at least regular) time in God's Word and Prayer.* Spending at least some time in the morning (before your day) is always advisable. Many find it best to rise early enough to do their main quiet time before the day really begins. However, some believers spend a portion of their time in the morning and then additional time in the afternoon or evening. Beyond our quiet times, it is vital to also cultivate the normal habit of prayer and communing with God as we go about our day (Matthew 6:6-9; 1 Thessalonians 5:17).

By all means let God guide you to the best quiet time pattern for you. Do not get caught in a condemnation trap about how much time you did or didn't spend each day. While consistent quiet time with God is *crucial*, do not view it as a legalistic trap. Praise God, we are indeed under grace, not law!

II.  *View your quiet time as an essential element of your love relationship with God, not just some legalistic duty* (Matthew 22:37; 1 Corinthians 13:1-3). Dear reader, never view your quiet time as something you "have" to do but rather a relationship you "get" to experience. Your prayer time is both talking and listening to God. While we do need discipline and self-control to guard our time with God, we do not view it as a chore but rather the heart of our intimate fellowship with God!

III.  *Let God guide you in a balanced practice of the five basic elements of relationship prayer with God.* Many dear saints at first may struggle with how to talk to God effectively. Some indeed wonder what to talk about other than their needs and desires. (Two excellent patterns to study are: the Lord's Prayer in Matthew 6:9-15 and Jesus' prayer in John 17:20-26.) Though you will not use these as a rigid formula, a general guide is to spend some time in the each of the five different prayer elements. The basic prayer elements are: (1) Praise, worship, exalting His name and glory. (2) A time of confession and repentance allowing God to search your heart. (3) Intercession for eternal kingdom issues (such as lost people, revival, evangelism, missions, healing of relationships, etc.) (4) Personal petitions (such as spiritual growth, personal desires, needs, wisdom, deliverance, protection, etc.) (5) Biblical study and meditative reflection and listening for God's voice. (In your prayer time, you make time to listen for God's voice as well as speak.)

Again, these five elements are a general rule but *not* a set formula you must rigidly follow each day. Your primary goal is to let the Holy Spirit guide you through these elements focusing attention where God leads. In general, you will first read and journal from God's Word, then let God guide you in each of the various elements of prayer. For further clarity, consider the following outline.

# A Simple Quiet Time Outline

(1) Spend a few moments in Scripture reading taking care to note any special impressions or insights. (2) Move into a few moments of praise, adoration and worship (3) Spend a few moments allowing God to search your heart, fully confessing and forsaking whatever sin He reveals (the next section provides help). (4) Pray for kingdom issues like evangelism, missions and revival (especially lost people). (5) Present your personal needs before God, and ask for spiritual protection and deliverance. (6) Ask the Lord to open your eyes. He wants you to know His voice in your heart. (7) Close with praise and ask for God's protection and fullness of the Holy Spirit.

Let me again stress there will be uniqueness in each person's pattern and schedule. You may or may not be led to pray all elements every day or in the same order. But make no mistake — at least some regularity in these elements is crucial to powerful fullness and growth in Christ. Simply ask God to guide you in the unique patterns and timing that is His will for you each day.

Dear reader, if you trust God and make reasonable efforts, you cannot fail! (Always feel free to just "talk to God." He does not require fancy language or exact formulas!) For more help, the next section gives far greater detail and instruction. Prayerfully read it and let God guide you in your own unique journey with Him. And remember, His grace is greater than our greatest weakness and we are **accepted** through the blood of Christ! "Let us therefore come boldly before the throne of grace to find help in time of need" (Hebrews 4:16).

# Part Two

# An Expanded Explanation of Powerful Daily Prayer and Closeness with God

**1. Make an absolute commitment to consistently spend significant time alone with God in His Word and prayer. (While we can and**

should talk to God in quick moments throughout the day, this cannot substitute for a special quiet time for significant cleansing and focused prayer.)

Believers, it is essential to give God *significant* time on a regular basis. *Two or three minute devotions are by no means the pattern of Jesus, the Early Church or anyone mightily used by God.* You must reject the false modern notion that you can develop a truly deep prayer life "on the run." Quiet time prayer of at least twenty to thirty minutes is a general starting suggestion for a vibrant daily prayer life. (That is 20-30 minutes of prayer in addition to reading the Word of God.) However, this does not have to all be at one time. Some believers spend a portion of their time in the morning and the rest in the afternoon or evening.

Many believers soon discover their time with God becomes so powerful it often goes long past the twenty to thirty minutes. When we get in God's manifest presence, we can easily lose all track of time. Please remember one great principle — the primary way we learn to pray is to "show up for practice." Of course, regular reading God's Word is crucial to prayer and closeness with Christ (Matthew 4:4). If you develop the habit of spending significant time alone with Jesus, He will utterly change your life! If you don't, your spiritual life will be very limited. Mark this well — a specific quiet time is not only Jesus' command, it is the consistent example of His life (Matthew 6:6; Mark 1:35; Luke 6:12; 9:18).

## Of Course We Also Pray Without Ceasing
### (1 Thessalonians 5:17)

In addition to closet prayer, we also embrace the glorious lifestyle of "prayer without ceasing" (1 Thessalonians 5:17). In other words, we learn to live every moment in the immediate awareness of God. By all means, we talk to God throughout the day. This too is very powerful prayer! And while we must be deeply committed to closet prayer time, we should never approach it as a legalistic bondage.

Dear reader, do not get caught in the "condemnation trap" concerning the exact form or length of your quiet time with God. If you occasionally miss your time with God, do not let Satan beat you up or tell you God won't hear you that day. Remember, through Jesus' name you can talk to God any time! Thank God we are under grace not legalism! Nonetheless, your special quiet time must be carefully guarded. It is the very heart of deeper closeness, maturity and power with God!

## 2. Approach your time in prayer and Scripture as a love relationship of talking and listening to God, not some formulaic, legalistic ritual.

True prayer is a relationship! It is not rigid formulas or programs, it is a love relationship with your God. *To view your prayer time as anything less is to miss the whole point of prayer.* More than anything else, God wants your personal love and this means making time to give Him your undivided attention. Modern saints especially need to reflect on the biblical story of Martha and Mary (Luke 10:38-42). Sadly, we have become a generation of Marthas! Many are so busy working *for* God, they neglect time alone *with* Him. This inevitably stunts our growth and short-circuits our spiritual power.

When you give appropriate time to approach prayer as a relationship, you will also learn to hear God's voice on a consistent basis. Not only will you talk to God, but He will talk to you! Make no mistake — true prayer involves much "listening" to God. In fact, genuine prayer always begins in the heart and mind of God! Prayer is not you trying to tell God what to do. It is discerning what God wants to do and aligning your prayers with His will. You most get clear discernment by spending significant time in prayer and meditative listening. As you learn to listen, you are then confident what you are asking is God's will. But saint, please *do not* let this sound difficult. By God's wonderful grace, you *can* learn to discern His voice! (John 10:27)

To hear God's voice, it is important to devote part of your prayer time to intentional reflection on Scripture. Obviously, reading Scripture is vital to hearing God! During your time of reading and study, write down key Scriptures and impressions God reveals. This form of journaling is invaluable to a powerful prayer life!

In many ways, learning to *hear* God is the greatest secret of answered prayer! In 1 John 5:14-15 (KJV), this truth is very clear. "And this is the confidence that we have in Him, that, if we ask any thing according to His will, we know He hears us: and if we know that He hears us, whatsoever we ask, we know that we have the petitions that we desired of Him." My friend, God wants you to hear His voice and know His will (John 10:27; Ephesians 5:17). If you will give Him some quality time, your spiritual hearing becomes keen and sharp.

## Loving God Means Loving His Word
### How to Embrace an Effective Pattern
### for Powerful Daily Reading

We cannot possibly discuss prayer and abiding in Christ without stressing the awesome importance of regularly reading and studying the Word of God. Prayer, hearing God and Scripture are inherently connected! "If you abide in Me, and My words abide in you, you will ask what you desire, and it shall be done for you" (John 15:7). So how do we effectively abide in God's Word? The Greek word "abide" (*anastrepho*) means "live in" which carries the idea of one's life totally centering in Christ.

In the biblical context of John 15, "abide in Me" is a term of close personal relationship. We must understand it is impossible to be close to anyone if we do not talk and listen to them a great deal. My friend, this is the exact purpose of your quiet time — deep talking, listening and surrender to Christ. Also central to your closeness with God, is your regular time in His Word. In Matthew 4:4, Jesus even said, "*We **live** by every word that comes from the mouth of God.*"

As far as a process for abiding in God's Word, let me say there is no rigid program we all must follow. However, I find three simple steps both essential and powerful.

## Three Steps to Life-Changing Daily Bible Reading

*A first step is to let God guide you to one of the many daily Bible reading patterns that will take you through the entire Bible at least once a year.* (Some double the one year reading schedule and go through God's Word twice a year.) Most reading plans are designed to expose you to different parts of the Bible each day. In that way, you consistently receive a variety of focus in your daily walk. Of course, just reading straight through the Bible a little each day is also very effective. I suggest that you choose a highly respected translation and not a paraphrase version of the Bible.

*Second, I strongly suggest that you keep a daily journal of impressions and truths God reveals as you read.* While this does not have to be elaborate or long, it will have enormous impact on your growth. Just a simple notebook is adequate. However many believers purchase attractive journals so they can permanently keep their written journey with God. Regular journaling is extremely advisable and helps you remember the key markers and dates in your life. A journal literally becomes a written chronicle of your relationship with God!

*Third, keep a concordance, Bible dictionary and quality Bible commentary handy so you can study key words that God quickens to your heart.* Furthermore, it is essential to read Bible verses in their *context!* A huge part of understanding what God is saying is to grasp the context to which He was speaking. Any good commentary will help you in that endeavor. My friend, these simple steps will grant you incredible closeness and clear hearing of God's voice. Remember our Lord promised the Holy Spirit would guide us into all truth (John 16:13). Do not be discouraged, the Holy Spirit lives within your heart. You really can learn to hear God's voice!

**3. Make a commitment to a biblically balanced prayer life by regularly practicing the five essential types of communication to God (especially regular cleansing, intercession and listening to God's voice).**

It is essential that our prayer life be far more than reciting a list of "needs and wants." God certainly wants His children to consistently experience great depths of personal praise and worship. Furthermore, we must experience daily cleansing to maintain the power of the Holy Spirit! He also wants to deepen our daily petitions and intercession. A further secret is learning to *listen* for God's voice as He prompts us in how and what to pray. We then learn to pray *His* agenda, not ours. Dear reader, please do not let this sound hard, mystical or out of reach. With these simple patterns, any child of God can easily experience God's closeness, power and guidance!

To summarize, a vibrant relationship with Jesus *requires* a fairly consistent practice of five basic types of prayer: *(1) Praise, thanksgiving and worship, (2) Thorough confession and repentance, (3) Biblical petition and supplication, (4) Intercession and (5) Meditative listening.* Obviously, you can only experience all these prayer types if you make significant daily time to be alone with God. It is virtually impossible to deeply experience all five types of prayer in only a two or three minute devotion. But believer, do not despair! Through God's grace, you *can* begin to experience all prayer types on a consistent basis. It is by no means complicated or out of reach.

## Learning to Let the Holy Spirit Guide Your Prayers

Let me also stress the vital importance of praying the various elements as the Holy Spirit leads and *not* in some rigid formula. In other words, your primary goal is not just "getting in all five prayer types" before you quit. The goal is letting Christ guide you as to *what* and *how* to pray. In other words, some days you may sense He is leading you to spend most of your time in worship or confession. On another day it may be far more petition. The point is — let Him guide! Prayer is a relationship, not a rote formula. However, it is advisable to consistently practice all five prayer elements with reasonable regularity. In that way, your walk with Christ is solid and mature.

Before closing the subject of balanced prayer, we need to address today's most crucial missing element for powerful closeness with God. For most believers, their failure to practice meaningful cleansing and surrender seriously blocks God's power and hinders their spiritual hearing. *But be encouraged, dynamic cleansing is not complicated and you can easily embrace these life-changing principles!*

## The Critical Important of
## Daily Cleansing and Surrender
### Today's Missing Element in Abiding

In your regular quiet time, it is crucial to do more than to always merely pray, "God forgive all my sins." While that prayer is fine occasionally, we must frequently allow God to do a deeper examination. The Psalmist says we are to let God "search our hearts" (Psalms 139:23-24). We are also commanded not only to confess but also to *forsake* our sins (Proverbs 28:13). In Lamentations 3:40, God says we are to "*examine*" our ways. In the Hebrew text, the words "search" (*baw-ka*) and "examine" (*khaw-ka*) both imply thorough spiritual cleansing, not some shallow surface prayer that is general.

My friend, it is impossible to truly forsake our sins if we don't get specific about identifying them! But let me assure you that deep cleansing is not complicated or out of reach. It does not take hours and neither are you required to legalistically do this every single day. Yet, the practice of consistent, thorough cleansing is absolutely crucial to living and praying in the power of the Holy Spirit.

## A Simple Pattern for
## Powerful Daily Cleansing and Fullness

For revolutionized closeness and power with God, follow this pattern or something similar. During some part of your prayer time, simply pause and ask God to search your heart. Ask Him to reveal anything you need to confess, surrender or work to change. To empower the process ask Him to search the different areas of your life one by one. The seven areas of our lives are: (1) *Thoughts*, (2) *Attitudes*, (3) *Speech*, (4) *Relationships*, (5) *Sins of Commission*, (6) *Sins of Omission*, and (7) *Avoiding the Cross and Full Surrender to Christ's Lordship.*

For example, you would simply pray "Father, do I have any *thoughts* or *attitudes* I need to confess and forsake?" Briefly pause and let Him speak. Next, you would pray, "Father, do I have any *words* I need to confess and forsake?" Pause and let Him speak. For thorough cleansing you could do that with each of the seven areas (though not necessarily all each day.) After you have asked god's cleansing, then surrender your heart and ask for the fullness and power of the Holy Spirit. He will surely grant your request! (Luke 11:13)

While we don't automatically have to go through all seven areas each day, this simple process gives God full access to your heart. (Of course, some do briefly pray through all seven areas.) Dear friend, when God has full access to your heart, He completely fills you with the Holy Spirit! When you are full of the Holy Spirit, there is clear hearing, enormous power and mighty answered prayer. And best of all, God's name receives great glory and honor!

Each believer will let God guide in their own preparation and pattern. One thing is certain — when consistent cleansing comes into your prayers, there will be a *dramatic* increase of God's presence and power. And best of all, it really is simple! For help with cleansing, we have a resource called *Drawing Near to God.* The tool is designed to provide any believer with a simple, Bible-centered pattern for daily cleansing and fullness of the Holy Spirit.

## 4. In your daily petitions, seek to focus more on issues of personal character and holiness than on temporal needs.

It is tragic when our prayer lives consist mainly of health, finances and other earthly personal issues. Though important, such issues are somewhat self-focused and temporary. God wants to focus most on that which is eternal and kingdom oriented. After all, God's great priority is to conform us to the image of Christ (Romans 8:29). He is deeply concerned about filling your thoughts and attitudes with His presence and holy power. If you are daily transformed in Spirit-empowered holiness, your prayers and personal soul winning will explode in new power. But you may well ask, "How can I effectively pray for such transformation in my own life?"

*A powerful Scriptural suggestion is to make the nine fruit of the Holy Spirit your daily personal prayer petition* (Galatians 5:22). The fruit of the Holy Spirit represents the very character and holiness of God Himself. As you daily ask God to fill you with each fruit, also ask Him to show you how you *don't* reflect that characteristic. When you thus pray the Word of God for your own life, He will miraculously transform every part of your being! As you are increasingly filled with these fruits, prayer and witnessing become as natural as breathing.

*The specific characteristics of the Beatitudes also provide excellent personal petitions* (Matthew 5). God will lead you to pray other biblical character words on a regular basis. Some examples of character words are: humility, zeal, discernment, wisdom, genuine worship, immovability, boldness, purity, proper motives, revelation, etc. Ask God to help you focus your personal petitions on character, purity and holiness. If you sincerely pray such prayers for your own heart, God will revolutionize your spiritual growth!

## 5. In your daily intercession, focus more on issues of evangelism, missions and revival than temporal earthly concerns.

It is tragic that so much modern intercession is mainly focused on health and other temporal issues. Without question, God's great priorities are the evangelization of the world and sweeping revival in the church (Matthew 28:18). If these are God's main priorities, should they not also be the primary focus of our intercession? Indeed they should! God does incredible things when we focus our intercession on lost people, missions and revival. Yet you may wonder, "How can I focus my intercession on God's great priorities?" Listed below are six powerful strategies based on biblical priorities.

(1) Develop a prayer list of lost people and intercede for them regularly.

(2) Develop a prayer list of the key leaders and ministry strategies of your church. Pray for them with consistency.

(3) Compile a prayer list of key spiritual and government leaders. Pray for them regularly.

(4) Regularly pray for vital mission strategies of your association, state and denomination. (You can get daily or weekly updates from your state and national denomination.)

(5) Daily intercede for revival and spiritual awakening in your city and nation. In my book, *How to Develop A Powerful Prayer Life*, I list twelve biblical prayers to help you effectively intercede for America and the world. (See resource mentioned below.)

(6) For all the various prayer subjects, develop a schedule to pray for certain items on particular days of the week. Otherwise it could be overwhelming. *However, always remain sensitive to God's promptings.* Don't become enslaved to any rigidly programmed schedule!

Dear friend, please do not feel that a powerful prayer life is out of your reach! If you are willing, God will revolutionize your praying and thus your walk with Him. For practical help, I have written the companion book, *How to Develop a Powerful Prayer Life*. It is designed to walk you step by step in a dynamic personal relationship with Jesus Christ. *How to Develop a Powerful Prayer Life* is designed to work hand in hand with this resource. In a very simple yet thorough way, it takes believers into the depths of a personal relationship with Jesus. This companion prayer tool is also priced so pastors can easily afford to order it for their whole congregations.

As we conclude this section, you now have a powerful tool for deep daily cleansing and mountain-moving prayer. The need for daily cleansing and growth is not something you will ever *outgrow*. Don't let anything keep you from walking in full cleansing and dynamic prayer. No matter how weak you have been, you *can* become a powerful, biblical intercessor. If God is for you, who can be against you? And believe me, dear saint, God *is* for you! (Romans 8:31)

# Appendix D

## Patterns for Conducting
## Transformation Prayer Groups

One of the most important elements of revival and powerful spiritual change in found James 5:16. "Confess your trespasses to one another, and pray for one another, that you may be healed. The effective, fervent prayer of a righteous man avails much." Indeed, a huge part of repentance and change is the practice of honest confession of sin and believers praying for one another. Yet in most modern churches, there is little or no place for this to occur. Even when churches do have functioning prayer groups, the elements of profound mutual confession, prayer and repentance are almost entirely missing. In other words, our churches are missing the most crucial element of spiritual power, fellowship and dynamic change!

*Releasing the Revival Flood* is designed to help restore the essential elements of deep conviction, united prayer, biblical fellowship and thorough repentance. That of course, releases the revival flood of God's holy presence. Transformation prayer or study groups will prove crucial to a mighty change in your life and church.

As entire churches or groups pray through *Releasing the Revival Flood*, I recommend that small groups meet weekly to discuss, pray and repent concerning the points of that week's material. Churches and groups are free to be flexible and follow God's leading in exactly how they do this. Most groups divide their session in some combination of discussion and prayer. Under the next heading, I list some basic suggestions.

## Basic Suggestions and Guidelines

1.  If at all possible, schedule at least 1 to 2 hours for group meeting times. This gives opportunity to encounter God without a sense of being rushed.

2. Each group (or church) will elect a facilitator who will be very familiar with that week's material and is prepared to lead in the discussion questions and prayer time.

3. Try to keep group size to ten or less. (So everyone can more fully participate.)

4. Each group member is responsible to thoroughly pray through that week's material and answer the study questions (in their own book).

5. The group time always begins with a strong season of prayer asking God to guide and empower all the discussion and prayer.

6. Move into the meeting by asking each member to share the impressions God revealed in that week's material. Also ask how God may have convicted and what steps of repentance they need to make (if any). Give other group members opportunity to share insights with each person. Spend time praying for the expressed needs and repentance of each member.

7. The facilitator will need to move the discussion along so most time is given to prayer and repentance. He or she will also need to pace the time so one or two people do not consume all the time.

8. At the start of each meeting, stress two things. (a) We deal with our own needs and avoid pointing out flaws in others. (b) All things shared are to be in confidence (unless otherwise agreed).

9. Keep the focus positive and major on praying for God's answers.

10. Pray for sweeping revival in the church, for God's name to be hallowed, and His kingdom exalted. Some churches will elect to have a group share time in the evening worship service. In that service, give time for complete confession and prayer guided by the pastor.

In summary, we simply ask God to lead these meetings into genuine confession, repentance and glorious transformation. Such prayer is all about God's kingdom and the growth of godly relationships. Each group is different so each facilitator must trust God for divine guidance, power and sensitivity to the Holy Spirit. For this reason, it is vital to choose facilitators of spiritual depth and maturity. Yet, let us approach these meetings in the confidence that God will surely lead us to Himself. Because of His marvelous grace, we cannot fail!

# Appendix E

## A Striking Analogy
### "Throwing Mud on a Bride"

One can only wonder how much of God's chastisement among believers is currently being blamed on simple bad health or even satanic attack. It would likely shock us to know the truth. According to Scripture, it is especially dangerous for anyone to sow anger and disunity in a local church! In Proverbs 6:16, God says divisiveness is not just a sin; He literally calls it an *abomination!* Dear saints, because God is so utterly serious about our abiding together in unity, we must *never* treat this issue lightly. One thing is certain — Christ does not view this lightly.

Regarding those who harm the purity or unity of a local church, consider a clear biblical analogy of a husband and wife. Husbands, what would you do if every time a particular person came around your wife, he (or she) would strike her or throw filth on her clothing? I have no doubt you would take extremely strong action if it happened even once, much less repeatedly. Perhaps you are thinking, "Who would be so foolish and wicked as to do something that outrageous?"

But wait a minute, dear saints, have we forgotten that the church *is* Christ's Bride? Without question, the analogy is *exactly* the same as with the husband protecting his wife! **So what is the direct and personal application?** *Anyone who harms a church by spreading anger, disunity or impurity is viciously striking Christ's very Bride.* He or she is literally throwing filth on the holy wedding gown of Christ's Bride! Could anything be more depraved, outrageous or spiritually dangerous? It is truly hard to imagine anything worse!

Based on the clear New Testament examples, anyone who persists in harming the love, unity or purity of a church should get their insurance in order. Let me quickly assure readers I am not trying to be cute, dramatic or harsh in making that statement. Such is the clear message of 1 Corinthians 11 and a whole host of Old and New Testament texts! This matter is so important that Jesus even said the world will know we are His by the "love and unity of His Church" (John 13:34-35; 17:21). Our Lord is deadly serious about the purity and unity of His Bride (the Church). Thus anyone who damages the loving unity of Christ's Bride directly attacks Christ and *He loses no battles*. One thing is for sure — being "under grace" is no defense for such behavior!

# Appendix F

## God's Strong Commands for Loving Fellowship and Unity
### An Expanded List of Relationship Scriptures

Proverbs 6:16 – "These six things doth the Lord hate: yea, seven are an **abomination** unto him: A proud look, a lying tongue, and hands that shed innocent blood, an heart that deviseth wicked imaginations, feet that be swift in running to mischief, a false witness that speaketh lies, **and he that soweth discord among brethren.**"

Matthew 5:9 – "Blessed are the peacemakers: for they shall be called the children of God."

Matthew 5:23-24; 6:14-15 – "Therefore if thou bring they gift to the altar, and there rememberest that thy brother hath ought against thee: leave there thy gift before the altar, and go thy way; first be reconciled to thy brother, and then come and offer thy gift…For if you forgive men their trespasses, your heavenly Father will also forgive you: But if you forgive not men their trespasses, neither will your Father forgive your trespasses."

Matthew 22:37-40 – "Jesus said unto him, Thou shalt love the Lord thy God with all thy heart, and with all thy soul, and with all thy mind. This is the first and great commandment. And the second is like unto it, Thou shalt love they neighbor as thyself. On these two commandments hang all the law and the prophets."

John 13:34-35 – "A new commandment I give unto you, that you love one another; as I have loved you, that you also love one another. By this shall all men know that you are my disciples if you have love one to another."

John 17:20-22 – "Neither pray I for these alone, but for

them also which shall believe on me through their word; That they all may be one as thou, Father, art in me, and I in thee, that they also may be one in us; that the world may believe that thou hast sent me. And the glory which thou gavest me I have given them; that they may be one, even as we are one."

Acts 2:1,42-47 – "And when the day of Pentecost was fully come, they were all with one accord in one place...And they continued steadfastly in the apostles' doctrine and fellowship, and in breaking of bread, and in prayers. And fear came upon every soul; and many wonders and signs were done by the apostles. And all that believed were together, and had all things common. And sold their possessions and goods, and parted them to all men, as every man had need. And they, continuing daily with one accord in the temple and breaking bread from house to house, did eat their meat with gladness and singleness of heart. Praising God, and having favor with all the people. And the Lord added to the church daily such as should be saved."

Romans 12:9(a),16-18 – "Let love be without dissimulation. Be of the same mind one toward another. Mind not high things, but condescend to men of low estate. Be not wise in your own conceits. Recompense to no man evil for evil. Provide things honest in the sight of all men. If it be possible, as much as lieth in you, live peaceably with all men."

Romans 15:5-7 – "Now the God of patience and consolation grant you to be likeminded one toward another according to Christ Jesus: That you may with one mind and one mouth glorify God, even the Father of our Lord Jesus Christ. Wherefore receive you one another, as Christ also received us to the glory of God."

1 Corinthians 1:10 – "Now I beseech you, brethren, by the name of our Lord Jesus Christ, that you all speak the

same thing, and that there be no divisions among you; but that you be perfectly joined together in the same mind and in the same judgment."

1 Corinthians 3:1-3 – "And I brethren, could not speak unto you as unto spiritual, but as unto carnal, even as unto babes in Christ. I have fed you with milk, and not with meat: for hitherto you were not able to bear it, neither yet now are you able. For you are yet carnal: for whereas there is among you envying, and strife, and divisions, are you not carnal, and walk as men?"

1 Corinthians 11:18,29-31 – "For first of all, when you come together in the church, I hear that there be divisions among you; and I partly believe it. For he that eateth and drinketh unworthily, eateth and drinketh damnation to himself not discerning the Lord's body. For this cause many are weak and sickly among you, and many sleep. For if we would judge ourselves, we should not be judged."

1 Corinthians 13:4-8(a) – "Love suffers long, and is kind, love envies not; love vaunts not itself, is not puffed up. Does not behave itself unseemly, seeks not her own, is not easily provoked, thinks no evil; Rejoices not in iniquity, but rejoices in the truth; bears all things, believes all things, hopes all things, endures all things. Love never fails."

Ephesians 4:3 – "With all lowliness and meekness and longsuffering, forbearing one another in love; Endeavoring to keep the unity of the Spirit in the bond of peace."

Ephesians 4:29-32 – "Do not let any unwholesome talk come out of your mouths, but only what is helpful for building others up according to their needs, that it may benefit those who listen. And do not grieve the Holy Spirit of God, with whom you were sealed for the day of redemption. Get rid of all bitterness, rage and anger, brawling and slander, along with every form of malice. Be kind and compassionate to one another, forgiving each other, just as in Christ God forgave you."

Philippians 4:8 – "Finally, brethren, whatsoever things are true, whatsoever things are honest, whatsoever things are just, whatsoever things are pure, whatsoever things are lovely, whatsoever things are of good report, if there be any virtue, and if there be any praise, think on these things."

Colossians 3:8;12-15 – "But now you also put off all these; anger, wrath, malice, blasphemy, filthy communication out of your mouth...Put on therefore, as the elect of God, holy and beloved, bowels of mercies, kindness, humbleness of mind, meekness, longsuffering; Forbearing one another and forgiving one another, if any man have a quarrel against any: even as Christ forgave you, so also do you. And above all these things put on love, which is the bond of perfectness. And let the peace of God rule in your hearts, to the which also you are called in one body; and be you thankful."

1 Thessalonians 5:13(b)-15 – "And be at peace among your-selves. Now we exhort you, brethren, warn them that are unruly, comfort the feebleminded, support the weak, be patient toward all men. See that none render evil for evil unto any man; but ever follow that which is good, both among yourselves, and to all men."

Titus 3:10-11 – "A man that is a slanderer after the first and second admonition reject; knowing that he that is such is subverted, and sinneth, being condemned of himself."

James 3:2-18 – "For in many things we offend all. If any man offend not in word, the same is a perfect man, and able also to bridle the whole body...Even so the tongue is a little member, and boasteth great things. Behold, how great a matter a little fire kindleth! And the tongue is a fire, a world of iniquity; so is the tongue among our members, that it defileth the whole body, and setteth on fire the course of nature; and it is set on fire of hell…Who is a wise man and endued with knowledge among you? Let him show out of a good conversation his works with meekness of wisdom. But if you have bitter envying and strife in your hearts, glory not, and lie not against the truth. This wisdom descendeth not from above, but is earthly sensual, devilish. For where envying and strife is, there is confusion and every evil work. But the wisdom that is from above is first pure, then peaceable, gentle, and easy to be entreated, full of mercy and good fruits, without partiality, and without hypocrisy. And the fruit of righteousness is sown in peace of them that make peace."

James 4:11-12 – "Speak not evil one of another, brethren. He that speaketh evil of his brother, and judgeth his brother, speaketh evil of the law, and judgeth the law: but if thou judge the law, thou art not a doer of the law, but a judge. There is one lawgiver, who is able to save and to destroy: who art thou that judgest another?"

James 5:9 – "Grumble not one against another, brethren, lest you be condemned; behold, the judge standeth before the door."

1 Peter 1:22 – "Seeing you have purified your souls in obeying the truth through the Spirit unto unfeigned love of the brethren, see that you love one another with a pure heart fervently."

1 Peter 4:8-9 – "And above all things have fervent love among yourselves: for love shall cover the multitude of sins. Use hospitality one to another without grudging."

1 John 2:9-11 – "He that saith he is in the light, and hateth his brother, is in darkness even until now. He that loveth his brother abideth in the light, and there is none occasion of stumbling in him. But he that hateth his brother is in darkness, and walketh in darkness and knoweth not

whether he goeth, because that darkness hath blinded his eyes."

1 John 3:10-15 – "In this the children of God are manifest, and the children of the devil: whosoever doeth not righteousness is not of God, neither he that loves not his brother. For this is the message that you heard from the beginning, that we should love one another…We know that we have passed from death unto life, because we love the brethren. He that loves not his brother abides in death. Whosoever hates his brother is a murderer: and you know that no murderer hath eternal life abiding in him."

1 John 4:7-8 – "Beloved, let us love one another: for love is of God; and every one that loveth is born of God, and knoweth God. He that loveth not knoweth not God; for God is love."

## The Biblical Commands of Loving Respect for Christian Leaders

Psalms 105:15 – "Touch not mine anointed, and do my prophets no harm."

1 Corinthians 1:10 – "I appeal to you, brothers, in the name of our Lord Jesus Christ, that all of you agree with one another so that their may be no divisions among you and that you may be perfectly united in mind and thought."

Ephesians 4:2-3 – "Be completely humble and gentle; be patient, bearing with one another in love. Endeavoring to keep the unity of the Spirit in the bond of peace."

1 Thessalonians 5:12-13 – "And we beseech you, brethren, recognize them which labor among you, and are over you in the Lord, and admonish you: and to esteem them very highly in love for their work's sake. And be at peace among yourselves."

1 Timothy 5:17 – "Let the elders that rule well be counted worthy of double honor, especially they who labor in the word and doctrine."

Hebrews 13:17 – "Obey them that have the rule over you, and submit yourselves: for they watch for your souls, as they that must give an account, that they may do it with joy, and not with grief; for that is unprofitable for you."

(All verses listed in King James Verion)

SDG